VEGETARIAN
COOKING FOR EVERYONE

VEGETARIAN
COOKING FOR EVERYONE

With more than 350 delicious and easy-to-follow
recipes illustrated in full color

edited by Susie Ward

CRESCENT BOOKS
New York

CONTENTS

INTRODUCTION

Vegetarian food is different, delicious, nourishing and fresh. It can turn cooking, as well as eating, into a daily pleasure. The simple goodness of fresh ingredients in a loaf of homemade bread and a bowl of soup often give more satisfaction than the most complicated concoction smothered in a butter-rich sauce. Learning to cook without meat and even most fish is something of a challenge, because most of us are so used to having one or the other as the main dish of the meal.

Vegetarianism and whole-food cooking are enjoying a new surge of popularity in the developed world as a reaction to the high-fat, high-sugar, high-starch junk foods that have so dominated our diets for the past 30 years.

The first pleasure of whole-food cooking is the goodness it brings to your table. The freshness and flavor of natural foods, unrefined and free from additives, offers a range of ingredients that is infinitely rich and subtle. But whole-food eating doesn't only satisfy the palate, it brings long-term health benefits, too.

Our Western diet tends to be soft, sweet and high in animal fats. Over-refined and processed foods contain fewer vitamins and minerals, and chemical additives can cause unpleasant side effects. The foods closest to nature - fresh fruit and vegetables, unrefined grains, nuts and dried beans - are high in vitamins and minerals, high in fiber and low in fat. They provide cheaper protein and satisfy at moderate calorie levels.

So vegetarianism also makes economic and ecological sense. A field of soy beans will yield 30 times as much protein as the same field given over to the rearing of beef cattle. Surprisingly though, it is still the case that agricultural land is devoted to feeding animals, far more than to growing crops. A further cruel reality is that economic pressures tend to encourage under-developed countries to export their grain as cattle feed for richer countries.

For many people, it is the slaughter of animals for food which has made them turn to a vegetarian life, as has the practise of keeping battery hens in tiny cages for the duration of their short lives. In addition, although modern food production methods have effectively made meat much cheaper than ever before, inevitably the taste of mass-produced meat, from animals reared on chemically treated feed and injected with hormones, suffers from a uniform blandness. A true free-range chicken is practically impossible to buy in the Western world – in America 98 percent of chickens are battery reared. Considerations such as this have given many a less ideological but as valid a reason to prefer a largely whole-food and vegetarian lifestyle.

Other healthy products - for instance yogurt, complement much vegetarian fare. It is perhaps the best known of all cultured milk products and has had an amazing rise from relative obscurity as an indigenous Middle Eastern food to a world-wide popularity - all within the last 20 or so years. It has been credited with extraordinary properties, particularly since scientists about 100 years ago became fascinated by the microbiological processes which take place in milk during fermentation. At that time a Russian scientist, Ilya Mechnikov, isolated the bacteria found in yogurt. It is recorded that ancient physicians used to prescribe sour milk for dysentery, tuberculosis, liver problems and various other illnesses. It was found that an acid milk is more easily digested than ordinary milk, and modern medical practitioners have used it to counteract the effect of some antibiotics which destroy beneficial intestinal flora. Today, aficionados of yogurt are able to enjoy a wide selection of the product and the truly devoted sleuth may be able to track down some very unusual varieties.

So you see, you don't have to be vegetarian to enjoy this book, but you might adopt a new attitude to eating. For instance, you could break away from the traditional three-course meal and serve several complementary dishes at once, as in Eastern countries, or you could serve one large salad as a main course and offer homemade bread and an assortment of dressings. The best thing about vegetarianism is that it is an adventure and opens new possibilities to the diner, and to the cook.

SOUPS

The goodness of soup has always appealed to those who appreciate real home cooking. Hearty and wholesome, soups preserve all the vitamins and nutrients of their cooked ingredients, but contain relatively few calories. And the country French say that you can always tell a true cook by her soup!

Cold tomato soup

Waste-nothing Vegetable Stock

INGREDIENTS *serves 4-6*
1-2 tbsp oil
2 large onions, chopped
1 clove garlic, chopped
2 carrots, sliced
2 sticks celery, sliced
juice of $\frac{1}{2}$ lemon
1 large potato, peeled and diced
$\frac{1}{2}$ cup lentils, presoaked
cabbage or cauliflower stems
outer leaves of cabbage, lettuce etc.
any vegetables past their prime, such as
    soft tomatoes or mushrooms
chopped fresh herbs
$8\frac{3}{4}$ cups water, including any leftover
    from cooking vegetables, tomato juice
    drained from cans etc.
salt and freshly ground black pepper
2-3 tbsp soy sauce

METHOD
Heat the oil in a large saucepan and stir-fry the onion and garlic until transparent.

Add the carrots, celery and lemon juice. Turn the heat to low, cover the pan and sweat, stirring occasionally, for 5-10 minutes.

Add the remaining vegetables and herbs and pour the water over. Season well and simmer, covered, for about 40 minutes, until the vegetables are mushy.

Blend the stock in a food processor or blender and add the soy sauce to taste. Keep in the refrigerator to use within a couple of days or freeze in ice cube trays.

Bean Soup

INGREDIENTS *serves 4-6*
1 cup field beans
1-2 tbsp oil
1 onion, chopped
1 clove garlic, chopped
2 carrots, chopped
2 stalks celery, sliced
$\frac{3}{4}$ cup peeled tomatoes (or a small can)
1 slice lemon
soy sauce
salt and freshly ground black pepper
parsley

METHOD
Soak the beans overnight. Bring to a boil in a large pan of water (about 5 cups) and simmer until tender.

Meanwhile, heat the oil in a skillet and cook the onion and garlic until soft. Add the carrots, celery and tomatoes, in that order, stirring all the while.

Tip the vegetables into the pan with the cooked beans. Add the slice of lemon and soy sauce. Taste and adjust seasoning. Heat through and serve sprinkled with chopped parsley. The soup may be partly blended if you like.

Beet and Cabbage Borscht

INGREDIENTS *serves 6-8*
butter or margarine
2 slices bacon, chopped
4 cups peeled and diced cooked beets
2 tbsp flour
2 tbsp vinegar
9 cups finely shredded red cabbage
1 bay leaf
1 clove garlic, crushed
1 tbsp sugar
8¾ cups vegetable stock
salt and freshly ground black pepper
⅔ cup sour cream

METHOD
Heat the butter and fry the bacon. Add the beet and toss it for 1 minute. Add the flour and stir well off the heat. Return to the heat and add the vinegar, mixing it in well.

Add the cabbage, bay leaf, garlic, sugar, stock, salt and pepper. Bring to a boil and then simmer, covered, for 1 hour, adding a little more stock, if necessary. Serve hot with a generous spoonful of sour cream in each bowl.

◄ Waste-nothing vegetable stock
► Beet and cabbage borscht

Harvest Soup

INGREDIENTS *serves 4-6*
1-2 tsp oil
1 onion, chopped
2¼ cups peeled and diced pumpkin
2 cups sliced carrots
2 potatoes
juice of ½ lemon
5 cups stock
salt and freshly ground black pepper
1 zucchini, sliced (optional)
⅓ cup sliced, runner beans (optional)
basil leaves to garnish

METHOD
Heat oil in a large saucepan and fry onion until translucent.

Add pumpkin, carrots and potatoes and pour over lemon juice. Sweat, covered, for 5 minutes.

Add stock and seasoning and simmer until potatoes are cooked. Blend or part-blend the soup.

If liked, add the zucchini and beans and simmer for a further 4 minutes. Check seasoning.

Serve garnished with basil leaves. This soup can also be served sprinkled with Parmesan cheese.

► Cream of cauliflower soup
► ▼ Garlic soup
▼ Harvest soup

Cream of Cauliflower Soup

INGREDIENTS *serves 4*
1 small cauliflower
salt and freshly ground black pepper
4 tbsp butter
¼ cup unbleached all-purpose flour
6 tbsp light cream
1-2 egg yolks
1 tbsp chopped chives

METHOD
Trim the outer leaves off the cauliflower and steam it whole in boiling salted water in a pan with the lid on until tender. Allow the cauliflower to cool and reserve the water.

Melt the butter in a saucepan and stir in the flour. Gradually stir in the cauliflower water, made up to 3¾ cups with fresh water.

Reserve some of the cauliflower flowerets for garnishing. Discard the tougher stems and purée the rest in a blender. Add to the saucepan.

Beat the cream and egg yolks together in a bowl. Beat in some of the soup, then return to the pan. Add reserved cauliflower flowerets. Heat through but do not boil. Season and add chopped chives. Serve with triangles of hot toast.

Garlic Soup

INGREDIENTS *serves 4-6*
5 cups vegetable stock
4 garlic cloves, crushed
3 level tsp paprika
3 level tsp cumin
salt and pepper
2 pieces bread, toasted
oil
6 eggs (optional)

METHOD
Pour chicken stock into a pan, add the garlic, paprika and cumin, and bring to a boil. Season.

Break the toast into cubes and put into hot soup bowls.

Place a pan on the heat, lightly oil and fry the eggs until the white forms. Tip out 1 egg into each soup bowl and pour the boiling soup over.

Cheese and Onion Soup

INGREDIENTS *serves 4-6*
1-2 tbsp oil
2 medium onions, sliced
5 cups stock
½lb potatoes
1½ cups grated cheddar cheese
salt
soy sauce

METHOD
Heat oil in a large saucepan and stir-fry onions until lightly browned. Add stock and bring to a boil.

Meanwhile, peel the potatoes and grate them into the saucepan. Turn down the heat and simmer until potatoes have cooked and soup has thickened.

Add the grated cheese, stirring to melt. Season to taste with salt and soy sauce. Serve with whole-wheat bread and a crisp green salad.

Butter bean and Mushroom Chowder

INGREDIENTS *serves 4-6*
1 cup dried butter beans soaked
  overnight in cold water
1 tsp olive oil
2 onions, chopped
2 stalks celery, sliced
1⅓ cup peeled and diced potatoes
2 cups sliced button mushrooms
½ cup whole corn kernels
1¼ cups skim milk
salt and freshly ground black pepper
2 tbsp chopped parsley

METHOD
Drain the beans and place in a large saucepan covered with fresh water. Boil fast for 10 minutes, then simmer for a further 35-40 minutes, or until soft.

Drain the beans and reserve 2 cups of the stock.

Heat the oil in a large saucepan and gently fry the onion. Add the celery and potato and cook for 2-3 minutes, stirring from time to time. Add the reserved stock and mushrooms, bring to a boil, cover and simmer for 10 minutes.

Add the beans, corn and milk, bring to a boil then simmer for 2-3 minutes. Season to taste.

Serve in individual soup bowls sprinkled with parsley. Serve slices of whole-wheat bread separately.

Curried Squash Soup

INGREDIENTS *serves 4*
oil
1 large onion, chopped
2 tbsp curry powder
1 small squash (about 1½lb), peeled and
    chopped
4¼ cups vegetable stock
⅔ cup yogurt
2 tbsp mango chutney

METHOD
Heat the oil, add the onion and cook until it has just softened but not browned. Stir in the curry powder and cook it for 1 minute. Add the squash and stir well.

Pour in the stock. Bring to a boil and then simmer until the squash is soft.

Blend the soup in a food processor or blender and return it to the pan.

Keep the soup warm while you mix the yogurt and chutney together. Stir into the soup and serve immediately.

NOTE If you prefer to make this in advance, don't add the yogurt mixture until you reheat it. You could serve a little shredded coconut with this and additional chutney, if desired.

◄▲ Cheese and onion soup
◄ Butterbean and mushroom chowder
► Curried squash soup

Bean Sprout Soup

INGREDIENTS *serves 4*
8oz fresh bean sprouts
1 small red bell pepper, cored and
    deseeded
2 tbsp oil
2 tsp salt
2½ cups water
1 scallion, finely chopped

METHOD
Wash the bean sprouts in cold water, discarding the husks and other bits and pieces that float to the surface. It is not necessary to trim each sprout.

Thinly shred the red bell pepper.

Heat a wok or large pot, add the oil and wait for it to smoke. Add the bean sprouts and red bell pepper and stir a few times. Add the salt and water.

When the soup starts to boil, garnish with finely chopped scallion and serve hot.

Tomato and Egg Flower Soup

INGREDIENTS *serves 6*
9oz tomatoes
1 egg
2 scallions, finely chopped
1 tbsp oil
4¼ cups water
2 tbsp light soy sauce
1 tsp cornstarch mixed with 2 tsp water

METHOD
Peel the tomatoes by dipping them in boiling water for a minute or so and then peel them. Cut into large slices.

Beat the egg. Finely chop the scallions.

Heat a wok or pan over a high heat. Add the oil and wait for it to smoke. Add the scallions to flavor the oil and then pour in the water.

Drop in the tomatoes and bring to a boil.

Stir in the soy sauce and very slowly pour in the beaten egg. Add the cornstarch and water mixture. Stir for a few minutes and serve.

◄ Bean sprout soup
► Tomato and egg flower soup

Chinese Cabbage Soup

INGREDIENTS *serves 4-6*
9oz Chinese cabbage
3-4 dried Chinese mushrooms, soaked in
    warm water for 30 minutes
2 tbsp oil
2 tsp salt
1 tbsp rice wine or dry sherry
3¾ cups water
1 tsp sesame seed oil

METHOD
Wash the cabbage and cut it into thin slices. Squeeze dry the soaked mushrooms. Discard the hard stems and cut the mushrooms into small pieces. (Reserve the water in which the mushrooms have been soaked for use later.)

Heat a wok or large pot until hot, add the oil and wait for it to smoke. Add the cabbage and mushrooms and stir.

Add the salt, wine, water and the mushroom soaking water. Bring to a boil.

Stir in the sesame seed oil and serve.

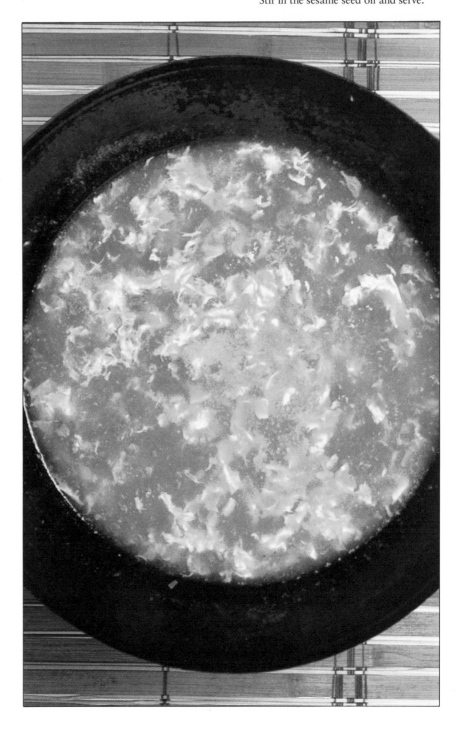

Cantonese Hot-and-Sour Soup

INGREDIENTS *serves 6*

3 dried Chinese mushrooms, soaked in
   warm water for 30 minutes
2 cakes tofu
½ cup Sichuan preserved vegetables
   (available from Oriental stores)
½ cup Chinese pickled vegetables, such
   as cucumber, cabbage or string beans
   (available from Oriental stores, or
   page 136)
2 scallions, finely chopped
2 slices ginger root, thinly shredded

3¾ cups water
1 tsp salt
2 tbsp rice wine or sherry
1 tbsp soy sauce
freshly ground pepper to taste
1 tsp sesame seed oil
1 tsp cornstarch blended with 2 tsp
   water

METHOD

Squeeze dry the mushrooms after soaking.
Discard the hard stems and cut mushrooms
into thin shreds. Reserve the water for use
later.

Thinly shred the tofu, Sichuan preserved
vegetables, pickled vegetables and ginger.
Finely chop the scallions.

In a wok or large pot, bring the water to a
boil. Add all the ingredients and seasonings
and simmer for 2 minutes.

Add the sesame seed oil and thicken the
soup by stirring in the cornstarch and water
mixture. Serve hot!

NOTE

A little vinegar can be added to the soup if
you find that the pickled vegetables do not
give a sour enough taste.

Chinese Mushroom Soup

INGREDIENTS *serves 4*
6 dried Chinese mushrooms
2 tsp cornstarch
1 tbsp cold water
3 egg whites
2 tsp salt
2½ cups water
1 scallion, finely chopped

METHOD
Soak the dried mushrooms in warm water for 25-30 minutes. Squeeze them dry, discard the hard stems and cut each mushroom into thin slices. Reserve the mushroom soaking water for use later.

Mix the cornstarch with the water to make a smooth paste. Comb the egg whites with your fingers to loosen them.

Mix the water and the mushroom soaking water in a pan and bring to a boil. Add the mushrooms and cook for about 1 minute. Now add the cornstarch and water mixture, stir and add the salt.

Pour the egg whites very slowly into the soup, stirring constantly.

Garnish with the finely chopped scallions and serve hot.

Corn and Asparagus Soup

INGREDIENTS *serves 4*
6oz white asparagus
1 egg white
1 tbsp cornstarch
2 tbsp water
2½ cups water
1 tsp salt
1 cup whole kernel corn
1 scallion, finely chopped, to garnish

METHOD
Cut the asparagus spears into small cubes.

Beat the egg white lightly. Mix the cornstarch with the water to make a smooth paste.

Bring the water to a rolling boil. Add the salt, corn and asparagus. When the water starts to boil again, add the cornstarch and water mixture, stirring constantly.

Add the egg white very slowly and stir. Serve hot, garnished with finely chopped scallions.

◄◄ Cantonese hot and sour soup
◄ Chinese mushroom soup

Red-hot Lentil Soup

INGREDIENTS *serves 6*
3 tbsp butter
1 large onion, chopped
1 clove garlic, chopped
1 slice fresh ginger root, unpeeled
1 slice lemon
1⅛ cups red lentils
7 cups water
salt
pinch of paprika
1 green chili, deseeded and chopped

METHOD
Heat 2 tbsp butter in a pan and add the onion, garlic, ginger and lemon. Sweat with the lid on over a low heat for 5 minutes.

Add the lentils and the water (small red lentils do not need to be presoaked) and season with salt and paprika. Cook for about 40 minutes until the lentils have thickened the soup.

Heat the remaining butter in a pan and quickly fry the chili. Serve the soup with chili topping.

Mushroom Soup

INGREDIENTS *serves 6*
butter or oil
1 large onion, sliced
6 cups sliced mushrooms
grated nutmeg
1 tbsp all-purpose flour
2 cups vegetable stock
1¼ cups yogurt
2 tbsp dry sherry (optional)

METHOD
Heat the butter and cook the onion until it has just softened but not browned. Add the mushrooms, stir and leave them to cook for 2 minutes. Add more butter if necessary.

Add the nutmeg and flour and stir well. Slowly add the stock, stirring until the mixture is smooth.

Bring the soup to a boil and then simmer for 5 minutes. Stir in the yogurt and just warm it through. Add the sherry. Serve hot.

Cream of Nettle Soup

INGREDIENTS *serves 6*
2lb young nettles
2 tbsp butter
1 small onion, chopped
¼ cup all-purpose flour
3¾ cups milk
salt and freshly ground black pepper
2 egg yolks
1 tbsp light cream
cream and croutons to serve

METHOD
Pick the young nettle leaves before the plants flower. Discard the stems, wash the leaves and press them into a pan with only the water that is clinging to them. Cover the pan and cook until soft (5-8 minutes). Purée in a blender.

Heat the butter in a pan and cook the onion until soft. Stir in the flour. Stir in a little milk and cook until thick. Stir in enough of the remaining milk to make a very thin sauce. Add the milk and the sauce to the nettles. Season well.

Beat the egg yolks with the cream. Stir in a little of the soup, then return to the pan. Heat through and check seasoning.

To serve, add a swirl of cream and some croutons to each individual bowl.

▲ ▲ Red-hot lentil soup
▲ Cream of nettle soup

Spinach Soup

INGREDIENTS *serves 4-6*
oil
1 large onion, sliced
$\frac{1}{2}$lb spinach, washed and picked over
1 clove garlic, crushed
$4\frac{1}{4}$ cups vegetable stock
$1\frac{1}{4}$ cups yogurt
salt and freshly ground black pepper

METHOD
Heat the oil, add the onion and cook until it has just softened but not browned. Add the spinach and garlic and stir.

Add the stock, bring to a boil and then simmer, covered, for 15 minutes.

Purée the soup, adding the yogurt slowly. Adjust the seasoning. Serve hot or cold.

NOTE
Use frozen spinach if you prefer, about 2 cups would do.

► Spinach soup

Pumpkin Soup

INGREDIENTS *serves 4-6*
1 tbsp sunflower oil
1 onion, chopped
12oz pumpkin or squash, peeled, seeds
   removed and diced
1$\frac{1}{3}$ cups diced carrots
2 potatoes, diced
2$\frac{1}{2}$ cups vegetable stock
2 small zucchini, thinly sliced
freshly ground black pepper
chopped parsley

METHOD
Place the oil and onion in a saucepan and cook for 2-3 minutes to soften.

Add the pumpkin or squash, carrots, potatoes and stock. Bring to a boil, cover and simmer for 15 minutes, or until the vegetables are nearly tender.

Add the zucchini and cook for 5 minutes more.

Purée half the soup, blend with the remaining soup and season with pepper to taste.

Reheat if necessary and serve in individual bowls. Make sure some of the zucchini float on the top to garnish.

Sprinkle with parsley to serve. The golden color of this soup, and its ingredients, make it an appropriately autumnal choice.

Watercress and Potato Soup

INGREDIENTS *serves 4-6*
butter or margarine
1 medium onion, chopped
3 cups peeled and sliced potatoes
2 bunches watercress
2$\frac{1}{2}$ cups vegetable stock
2 cups yogurt
1 egg
salt and freshly ground black pepper

METHOD
Heat the butter, add the onion and cook until it has just softened but not browned.

Add the potatoes and watercress and stir and leave on a low heat for 3 minutes. Pour in the stock and simmer for 20 minutes.

Mix the yogurt with the egg. When the potatoes are soft, purée the soup, adding the yogurt mixture slowly, as the machine is running. If you wish to serve warm, return to the saucepan, and stir over low heat to avoid curdling.

If you prefer the soup cold, chill for about 1 hour, then serve garnished with thinly sliced radish.

Chilled Apple Soup

INGREDIENTS *serves 6*
3 medium cooking apples, peeled and
   cored
$\frac{2}{3}$ cup water
$\frac{1}{3}$ cup sugar
juice of $\frac{1}{2}$ lemon
1 tbsp ground cinnamon
2 cloves
salt
1 tbsp white wine
scant 2 cups yogurt
$\frac{2}{3}$ cup sour cream (optional)

METHOD
Cube the apples and cook them with the water, sugar, lemon juice, cinnamon, cloves and salt to taste until they are soft. Remove the cloves and mash the apples and leave them to cool.

Add the wine and yogurt to the apples and mix together well. Serve, well chilled, with the sour cream if desired.

VARIATION
This Hungarian soup can be made with plums, pears, peaches or cherries. Reserve a little of the chosen fruit to garnish the soup.

These fruit "soups" – really purées – are traditionally served before meals of duck or goose, favorite Hungarian main courses. The sweet acid of the fruit complements the flavor of the birds and helps to cut their fatty richness.

◄ Pumpkin soup
► Chilled apple soup

Watercress Soup

INGREDIENTS *serves 4*
butter
1 large onion, chopped
1¹/₃ cups potatoes, peeled and diced
5 cups stock
salt and freshly ground black pepper
3 bunches watercress
cream

METHOD
Melt the butter in a large saucepan, add the
onion and cook, stirring, until transparent.

Add the potatoes, stock and seasoning.
bring to a boil, then simmer until potatoes
can be mashed with a fork.

Wash the watercress and discard tough
stems and yellow leaves. Reserve a few
sprigs for garnish, roughly chop the rest and
add to the soup. Continue cooking for 2
minutes.

Allow the soup to cool slightly, then
purée in a blender. Allow to cool completely.
Taste and adjust seasoning. Chill and serve
with sprigs of watercress to garnish and a
swirl of cream.

◀ Watercress soup
▶ Gazpacho

Carrot and Coriander Soup

INGREDIENTS *serves 6-8*
oil or butter
1 medium onion, sliced
9 cups sliced carrots
1 tsp ground coriander
3¾ cups vegetable stock
⅔ cup sour cream
salt and freshly ground black pepper
parsley to garnish

METHOD
Heat the oil, add the onion and cook until it has just softened but not browned. Add the carrots and coriander and stir well. Leave the carrots to cook gently for 3 minutes.

Pour in the stock and bring the mixture to a boil, then simmer, covered, for 25 minutes.

Purée the soup, adding the sour cream. Adjust the seasoning. Serve very cold, garnished with parsley.

Gazpacho

INGREDIENTS *serves 4-6*
1lb large ripe tomatoes
1 large onion
2 cloves garlic
1 green bell pepper
1 red bell pepper
½ cucumber
2 slices whole-wheat bread
3 tbsp olive oil
3 tbsp wine vinegar
1¼ cups tomato juice
1¼ cups water
salt and freshly ground black pepper

METHOD
Peel tomatoes, discard seeds and juice and chop the flesh. Peel and finely chop the onion and garlic. Remove pith and seeds from peppers and dice. Peel and dice the cucumber. Cut the crusts from the bread and dice.

Put vegetables and bread in a large bowl, pour over the remaining ingredients, stir and season. Chill well — overnight is best for a good tasty soup.

You can partly blend the soup if you wish, or blend all of it, in which case offer small bowls of chopped onions, tomatoes, peppers, cucumber and croutons as accompaniments.

Broccoli and Orange Soup

INGREDIENTS *serves 6*
1 medium onion, chopped
1 tbsp oil
1lb broccoli, chopped
juice of 2 oranges
2½ cups vegetable stock
1¼ cups yogurt
1 tbsp cornstarch
2 tbsp water
salt and freshly ground black pepper

METHOD
(Reserve some small pieces of broccoli for garnish, together with a little grated orange zest.) Heat the oil and cook the onion until it has just softened but not browned. Add the broccoli and stir around. Cook, covered, for a few minutes and then add the orange juice and stock. Bring to a boil, cover and simmer for about 20 minutes, until the broccoli is soft. Purée the soup in a blender. Mix the cornstarch and water to a smooth paste and stir into the soup with salt and pepper to taste. Return the soup to the heat and cook for a further 5 minutes. Serve, garnished with the reserved broccoli and the orange zest.

Use frozen broccoli if fresh is not available. Serve cold if preferred.

Persian Cucumber Soup

INGREDIENTS *serves 6*
1 large cucumber, finely grated
2½ cups yogurt
2 tbsp tarragon vinegar
dill
2 tbsp raisins soaked in 2 tbsp brandy
　for a few hours
2 hard-boiled eggs, finely chopped
1 large clove garlic, crushed
1 tsp sugar
⅔ cup cream
salt and freshly ground black pepper

METHOD
Combine all the ingredients and stir thoroughly. Refrigerate for a minimum of 3 hours and serve very cold.

VARIATION
John Tovey of the Miller Howe Hotel in the English Lake District has his own special twists to this classic Persian soup. He suggests adding or subtracting ingredients as you like. You may prefer mint or tarragon to dill, and chopped apples, celery, fennel, radishes can all be included.

Avocado Soup

INGREDIENTS *serves 4*
2 large ripe avocados
2½ cups yogurt
1 clove garlic, crushed
juice of 1 lemon
salt and freshly ground black pepper

METHOD
Halve the avocados, remove the seeds and peel the avocados. Blend all the ingredients together. Serve very well chilled, garnished with chives if desired.

NOTE
The thickness of the soup will depend as much on the size of the avocados as the thickness of the yogurt used. You can thin it down with a little milk or cream, if you need to.

Cold Tomato Soup

INGREDIENTS *serves 6-8*
2½ cups tomato juice
2½ cups yogurt
3 scallions, chopped
1 green bell pepper, chopped
1 large tomato, peeled and chopped
salt and freshly ground black pepper

METHOD
Blend the juice and yogurt and pour the mixture into a large bowl. Add the onions, pepper and tomato and season to taste. Serve well chilled, with some ice cubes floating in the soup.

VARIATION
You can add or subtract ingredients to this according to what you have handy. Try sliced avocados; shrimps; fresh basil; chopped olives; cucumber cut into fine dice; raw sliced mushrooms; chopped fennel; fried croutons.

▼ Persian cucumber soup

26

HORS D'ŒUVRES
AND APPETIZERS

International cuisine offers a wide selection of vegetarian and whole-food hors d'œuvres and appetizers. Vegetable pastes and pâtés take a variety of forms, from Greek hummus and Egyptian fava bean pâté to Mexican avocado guacamole and Italian-inspired zucchini molds. Stuffed vegetables – like eggplants and artichokes – and deep-fried mouthfuls, including Indian samosas, Chinese egg rolls and Bulgarian eggs, tempt from the four corners of the world.

Samosas

Hummus

INGREDIENTS *serves 4*
1⅓ cups garbanzo beans, soaked
   overnight
1 bouquet garni
1 small onion, sliced
2 cloves garlic, crushed
juice of 2 lemons
4 tbsp tahini paste
3 tbsp olive oil
salt and freshly ground black pepper
1 tomato, sliced
sprig of parsley

METHOD
Drain the garbanzo beans and place in a large saucepan with plenty of water, the bouquet garni and onion. Bring to a boil, then simmer gently for 1¾-2 hours, or until tender.

Drain, reserving a little of the cooking liquid. Discard the onion and bouquet garni.

Place the garlic, lemon juice, tahini, olive oil and seasoning in a food processor or blender. Add the cooked garbanzo beans and process to a smooth paste.

Add a little of the reserved cooking liquid if the paste is too thick, and stir rapidly.

Arrange the hummus in a dish, edge with halved tomato slices and garnish with parsley. Serve with warmed pita bread.

Guacamole

INGREDIENTS *serves 2-4*
2 large ripe avocados
2 large ripe tomatoes
1 bunch scallions
1-2 tbsp olive oil
1-2 tbsp lemon juice
salt and freshly ground black pepper
2 green chilies

METHOD
Remove the flesh from the avocados and mash. Peel the tomatoes, remove the seeds and chop finely. Chop the scallions.

Mix vegetables together with olive oil and lemon juice and season to taste. Garnish with chopped green chilies and serve, chilled, as a dip or with hot pita bread (see page 151).

Israeli Avocado Cream

INGREDIENTS *serves 4*
1 large avocado
⅓ cup cream cheese
½ small onion, finely chopped
dash Tabasco sauce
2 tbsp lemon juice
salt and freshly ground black pepper

METHOD
Mash the flesh of the avocado. Add the remaining ingredients, mixing them in very well. Spoon the mixture into a serving dish and cover it well. Refrigerate until required. Do not make this too long before you intend to serve it, as avocado discolors easily.

NOTE
Serve with raw vegetables or crackers as a dip or spread.

Yogurt and Tahini Dip

INGREDIENTS *serves 4-6*
2 cloves garlic, crushed
⅔ cup tahini paste
⅔ cup yogurt
juice of 2 lemons
salt and freshly ground black pepper
chopped parsley

METHOD
Blend everything together except the parsley until smooth. Taste and add more lemon juice and seasoning if necessary. Turn into a bowl and garnish with the chopped parsley.

NOTE
Serve as a dip, with pita or crackers, or as an accompaniment to vegetables, salads or meat or fish dishes.

◀ ▲ Hummus
◀ Guacamole
▶ Israeli avocado cream

Blue Cheese Pâté

INGREDIENTS *serves 4*
1¼ cups yogurt
1 cup crumbled blue cheese
2-4 tbsp light or heavy cream

METHOD
Drain the yogurt for about 5 hours. Remove the resulting cheese from the cloth carefully.

Purée the drained yogurt with the blue cheese and just enough cream to reach the required consistency. Refrigerate the mixture until required. It will firm up considerably.

NOTE
This mixture is useful as a filling for fruit (especially good with pears) or choux pastry, for stuffed tomatoes or celery, or as a salad dressing, in which case add more cream or creamy milk. Use ⅔ cup cottage cheese or low-fat cream cheese instead of the drained yogurt.

▶ Blue cheese pâté

Celery Mousse

INGREDIENTS *serves 4-6*
1 tbsp unflavored gelatin
2 tbsp hot water
1 medium head of celery with leaves,
   roughly chopped
$\frac{7}{8}$ cup yogurt
squeeze lemon juice
1 small onion
parsley
$\frac{3}{4}$ cup farmer's cheese
salt and freshly ground black pepper

METHOD
Dissolve the gelatin in the hot water. Blend all the remaining ingredients, except the farmer's cheese, feeding them into a blender or food processor a little at a time.

Add the dissolved gelatin and farmer's cheese and blend it into the mixture. Turn into a moistened mold (a small ring mold looks nice). Refrigerate until set. Unmold and serve as a part of a cold buffet, an accompaniment to cold meat or chicken or fish.

NOTE
For a richer version, substitute mayonnaise for the yogurt.

Fava Bean Pâté

INGREDIENTS *serves 4*
1½ cup shelled fava beans
about 1 cup cream cheese
salt and freshly ground black pepper
mint sprigs

METHOD
If the beans are old, remove the skins before or after cooking. Boil lightly in salted water until tender.

Mash or put through a vegetable mill with enough cream cheese to make a thick paste. Season with salt and pepper. Press into individual dishes and garnish each with a sprig of mint. Serve with triangles of whole-wheat toast.

 ▲ ▶ Celery mousse
▶ Fava bean pâté

Tarama Salad

INGREDIENTS *serves 6-8*
3 large potatoes
3 tbsp milk
4oz red caviar or red lumpfish roe
6 tbsp water
4 tbsp fresh lemon juice
1 small onion, finely chopped
¾ cup pure olive oil

METHOD
Peel the potatoes. Cook them in boiling water until very soft, about 20 minutes. Drain the potatoes and put them in a mixing bowl. By hand or with an electric mixer, mash the potatoes, slowly adding the milk, until smooth. Add the caviar and water to the potatoes. Mix well.

Stir the lemon juice and onion into the mixture and mix briefly. Slowly beat in the olive oil. Continue to beat until a smooth paste is formed.

Transfer to a serving bowl. Arrange *crudités* around the dip and serve.

Stuffed Peppers

INGREDIENTS *serves 4*
2 large green bell peppers (or 1 red and
   1 green)
1½ cups ricotta cheese
1 small pickled cucumber, finely
   chopped
1 tbsp chopped parsley
1 tbsp chopped dill (or half or dried)
salt and freshly ground black pepper
crisp lettuce to serve

METHOD
Remove the stem end of the peppers and discard the seeds. Mix the ricotta with the pickled cucumber, parsley, dill and salt and pepper.

Stuff the mixture into the peppers and refrigerate for several hours.

With a very sharp knife, cut the peppers into slices about ½in thick. Serve the pepper slices on a bed of crisp lettuce.

NOTE
Use cottage cheese if you prefer instead of the ricotta, or a mixture of low-fat soft cheeses.

▼ Tarama salad

Stuffed Tomatoes

INGREDIENTS *serves 4*
8 small tomatoes, or 3 large tomatoes
4 hard-boiled eggs, cooled and shelled
6 tbsp mayonnaise
1 tsp garlic paste
salt and freshly ground black pepper
1 tbsp chopped parsley
1 tbsp white bread crumbs for the large
   tomatoes

METHOD
Peel the tomatoes, first by cutting out the core with a sharp knife and making a '+' incision on the other end of the tomato. Then place in a pan of boiling water for 10 seconds, remove and plunge into a bowl of iced or very cold water (this latter step is to stop the tomatoes from cooking and going mushy).

Slice the tops off the tomatoes, and just enough of their bases to remove the rounded ends so that the tomatoes will sit upright on the plate. Keep the tops if using small tomatoes, but not for the large tomatoes.

Remove the seeds and inside, either with a teaspoon or small, sharp knife. Mash the eggs with the mayonnaise, garlic paste, salt, pepper and parsley.

Fill the tomatoes, firmly pressing the filling down. With small tomatoes, replace the lids at a jaunty angle. If keeping to serve later, brush them with olive oil and black pepper to prevent from drying out. Cover with plastic wrap and keep.

NOTE
For large tomatoes, the filling must be very firm, so it can be sliced. If you make your own mayonnaise, thicken it by using more egg yolks. If you use store-bought mayonnaise, add enough white bread crumbs until the mixture is the consistency of mashed potatoes. Season well, to taste. Fill the tomatoes, pressing down firmly until level. Refrigerate for 1 hour, then slice with a sharp carving knife into rings. Sprinkle with chopped parsley.

Tonno e Fagioli

INGREDIENTS *serves 4*
1½ cups canned red kidney beans,
   drained
1 onion chopped
7oz can tuna fish
handful chopped parsley
dash lemon juice
freshly ground black pepper

METHOD
Mix the beans with the onion. Drain the tuna fish, reserving the oil. Flake and add to the salad.

Add the parsley, a dash of lemon juice and plenty of black pepper. Toss and add some of the reserved fish oil and more lemon and pepper to taste.

▲ ◄ Stuffed tomatoes
◄ Tonno e fagioli

Zucchini Molds

INGREDIENTS *serves 4*
1lb zucchini, sliced
1 onion, chopped
2 tbsp lemon juice
2 tsp chopped fresh cilantro leaves
1/2 cup fromage blanc
salt and freshly ground black pepper
1 envelope unflavored gelatin
2/3 cup lowfat yogurt
5 tbsp skim milk
1 egg yolk
1 tsp curry paste

METHOD
Place the zucchini and onions in a saucepan with 2 tbsp water and the lemon juice. Cover and cook over a gentle heat for 8-10 minutes, or until softened.

Cool slightly and purée in a food processor or blender. Add the cilantro leaves, cheese and seasoning and purée until smooth. Leave until lukewarm.

Sprinkle the gelatin over 2 tbsp water in a cup. Stand in a saucepan of hot water and stir to dissolve. Add to the purée and pour into four 2/3 cup ramekin dishes. Chill for 1-1½ hours, until set.

Meanwhile, mix the yogurt, milk, egg yolk and curry paste together and heat gently until slightly thickened. Do not boil. Leave to cool.

Pour the sauce across the base of a serving dish, loosen the molds and turn out onto the dish. Garnish the tops of the molds with chervil and serve.

Mozzarella and Avocado Bees

INGREDIENTS *serves 2*
1 ripe avocado
4oz Mozzarella cheese
1 tbsp olive oil
1 tbsp tarragon vinegar
salt and freshly ground black pepper

METHOD
Cut the avocado in half and remove the seed. Carefully remove the skin from each half of the avocado. Lay the avocado halves flat-side downwards and cut horizontally into 1/4-1in slices.

Cut semi-circular slices from the Mozzarella, with 4 extra semi-circles for wings.

Arrange the cheese slices between the avocado slices to form the striped body of the bee, and arrange the wings at the sides.

Mix the oil and vinegar together and season well. Pour over the bees and serve.

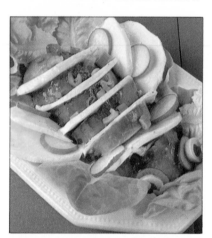

Vegetables in Aspic

INGREDIENTS *serves 4*
2½ cups aspic or equivalent
1 cup peeled and diced carrot
1 cup trimmed and sliced green beans
1 tbsp walnut oil
1 cup sliced button mushrooms
1 tbsp sliced stuffed olives
2/3 cup thick mayonnaise

METHOD
Prepare the aspic or equivalent and allow it to cool. Chill a mold. Wet the mold and when the aspic is almost set, line the mold with it. Place in the refrigerator to set.

Meanwhile, cook the carrot and green beans in salted water until tender. Refresh in cold water. Heat the walnut oil in a pan and gently sauté the mushrooms. Allow to cool.

Mix the vegetables together with the olives, mayonnaise and the remaining aspic and fill the mold. Chill until set.

Dip the mold into hot water and turn out onto a plate. Cut into wedges and serve each wedge with a crisp lettuce leaf and a triange of whole-wheat toast.

▶ Vegetables in aspic
◀ Mozzarella and avocado bees
▼ Zucchini molds

Summer Bouquet Mousse

INGREDIENTS *serves 4-6*
2 envelopes unflavored gelatin
2 tbsp warm water
2 eggs, separated, plus 1 egg white
²/₃ cup heavy cream
1 cup crumbled Roquefort cheese
3 tbsp sour cream
salt and freshly ground white pepper
few drops Tabasco sauce

THE BOUQUET
nasturtium flowers and leaves
borage flowers and leaves
summer savoury
sprigs of mint, fennel and dill

METHOD
Put the gelatin and water into a small bowl and stand it in a pan of simmering water. Stir well until the gelatin has dissolved.

Beat the egg yolks with half the heavy cream, the sour cream and the gelatin. Mash in the cheese. Whip the remaining heavy cream, fold into the mixture, season and add Tabasco sauce. Chill.

▲ Melon and Ugli fruit with lemon sauce

Beat the egg whites until soft peaks form. Fold them into the mixture. Oil a ring mold, pour in the mousse and chill until set.

Dip the mold into hot water, invert a plate over it and turn the mousse out. Fill the center with a pozy of edible flowers and delicate leafy herbs. This dish can form the centerpiece of a summer lunch in the garden. Serve with whole-wheat bread.

Melon and Ugli Fruit with Lemon Sauce

INGREDIENTS *serves 4*
2 Charentais melons
2 ugli fruit (or grapefruit) pith removed
   and segmented
2 tsp light brown unrefined sugar
juice of 2 lemons
grated zest of ¹/₂ lemon
lemon peel twists

METHOD
Halve the melons, remove the seeds and scoop out balls of flesh using a vegetable baller, leaving some flesh for later.

Cut the ugli fruit (or grapefruit) segments in half, if large, and mix with the melon.

Scoop out the remaining melon flesh from the skins and place in a food processor or blender. Add the sugar, lemon juice and rind and blend.

Pour over the fruit and chill until required. To serve, divide the fruit between 4 tall individual glass dishes. Decorate the glass sides with twists of lemon peel.

Date and Cream Cheese Spread

INGREDIENTS *makes 1 cup*
¼ cup cream cheese
2 tbsp milk
1½ cups finely chopped fresh dates
1 tbsp finely grated lemon zest.

METHOD
Mix the cheese with the milk to a smooth cream. Add the dates and lemon zest and mix together well.

NOTE
Fresh dates are so different from the more widely known semi-dried variety, familiar to us at Christmas time. They are not as sweet as the boxed ones and lend themselves to interesting combinations. This spread can be used on bread (try whole-wheat) or as a cocktail appetizer on small crackers.

VARIATION
Another delicious way to use fresh dates is to make a stuffing of cream cheese, with chopped raisins, chopped ginger or chopped nuts and fill the dates, which are left whole but with the pits removed.

Tomato and Mozzarella Salad

INGREDIENTS *serves 4*
2-3 large tomatoes, thinly sliced
4oz fresh Mozzarella cheese, thinly sliced
2 tbsp fresh shredded basil
6 tbsp extra virgin olive oil
salt and freshly ground black pepper

METHOD
Arrange the tomatoes and Mozzarella in alternating layers in a serving dish.
    Garnish the salad with the basil.
    Sprinkle the salad with the olive oil and with the salt and pepper. Serve.

◄ Summer bouquet mousse
► Date and cream cheese spread

Crudités with Hot Anchovy Dip

INGREDIENTS *serves 6-8*
a selection of crisp raw vegetables, cut
   into manageable pieces:
   carrots
   celery
   green, red and yellow bell peppers
   cucumber
   cauliflower flowerets
   radishes
   mushrooms

DIP
½ cup butter
2 cloves garlic, crushed
8 anchovy fillets
1¼ cups heavy cream

METHOD
Prepare the vegetables and arrange them on
a serving platter. Keep chilled.

Prepare the dip. Heat the butter in a pan
and add the garlic. Drain the anchovy fillets
and pat dry with paper towels. When the
garlic has softened, pound the anchovies
into the pan until you have a smooth paste.

Beat in the cream and bring back to a boil.
Cook, stirring until the dip has thickened.
Serve hot. If you use a small copper pan or a
fondue pan, you can serve the dip in the pan
you cooked it in.

▲ ▶ Garlic mushrooms
◀ Crudités with hot anchovy dip

Garlic Mushrooms

INGREDIENTS *serves 4-6*
6 tbsp butter
1½lb mushrooms, button or cap
few drops lemon juice
salt and freshly ground black pepper
2 cloves garlic, crushed
1 tbsp chopped cilantro or parsley

METHOD
Heat the butter in a large pan. Add the mushrooms and sweat gently, covered, for 5 minutes, shaking occasionally.

Add the lemon juice, salt and pepper. Increase the heat, tossing the mushrooms well. Add the garlic, toss and cook for 2 minutes.

Add the cilantro or parsley and cook for 1 minute. Remove from the heat and serve.

Stuffed Garlic Mushrooms

INGREDIENTS *serves 4*
16 open mushrooms, about 1½in across
2 slices whole-wheat bread, crumbled
²⁄₃ cup warm milk
4 cloves garlic
1 cup chopped fresh mixed herbs
oil
salt and freshly ground black pepper
few sprigs watercress

METHOD
Preheat the oven to 350°F.

Wipe the mushroom caps clean. Remove, chop and reserve stems. Soak the bread crumbs in milk until soft, then squeeze out the excess milk.

In a mortar, pound the garlic with herbs and enough oil to make a paste. Pound in the stems. Mix together with the bread crumbs and season well with salt and pepper.

Spoon the filling into the mushroom caps and arrange them in a lightly oiled baking dish. Bake for about 15 minutes until mushrooms are soft and juicy and filling has crisped a little on the top. Serve hot with sprigs of watercress.

Vegetarian Egg Rolls

INGREDIENTS *serves 4*
20 frozen egg roll skins
8oz fresh bean sprouts
8oz young tender leeks or scallions
4oz carrots
4oz white mushrooms
oil for deep-frying
1½ tsp salt
1 tsp sugar
1 tbsp light soy sauce

METHOD
Take the egg roll skins out of the package and leave them to defrost thoroughly under a damp cloth.

Wash and rinse the bean sprouts in a bowl of cold water and discard the husks and other bits and pieces that float to the surface. Drain.

Cut the leeks or scallions, carrots and mushrooms into thin shreds.

Heat 3-4 tbsp of oil in a preheated wok or skillet and stir-fry all the vegetables for a few seconds. Add the salt, sugar and soy sauce and continue stirring for 1-1½ minutes. Remove and leave to cool a little.

Cut each egg roll in half diagonally. Place about 2 tsp of the filling on the skin about a third of the way down, with the triangle pointing away from you. Lift the lower flap over the filling and roll once, then fold in both ends and roll once more.

Brush the upper edge with a little flour-and-water paste and roll into a neat package. Repeat until all filling is used up.

Heat about 6⅓ cups oil in a wok or deep-fryer until it smokes. Reduce the heat or even turn it off for a few minutes to cool the oil a little before adding the egg rolls. Deep-fry 6-8 at a time for 3-4 minutes or until golden and crispy. Increase the heat to high again before frying each batch. As each batch is cooked, remove and drain it on paper towels. Serve hot with a dip sauce such as soy sauce, vinegar, chili sauce or mustard.

NOTE
These egg rolls are ideal for a buffet-style meal or as cocktail snacks. (They can also be frozen for up to 3 months.)

Sichuan-style Cucumber

INGREDIENTS *serves 4*
1 cucumber
1 tsp salt
2 tbsp sugar
2 tbsp vinegar
1 tbsp chili oil

METHOD
Split the cucumber in two lengthwise and then cut each piece into strips rather like French fries. Sprinkle with the salt and leave for about 10 minutes to extract the bitter juices.

Remove each cucumber strip. Place it on a firm surface and soften it by gently tapping it with the blade of a cleaver or knife.

Place the cucumber strips on a plate. Sprinkle the sugar evenly over them and then add the vinegar and chili oil just before serving.

▶ Crispy seaweed
▼ Vegetarian egg rolls

Crispy Seaweed

INGREDIENTS *serves 4*
1¾lb spring greens
2½ cups oil for deep-frying
1 tsp salt
1 tsp sugar

METHOD
Wash and dry the spring green leaves and shred them with a sharp knife into the thinnest possible shavings. Spread them out on paper towels or put in a large colander to dry thoroughly.

Heat the oil in a wok or deep-fryer. Before the oil gets too hot, turn off the heat for 30 seconds. Add the spring green shavings in several batches and turn the heat up to medium high. Stir with a pair of cooking chopsticks.

When the shavings start to float to the surface, scoop them out gently with a slotted spoon and drain on paper towels to remove as much of the oil as possible. Sprinkle the salt and sugar evenly on top and mix gently. Serve cold.

VARIATION
Deep-fry ½ cup split almonds until crisp and add to the "seaweed" as a garnish, to give the dish a new dimension.

Devilled Eggs

INGREDIENTS *serves 4*
4 hard-boiled eggs, cut in half,
    lengthwise
1½ tbsp finely chopped onions
2 green chilis, finely chopped
1 tbsp chopped fresh cilantro leaves
½ tsp salt
2 tbsp mashed potatoes
oil for deep frying
1 tbsp all-purpose flour
¼ cup water

METHOD

Remove the yolks and mix with the onions, chilis, cilantro leaves, salt and mashed potatoes. Put the mixture back into the egg whites. Chill for 30 minutes.

Heat the oil in a karai or wok over high heat. While the oil is heating up make a batter with the flour and water. Be careful not to allow the oil to catch fire.

Dip the eggs into the batter and slip into the hot oil. Fry until golden, turning once.

Stuffed Eggplants

INGREDIENTS *serves 4-8*
4 eggplants
olive oil
1 large onion, chopped
2-3 cloves garlic, crushed
4 large tomatoes, peeled and chopped
2 tbsp chopped fresh herbs
salt and freshly ground black pepper
4oz Mozzarella cheese
4 tbsp whole-wheat bread crumbs
a little butter

METHOD

Preheat the oven to 400°F. Wash the eggplants. Cut in half lengthwise and score the cut surface deeply with a knife. Sprinkle with salt and leave, cut surface down, for 30 minutes.

Meanwhile, heat 1-2 tbsp oil in a pan and fry the onion and garlic until translucent. Transfer to a bowl and mix in the tomatoes and chopped herbs.

Add more oil to the pan. Rinse the eggplants and pat dry. Place them cut surface down in the pan and cook gently for about 15 minutes. They absorb a lot of oil,

▼ Stuffed eggplants   ▲ Devilled eggs

so you will need to keep adding a little more.

Scoop some of the flesh out of the eggplants, mash and mix it with the rest of the filling. Season well. Pile the filling onto the eggplants and top with thinly sliced Mozzarella. Sprinkle with bread crumbs and dot with butter. Place eggplants in a greased baking dish and bake for 20 minutes until the cheese has melted and the bread crumbs are crispy.

Bulgarian Eggs

INGREDIENTS *serves 4*
1¼ cups yogurt
1 small clove garlic, crushed
salt and freshly ground black pepper
2 tbsp butter, melted
½ tsp paprika

METHOD
Softly poach the eggs. Mix the yogurt with the garlic, salt and pepper and warm it through gently but don't let it boil. Spoon it into 4 shallow dishes. Place 1 egg, well drained, into each dish. Add the paprika to the melted butter and drizzle it onto the eggs. Serve immediately, with hot French bread or pita.

▼ Artichokes with Tomato Sauce

NOTE
This amount makes a good appetizer or very light supper dish. Double the quantity for a more substantial meal.

Artichokes with Tomato Sauce

INGREDIENTS *serves 4*
4 large artichokes
1-2 tbsp oil
1 large onion, chopped
2 cloves garlic, chopped
1½ cups mashed tomatoes
1 tbsp tomato paste
2 tsp chopped fresh oregano
lemon juice
salt and freshly ground black pepper

METHOD
Rinse the artichokes thoroughly under cold water and leave them upside down to drain. Bring a very large pan of salted water to a boil, put the artichokes in and boil fast for 30-50 minutes, depending on the size. When an outer leaf comes away at a gentle tug, the artichokes are ready.

Meanwhile, make the sauce. Heat the oil in a pan and fry the onion and garlic until transparent. Add the tomatoes, tomato paste and oregano and reduce until the sauce is of pouring consistency but not sloppy. Season with salt and pepper and a dash of lemon juice to taste.

Drain the artichokes. When cool, pull out the tiny inner leaves together with the hairy inedible choke. Spoon in some tomato sauce. Stand each artichoke in a pool of sauce on an individual dish and serve.

Pakoras

INGREDIENTS *makes enough for 1lb vegetables*
4 tbsp garbanzo bean flour
2 tsp oil
1 tsp baking powder
½ tsp salt
6 tbsp water
Any of the following vegetables can be used:
   eggplants, cut into very thin rounds
   onions, cut into ⅛in rings

potatoes, cut into very thin rounds
cauliflower, cut into ¾in flowerets
chili, left whole
pumpkin, cut into thin slices
green bell pepper, cut into thin strips
oil for deep frying

METHOD

Mix all the batter ingredients together and beat until smooth. Wash the slices of vegetables and pat dry.

Heat the oil in a karai or wok till very hot. Dip a slice of the vegetable in the batter and put into the hot oil. Place as many slices as you can in the oil. Fry till crisp and golden. Drain and serve with mint or cilantro chutney (page 134).

Samosas

INGREDIENTS *serves 4-6*
3 tbsp oil
¼ tsp whole cumin seeds
4 cups potatoes cut into ½in cubes
1 green chili, finely chopped
pinch turmeric
½ tsp salt
scant ½ cup peas
1 tsp ground roasted cumin (oven-roasted for 5 minutes)

DOUGH

2¼ cups all-purpose flour
1 tsp salt
3 tbsp oil
scant ½ cup oil for deep frying

METHOD

Heat the oil in a karai over medium high heat and add the cumin seeds. Let them sizzle for a few seconds.

Add the potatoes and green chili and fry for 2-3 minutes. Add the turmeric and salt and, stirring occasionally, cook for 5 minutes.

Add the peas and the ground roasted cumin. Stir to mix. Cover, lower heat and cook a further 10 minutes until the potatoes are tender. Cool.

Meanwhile, sift together the flour and salt. Rub in the oil. Add enough water to form a stiff dough. Knead for 10 minutes until smooth.

Divide into 12 balls. Roll each ball into a circle of about 6in across. Cut in half. Pick up one half, flatten it slightly and form a cone, sealing the overlapping edge with a little water. Fill the cone with 1½ tsp of the filling and seal the top with a little water. In a similar way make all the samosas.

Heat oil in a karai or wok over medium heat. Put in as many samosas as you can into the hot oil and fry until crisp and golden. Drain. Serve with a chutney.

◄ Pakoras

SALADS

Salads today have come far beyond the tossed green version. All kinds of vegetables – and fruit – homely and exotic, have joined the cast list in the modern salad repertoire. The influence of Californian and nouvelle cuisines vie with that of the East to make your choice as interesting as possible.

Pear salad

Tomato Salad with Modern Vinaigrette

INGREDIENTS *serves 4*
3 large tomatoes
½ onion, finely sliced
few ripe olives
1¼ cups Modern Vinaigrette (see page 128)

METHOD
Slice the tomatoes horizontally. Arrange either in a large bowl with onion in between layers, or on a large plate. Sprinkle with ripe olives.

Dredge the tomatoes with the dressing and serve.

NOTE
If keeping to serve later, add the dressing 20 minutes before required.

▲ Tomato Salad with Modern Vinaigrette

Swedish Tomato Salad

INGREDIENTS *serves 6*
6 large tomatoes, seeded and halved
¾ cup walnut oil
6 tbsp white-wine vinegar
2 garlic cloves, crushed
¾ tsp dried dill
¼ tsp sugar
¼ tsp honey
½ tsp Dijon-style mustard
2 tbsp chopped fresh chives
½ tsp salt
¼ tsp freshly ground black pepper
6 to 8 lettuce leaves
6 fresh parsley sprigs

METHOD
Put the tomatoes, cut-side down, in a shallow dish.

Put the walnut oil, vinegar, garlic, dill, sugar, honey, mustard, chives, salt and pepper in a jar with a tightly fitting lid. Cover tightly and shake vigorously until all the ingredients are blended.

Pour the dressing over the tomatoes. Chill the salad for 2½ hours. Spoon the dressing over the tomatoes every 30 minutes.

Line a serving dish with lettuce leaves. Remove the tomatoes from the dressing and place them on the lettuce leaves. Pour the dressing over the tomatoes. Garnish with the parsley sprigs and serve.

Italian Fontina Cheese Salad

INGREDIENTS *serves 6*
2 large sweet yellow bell peppers, seeded and halved
2 large sweet red bell peppers, seeded and halved
8oz Fontina cheese, diced
2oz pitted green olives, thinly sliced
6 tbsp pure olive oil
1½ tsp Dijon-style mustard
3 tbsp light cream
1 tbsp chopped scallion
¾ tsp salt
1 tsp freshly ground black pepper
1 tbsp chopped fresh parsley

METHOD
Preheat the broiler. Place the yellow and red peppers on a cookie tray and broil until the skins are blistered and slightly blackened, about 10-15 minutes. Remove the peppers from the heat.

When the peppers are cool enough to handle, remove the blistered skin. Cut the peppers into strips about ⅛in wide. Put the pepper strips, Fontina cheese and olives in a serving bowl.

Put the olive oil, mustard, cream, scallion, salt and pepper in a jar with a tightly fitting lid. Cover tightly and shake until well blended.

Pour the dressing over the salad and toss. Chill the salad for 1 to 2 hours. Garnish with the chopped parsley and toss again lightly before serving.

Japanese Cucumber Salad

INGREDIENTS *serves 4*
2 medium-sized cucumbers, thinly sliced
1 tsp salt
4 tbsp rice wine vinegar
2 tbsp soy sauce
1 tsp sugar
2 tsp white sesame seeds

METHOD
Put the cucumber slices in a colander. Sprinkle with the salt. Let the cucumber slices drain for 30 minutes.

Remove the cucumber slices from the colander. Put the slices between two layers of paper towels and pat them dry.

Into a jar with a tightly fitting lid, put the vinegar, soy sauce and sugar. Cover tightly and shake well until the sugar dissolves.

Put the cucumber slices in a salad bowl. Add the dressing and toss lightly.

Toast the sesame seeds in a dry skillet over a high heat, shaking the pan frequently. When the seeds begin to jump, remove them from the pan and crush them with a pestle. Sprinkle the crushed sesame seeds on the salad and serve.

▲ Japanese cucumber salad

Pine Nuts and Watercress

INGREDIENTS *serves 4*
2 tbsp pine nuts
2 large bunches watercress
2 cups finely chopped fresh parsley
1 cup finely chopped fresh chives
¾ cup Lemon Dressing (see page 131)

METHOD
Preheat the oven to 350°F. Put the pine nuts on a cookie sheet and toast them in the oven until browned, about 8-10 minutes.

Put the watercress, parsley and chives in a salad bowl. Add the Lemon Dressing and toss. Add the pine nuts and toss again.

Orange and Walnut Salad

INGREDIENTS *serves 4*
3 plump heads Belgian endive
2 large sweet oranges, peel and pith
    removed, segmented
¾ cup chopped walnuts

MUSTARD DRESSING
2 tbsp walnut oil
pinch mustard powder
1 tbsp orange juice
1 tbsp lemon juice

METHOD
Mix the endive slices, oranges and half the
walnuts together and place in a serving dish.
    Sprinkle the remaining walnuts over.
    Beat the walnut oil and mustard powder
together, then gradually beat in the orange
and lemon juices.
    Pour the dressing over the salad and serve
immediately.

Mixed Greens and Mushrooms with Raspberry Vinaigrette

INGREDIENTS *serves 4*
4 tbsp pine nuts
2 heads cabbage lettuce or other soft
    lettuce
2 heads Belgian endive
1 small head radicchio
8oz stemmed small mushrooms

RASPBERRY VINAIGRETTE
4 tbsp olive oil
2 tbsp raspberry vinegar
1 finely chopped shallot
1 tsp Dijon-style mustard
2 tsp light cream
salt and freshly ground black pepper to
    taste

METHOD
Preheat the oven to 350°F. Place the pine
nuts in a shallow baking dish and toast them
in the oven until lightly browned, about 5
minutes. Remove from oven and set aside.
    Wash and gently dry the cabbage lettuce,
endive and radicchio. Tear the lettuce and
radicchio into bite-sized pieces. Cut the
endive into thin slices. Put the greens into a
large salad bowl. Add the mushrooms and
toasted pine nuts.
    In a mixing bowl combine the olive oil,
vinegar, shallot, mustard, cream, salt and
pepper. Whisk until the vinaigrette is
smooth and well blended.
    Pour the vinaigrette over the greens and
toss well. Serve at once.

▲◄ Orange and walnut salad
◄ Mixed greens and mushroom salad
with raspberry vinaigrette

Orange and Mixed Green Salad

INGREDIENTS *serves 4*
1/2 head cabbage lettuce or mignonette lettuce
2 large navel oranges
1 1/3 cups carrots cut in strips
1/3 cup golden raisins or currants
3/4 cup Cheese Herb Dressing (see page 130)

METHOD
Tear the lettuce into bite-sized pieces. Arrange them in a salad bowl. Peel the oranges and divide them into segments. Cut each segment into halves or thirds. Add the pieces to the salad bowl. Add the carrots and raisins to the salad bowl and toss. Pour on the Cheese Herb Dressing and toss.

Garden Mixed Green Salad

INGREDIENTS *serves 6-8*
1 head cabbage lettuce or garden lettuce
1 medium-sized head romaine lettuce
3 heads Belgian endive
1 stalk celery, chopped
3 hard-boiled eggs, sliced
4oz watercress, thick stems removed, coarsely chopped
1/2 medium-sized onion, sliced into rings
2 large tomatoes, peeled and cut in to wedges
2/3 cup pickled beet, cut in strips
2 tbsp chopped fresh parsley
1 1/4 cups Rich French Dressing (see page 129)

METHOD
Line the salad bowl with some leaves of the cabbage or garden lettuce.

Tear the remaining cabbage lettuce and the romaine lettuce into bite-sized pieces. Add them to the salad bowl.

Cut the endive into bite-sized pieces. Add them to the salad bowl.

Add the celery, eggs, watercress, onion rings and tomatoes to the salad bowl. Toss gently. Refrigerate until ready to serve.

Before serving, add the beet, parsley and Rich French dressing. Toss and serve.

▼ Orange and mixed green salad

Chicory and Alfalfa Salad

INGREDIENTS *serves 4-6*
½ small chicory, torn into pieces
4oz alfalfa sprouts
2oz small button mushrooms, thinly
    sliced
½ red bell pepper, sliced

DRESSING
juice of 1 lemon
2tsp olive oil
1 small onion, grated
¼tsp Chinese five-spice powder

METHOD
Arrange the chicory on a large serving plate
or 4 individual plates.

Mix the alfalfa sprouts, mushrooms and
pepper together in a bowl.

Mix the dressing ingredients together
and add to the bowl of vegetables. Toss well
and arrange on top of the lettuce.

California Waldorf Salad

INGREDIENTS *serves 6*
3½oz mung bean sprouts or alfalfa
    sprouts
3 tart apples, cored and diced but not
    peeled
2⅔ cup chopped celery
½ cup slivered almonds
3 large mushrooms, coarsely chopped
1 cup Yogurt Mayonnaise (see page 131)
10 lettuce leaves
3½oz seedless grapes, halved

METHOD
Blanch the bean sprouts in a pan of boiling
water for 45 seconds. Drain and rinse in
cold water. Drain well again. Coarsely chop
the bean sprouts.

Put the apple, celery, almonds and
mushrooms in a large mixing bowl. Mix
well with a wooden spoon.

Add the Yogurt Mayonnaise and mix
thoroughly.

Line a serving platter with the lettuce
leaves. Mound the bean sprouts in the
center. Transfer the mixed ingredients to the
platter and garnish with the halved grapes.

Classic Waldorf Salad

INGREDIENTS *serves 2 - 4*
8 stalks crisp celery
2 rozy-skinned dessert apples
lemon juice
½ cup walnuts
6 tbsp good mayonnaise
salt and freshly ground black pepper

METHOD
If the celery is not crisp, immerse it in ice-
cold water. It will soon freshen up. Pat dry
and slice.

Core the apples but do not peel - the pink
skin will give color contrast to the salad.
Slice and sprinkle with lemon juice to
prevent discoloring. Toss all the ingredients
in the mayonnaise and season well.

VARIATION
This salad also tastes good with blue cheese
dressing. Blend the mayonnaise with 1 tbsp
blue cheese before adding to the salad.

▲ ▲ Chicory and alfalfa salad
▲ California Waldorf salad
▶ Waldorf salad

50

Greek Salad

INGREDIENTS *serves 4*
1 head crunchy lettuce, shredded
2 Mediterranean tomatoes, sliced
½ cucumber, thinly sliced
1 onion, coarsely chopped
handful ripe olives
1½ cup cubed feta cheese
olive oil
salt and freshly ground black pepper

METHOD
Combine the vegetables and cheese in a
large bowl. Pour over enough olive oil to just
coat the salad. Season well and toss.

Chill for 1 hour. Toss again, check
seasoning and serve.

Strawberry and Avocado Salad

INGREDIENTS *serves 2*
1 ripe avocado
6oz strawberries
1 tbsp strawberry vinegar
1 tbsp olive oil
freshly ground black pepper

METHOD
Cut avocado in half lengthwise and remove
the seed. Carefully remove the flesh from the
skin in one piece, using a metal spoon or
spatula. Cut each half into slices and
arrange around the edge of the serving
plate.

Hull and slice the strawberries. Pile in the
middle of the plate.

Mix together the strawberry vinegar and
olive oil and pour over salad. Season with
lots of black pepper.

▶ Greek salad

Avocado and Grapefruit Salad

INGREDIENTS *serves 6*
1 ripe avocado
2 tbsp fresh lemon juice
1 head romaine lettuce
3½ cups seeded grapefruit segments
1 red onion, thinly sliced
1 cup Rich French Dressing (see page 128)

METHOD
Peel the avocado and cut it into slices. Put the slices in a bowl and sprinkle with the lemon juice.

Tear the lettuce into bite-sized pieces. Put the lettuce in a salad bowl. Add the grapefruit, avocado and onion to the salad bowl. Pour the French dressing over. Refrigerate for 30 minutes before serving.

Russian Radish and Cucumber Zakusky

INGREDIENTS *serves 4-6*
2 hard-boiled eggs, shelled
1 cup sour cream
¾ tsp salt
1 tsp freshly ground black pepper
3 tbsp chopped fresh dill
2 cups thinly sliced radishes
1 large cucumber, peeled, seeded and thinly sliced

METHOD
Remove the yolks from the eggs. Put them in a small mixing bowl and mash well with a fork. Chop the whites and set them aside.

Add the sour cream, salt, pepper and 2 tbsp of the dill to the mixing bowl. Stir until well blended.

Arrange the radishes and cucumber slices on a serving platter. Add the egg yolk and sour cream mixture. Garnish with the remaining dill and the chopped egg whites, and serve with black bread and small glasses of vodka in the Russian manner.

▼ Avocado and grapefruit salad

Cauliflower, Blue Cheese and Yogurt Salad

INGREDIENTS *serves 4*
1 head cauliflower
4 tbsp yogurt
2 tbsp blue cheese, softened
4 tbsp chopped fresh parsley
salt and freshly ground black pepper

METHOD
Cut the cauliflower into tiny flowerets - reserve the stems for use in a soup.

Cream the yogurt and blue cheese together. Toss the cauliflower and parsley in the dressing and season well.

Summer Macaroni Salad

INGREDIENTS *serves 6 - 8*
¾ cup mayonnaise
2 tsp Dijon-style mustard
1 tbsp white-wine vinegar
¼ tsp celery seeds
4 cups cooked macaroni
3½oz chopped celery
¾ cup chopped carrots
2oz sliced radishes
3 tbsp chopped pimiento-stuffed green olives
3 tbsp chopped red bell pepper
5 tbsp chopped scallions
2 tbsp chopped fresh parsley
¾ tsp salt
¼ tsp freshly ground black pepper

METHOD
Put the mayonnaise, mustard, vinegar and celery seeds in a small mixing bowl. Beat with a fork or an electric mixer until well blended.

Put the macaroni in a large serving bowl and add the mayonnaise mixture. Toss until the macaroni is well coated. Add the celery, carrots, radishes, olives, red peppers, scallions and parsley. Toss well. Add the salt and pepper. Toss lightly.

Cover the bowl and chill for 1½ hours. Remove from the refrigerator and serve.

▲ ◄ Cauliflower, blue cheese and yogurt salad
◄ Summer macaroni salad

Mild Cheddar Salad

INGREDIENTS *serves 2*
4oz mild cheddar cheese
1 bunch watercress
2 handfuls young spinach leaves
2 large Mediterranean tomatoes
1 cup mushrooms
6-8 scallions
2 tbsp olive oil
1 tbsp wine vinegar
1-2 tsp mustard powder
salt and freshly ground black pepper

METHOD
Cube the cheese. Wash the spinach and watercress, discarding stems and any tough or yellow leaves. Immerse the tomatoes in boiling water until their skins split, then refresh with cold water, peel and roughly chop. Slice the mushrooms. Trim the scallions; make several lengthwise cuts around each into the onion and spread out the layers in a decorative fashion.

Make the dressing by combining the oil, vinegar, mustard and seasonings.

Combine the watercress, spinach, tomatoes and mushrooms in a salad bowl, add the dressing and toss. Top with the cheese and onions.

Coleslaw

INGREDIENTS *serves 6*
1 small crisp head white cabbage
8oz carrots
2 tbsp chopped chives
$\frac{1}{3}$ cup golden raisins
1 tbsp sesame seeds
$\frac{1}{2}$ cup Mayonnaise (see page 128)

METHOD
Shred the cabbage finely, discarding the core. Grate the carrots.

Toss all the ingredients together in the Mayonnaise and mix well. Taste and adjust seasoning. Chill overnight in the refrigerator. Mix well again before serving.

▶ ▲ Mild Cheddar salad

Middle Eastern Coleslaw

INGREDIENTS *serves 4-6*
6 cups coarsely shredded cabbage
2 - 3 tbsp salt
1 cup fresh orange juice
3 tbsp fresh lemon juice
$\frac{1}{4}$ tsp sugar
$\frac{1}{2}$ tsp honey
1 tsp hot red-pepper flakes
2 tsp white-wine vinegar
$\frac{1}{2}$ tsp salt

METHOD
Put the shredded cabbage in a colander. Sprinkle the 2-3 tbsp of salt over the cabbage and let stand for 1 hour.

Rinse the salt from the cabbage. Drain. Wrap the cabbage in a dish towel and squeeze as much liquid from it as possible.

Put the orange juice, lemon juice, sugar, honey, hot red-pepper flakes, vinegar and salt in a salad bowl. Stir until mixed. Add the cabbage to the salad bowl and toss well.

Potato Salad with Horseradish

INGREDIENTS *serves 4*
1¹/₂lb new potatoes
²/₃ cup sour cream
3 tbsp finely grated horseradish
pinch paprika
¹/₂ tsp honey
salt and freshly ground black pepper
bunch scallions or chives
handful chopped fresh parsley

METHOD
Wash the potatoes, but do not peel. Boil in salted water until tender.

Meanwhile, make the dressing. Combine the sour cream with the horseradish, paprika and honey. Mix well and season with salt and pepper.

Trim the scallions and slit down the stems so that they curl outwards. Chop the chives.

When the potatoes are done, slice them while still hot and mix into the dressing with the parsley. Toss in the onions or chives. Serve immediately, or chill and serve cold.

Traditional Potato Salad

INGREDIENTS *serves 4-6*
7 medium-sized potatoes, peeled, cooked and diced
1 medium-sized onion, finely chopped
2 tbsp finely chopped pimiento-stuffed green olives
1¹/₃ cup sliced celery
2 hard-boiled eggs, chopped
³/₄ cup mayonnaise
2 tbsp wine vinegar
¹/₂ tsp salt
1 tsp freshly ground black pepper
2 tbsp chopped fresh parsley

METHOD
In a salad bowl, put the potatoes, onion, olives, celery and eggs. Mix lightly.

Add the mayonnaise, vinegar, salt and pepper. Toss to coat all the ingredients. Garnish with parsley and serve.

Italian Zucchini Salad

INGREDIENTS *serves 4*
2 medium-sized zucchini
8 tbsp pure olive oil
3 tbsp red-wine vinegar
1 scallion, white part only, finely chopped
¹/₂ tsp dried basil
large pinch dried oregano
large pinch dried marjoram
1 garlic clove, crushed
¹/₄ tsp salt
2 tbsp chopped fresh parsley
¹/₂ tsp freshly ground black pepper

METHOD
Cook the zucchini in a pot of salted boiling water for 7-8 minutes. Drain well and rinse in very cold water for 5 minutes. Drain again. Slice the zucchini thinly.

Put the olive oil, vinegar, scallion, basil, oregano, marjoram, garlic and salt in a jar with a tightly fitting lid. Cover tightly and shake until well blended.

Put the zucchini and the dressing in a salad bowl. Toss very gently. Let stand for 15-20 minutes. Sprinkle with parsley and pepper and serve.

German Potato Salad

INGREDIENTS *serves 6*
6 large potatoes or 2lb small potatoes
4 whole scallions, finely chopped
1 garlic clove, finely chopped
1 tsp drained capers
2 tbsp chopped fresh dill
2 tbsp chopped fresh parsley
1 tsp salt
1 tsp freshly ground black pepper
5 tbsp pure olive oil
3 tbsp wine vinegar
1 tbsp vegetable stock (optional)
$\frac{1}{2}$ tsp sugar

METHOD
Cook the potatoes, in their skins, in a large pot of lightly salted boiling water. Drain well, peel while warm and dice. (Leave small potatoes whole and unpeeled, if you prefer.)

Put the potatoes in a salad bowl and add the scallions, garlic, capers, dill and parsley. Toss lightly.

Into a jar with a tightly fitting lid, put the salt, pepper, olive oil, vinegar, vegetable stock and sugar. Cover and shake until blended.

Pour the dressing over the potato salad and toss lightly. Let stand at room temperature for $1\frac{1}{2}$ hours before serving.

▲ ◄ Potato salad with horseradish
► German potato salad

Lentil and Feta Cheese Salad

INGREDIENTS *serves 6*
2 cups brown lentils
1 bay leaf
1/2 tsp dried basil
2 garlic cloves, crushed
1 stalk celery, finely chopped
1 small onion, chopped
3 tbsp chopped fresh chives
1 1/2 cups crumbled feta cheese
6 tbsp virgin olive oil
3 tbsp wine vinegar
large pinch dried oregano
salt and freshly ground black pepper

METHOD
Put the lentils in a bowl. Add 3 cups cold water and soak the lentils for 2 hours. Drain.

Put the lentils in a saucepan and add enough cold water to cover them completely. Add the bay leaf, basil and 1 garlic clove. Bring to a boil and simmer, covered, for 20 minutes.

Add the celery and onion. Add enough additional water to cover the lentils. Cover the saucepan and simmer for 10 more minutes.

Drain the lentils, celery and onion and discard the bay leaf and garlic clove. Put the lentils, celery and onion in a serving bowl. Add the chives and feta cheese. Toss.

Put the olive oil, vinegar, oregano, remaining garlic clove, salt and pepper in a jar with a tightly fitting lid. Cover tightly and shake until well blended.

Pour the dressing over the lentil salad and toss. Let the salad stand for 2 hours, tossing occasionally, before serving.

Egg and Pasta Salad

INGREDIENTS *serves 4*
1 cup green or whole-wheat pasta
  shapes
2 tsp oil
4 eggs
1 cup green beans
2 stalks celery
1 dessert apple
1/2 cup walnuts
Mayonnaise (see page 128)
salt and freshly ground black pepper
1-2 tbsp chopped fresh dill
sliced chicken meat, optional

METHOD
Cook the pasta in plenty of boiling salted water, to which you have added oil, until al dente. Drain and allow to cool.

Hard boil the eggs, shell under cold running water and allow to cool. Cut into quarters.

Top and tail the beans and cut into manageable lengths. Simmer in salted water until cooked but not soft. Drain and allow to cool.

Chop the celery. Peel, core and dice the apple. Toss all the ingredients except the eggs together in the Mayonnaise. Season and garnish with eggs and dill. Meat eaters can add sliced chicken to this dish.

Navy Bean Salad

INGREDIENTS *serves 4*
1 cup dried navy beans, soaked
  overnight
2 cloves garlic, crushed
2 tbsp wine vinegar
2 tbsp olive oil
1 tsp French mustard
salt and freshly ground black pepper
1 red bell pepper, deseeded and thinly
  sliced
1 leek, thinly sliced
2 scallions, green and white parts
  chopped separately

METHOD
Place the beans in a large saucepan and cover with fresh water. Bring to a boil and boil fast for 10 minutes, then cover and simmer for 40-50 minutes or until tender. Drain.

Combine the garlic, vinegar, olive oil, mustard and seasoning in a screw-top jar, seal and shake well.

Pour over the hot beans and leave to cool. Stir in the pepper, leek and white parts of the scallions and place in a serving dish.

Sprinkle with green chopped scallion and serve.

▲ Bean salad
▶ Egg and pasta salad

58

Ossum Salad

INGREDIENTS *serves 6*
1 cup dried red kidney beans, soaked
  overnight and drained
3 tbsp Modern Vinaigrette (see page
  128)
1 small onion, finely chopped
3 hard-boiled eggs, chopped
1 small head celery, chopped, or 1 small
  cauliflower, chopped
3 tbsp brown or mustard pickle
5 anchovy fillets, chopped (optional)
²⁄₃ cup sour cream
salt and pepper

METHOD
Bring the soaked beans to the boil in fresh
water and boil rapidly for 10 minutes, then
cook for 1-1¹⁄₂ hours, until they are tender
but not soft. Drain them and pour the
Modern Vinaigrette and onion over while
the beans are still warm.

When the beans are cold, add the
remaining ingredients, mixing everything
together well. Use yogurt instead of sour
cream if preferred. Refrigerate and serve
cold.

◄ *Ossum Salad*

Barbecue Salad

INGREDIENTS *serves 4*
3 large tomatoes, quartered
2 large green bell peppers, deseeded
  and quartered
1 red bell pepper, deseeded and
  quartered
1 large eggplant, peeled and quartered
2 large onions, halved
1 cup Herb Dressing or Touch of Asia
  Dressing (see page 131)

METHOD
Thread the tomato, green pepper, red
pepper and eggplant quarters and the onion
halves onto 6 (or more) long skewers.

Lay the skewers on the barbecue grill over
white coals or place them under an oven
broiler at a high heat. Cook for 12-15
minutes, turning frequently.

Remove the skewers from the grill.
Remove the vegetables from the skewers.
Put the eggplant and tomato pieces in a
bowl.

While still hot, peel the skin from the
pepper pieces. Add the pieces to the salad
bowl. Coarsely chop the onions and add
them to the salad bowl. Add the dressing
and toss. Refrigerate for 30 minutes before
serving.

Kidney Bean, Garbanzo and Corn Salad

INGREDIENTS *serves 4*
1 cup dried red kindney beans
1 cup dried garbanzo beans
1 cup corn kernels, cooked
6 scallions
2 very large tomatoes
Tofu Dressing (see page 128)

METHOD
Soak the kidney beans and the garbanzo
beans separately overnight. Drains each
and cook separately in fresh water to cover.
Bring to the boil for 10 minutes, then
simmer until tender but not mushy. Drain
and cool.

Chop the scallions and slice the
tomatoes.

Toss all the ingredients in tofu dressing
and serve at room temperature with hot pita
bread.

▲ *Kidney Bean, Garbanzo and Corn Salad*

Green Bean and Pepper Salad

INGREDIENTS *serves 4*

8oz thin green beans

1 medium or 2 small red bell peppers, cored and deseeded

2 slices fresh ginger root, thinly shredded

1½ tsp salt

1 tsp sugar

1 tbsp sesame seed oil

METHOD

Wash the green beans, snip off the ends and cut into 1-2in pieces. Cut the red bell peppers into thin shreds. Blanch them both in boiling water and drain.

Put the green beans, red bell peppers and ginger into a bowl. Add the salt, sugar and sesame seed oil. Toss well and serve.

Tomato Salad with Scallions and Oil Dressing

INGREDIENTS *serves 4*

2 large firm tomatoes

1 tsp salt

1 tsp sugar

3-4 scallions, finely chopped

3 tbsp salad oil

METHOD

Wash and dry the tomatoes. Cut them into thick slices. Sprinkle with salt and sugar. Leave to marinate for 10-15 minutes.

Place the finely chopped scallions in a heatproof bowl. In a pan, heat the oil until quite hot and pour over the scallions. Add the tomatoes, toss well and serve.

NOTE

Other vegetables such as cucumber, celery and green bell peppers can be served in the same way.

Chinese Cabbage Salad

INGREDIENTS *serves 4*

1 small Chinese cabbage

2 tbsp light soy sauce

1 tsp salt

1 tsp sugar

1 tbsp sesame seed oil

METHOD

Wash the cabbage thoroughly, cut into thick slices and place in a bowl.

Add the soy sauce, salt, sugar and sesame seed oil to the cabbage. Toss well and serve.

NOTE

Green or red bell peppers (or both) can be added to the cabbage.

▶ Chinese cabbage salad
◀▲ Green bean and pepper salad
▲ Tomato salad with scallions

62

Bean Sprout Salad

INGREDIENTS *serves 4*
1lb fresh bean sprouts
1 tsp salt
2¹⁄₂ quarts water
2 tbsp light soy sauce
1 tbsp vinegar
2 scallions, finely shredded

METHOD
Wash and rinse the bean sprouts in cold water, discarding the husks and other bits and pieces that float to the surface. It is not necessary to trim each sprout.

Blanch the sprouts in a pan of salted boiling water. Pour them into a colander and rinse in cold water until cool. Drain.

Place the sprouts in a bowl or a deep dish and add the soy sauce, vinegar and sesame seed oil. Toss well and garnish with thinly shredded scallions just before serving.

Sweet-and-Sour Cucumber Salad

INGREDIENTS *serves 4*
1 cucumber
2 tsp finely chopped fresh ginger root
1 tsp sesame seed oil
2 tbsp sugar
2 tbsp rice vinegar

METHOD
Select a dark green and slender cucumber; the fat pale green ones contain too much water and have far less flavor. Cut it in half lengthwise, then cut each piece into slices. Marinate with the ginger and sesame seed oil for about 10-15 minutes.

Make the dressing with the sugar and vinegar in a bowl, stirring well to dissolve the sugar.

Place the cucumber slices on a plate. Just before serving, pour the sugar and vinegar dressing evenly over them and toss well.

Celery Salad

INGREDIENTS *serves 4*
1 celery
1 tsp salt
7¹⁄₂ cups water
2 tbsp light soy sauce
1 tbsp vinegar
1 tbsp sesame seed oil
2 slices fresh ginger root, finely shredded

METHOD
Remove the leaves and tough outer stems of the celery. Thinly slice the tender parts diagonally. Blanch them in a pan of boiling, salted water. Then pour them into a colander and rinse in cold water until cool. Drain.

Mix together the soy sauce, vinegar and sesame seed oil. Add to the celery and toss well.

Garnish the salad with finely shredded ginger root and serve.

▲▲ Bean sprout salad
▲ Celery Salad

▶ Caribbean fruit salad

64

Caribbean Fruit Salad

INGREDIENTS *serves 6-8*
1½ cups blueberries or black currants
2 peaches, pitted and thinly sliced
¾ cup halved green and black seedless
  grapes
1 cup fresh pineapple chunks
1 cup diced honeydew melon
5 tangerines, peeled, white membrane
  removed, segmented and seeded
1 cup diced cantaloupe
1 cup cubed Gruyère cheese
8oz fresh dates
1 cup Yogurt Mayonnaise (see page 131)
1 tbsp honey
2 tbsp rum
2 large bananas, halved
¾ cup finely chopped almonds

METHOD
Arrange the blueberries, peaches, grapes, pineapple, honeydew melon, tangerines, cantaloupe, cheese and dates on a large serving platter.

In a small mixing bowl, add the honey and rum to the Yogurt Mayonnaise and stir until well mixed. Place the dressing in a separate bowl in the center of the platter.

Lightly roll the banana pieces in the chopped almonds and add them to the rest of the fruit. Let each guest take some fruit and dressing and toss the salad on individual plates.

South Seas Fruit Salad

INGREDIENTS *serves 6-8*
2 ripe papayas, peeled, seeded and
  cubed
2 large bananas, peeled and diced
½ cuphalved seedless green grapes
1 cup cubed pineapple
3 tangerines, peeled, white membrane
  removed, segmented and seeded
5 tbsp peanut oil
1 tbsp sesame oil
4 tbsp fresh lime juice
¼ tsp salt
2 tsp sugar

METHOD
Arrange the papaya, banana, grapes, pineapple and tangerine segments in serving bowls.

Into a blender or food processor, put the peanut oil, sesame oil, lime juice, salt and sugar. Blend until well mixed.

Pour the dressing over the salad. Cover the bowls and chill for 1-2 hours before serving.

Melon Salad with Ginger Sauce

INGREDIENTS *serves 6-8*
¾ cup heavy cream
1 tsp fresh lemon juice
1 tbsp confectioner's sugar
large pinch cayenne pepper
3 large pieces preserved ginger, finely chopped
⅓ cup chopped almonds
2 large melons of your choice, peeled, seeded and cubed

METHOD

Put the cream, lemon juice, sugar and cayenne pepper in a mixing bowl. Beat the cream until it becomes thick but not stiff. Add the ginger and the almonds, reserving 1 tbsp of the almonds. Continue to beat until the cream becomes stiff. Cover the bowl and chill until ready to serve.

Put the melon in a serving dish and chill until ready to serve. Just before serving, top the melon cubes with the ginger cream. Sprinkle the remaining almonds on top.

Persimmon Salad

INGREDIENTS *serves 4*
4 very ripe persimmons
4 crisp lettuce leaves
4 tbsp plain yogurt or sour cream
1 tsp lemon juice
¾ cup chopped raw cashews

METHOD

Place the persimmons stem-side down on a flat surface. Carefully cut an "X" into the top surface of the skin. Gently peel the skin away from the pulp, a little bit at a time, about halfway down the side of the persimmon. Keeping the skin intact, loosen the remaining pulp from the skin with a spoon. Place each persimmon on a lettuce leaf.

In a small bowl, combine the yogurt and lemon juice. Spoon equal amounts over each persimmon and sprinkle with the chopped nuts. Serve immediately or chill briefly.

Pear Salad

INGREDIENTS *serves 4*
4 dessert pears
1 clove garlic, crushed
1 tsp salt
1½ tsp sugar
½ tsp dried tarragon, crumbled
½ tsp dried basil, crumbled
2½ tbsp red-wine vinegar
2½ tbsp olive oil
2½ tbsp water
1 tbsp sherry
⅔ cup coarsely chopped celery
⅔ cup coarsely chopped green pepper
3 scallions, sliced
2 large ripe tomatoes, finely chopped
4 romaine lettuce leaves, chilled

METHOD

Wash the pears and refrigerate. In a bowl mix together the garlic, salt and sugar. Add the tarragon, basil, vinegar, oil, water and sherry. Beat until well blended. Transfer to a 16oz jar, cover, and let stand for 1-1½ hours.

Place the celery, green pepper, scallions and tomatoes in a bowl. Chill for 1 hour.

Remove the vegetables and pears from the refrigerator. Shake the dressing to mix well. Pour half the dressing over the vegetables and toss.

Place 1 lettuce leaf on each of 4 serving plates. Halve and core the pears. Arrange 2 pear halves, cut-side up, on each lettuce leaf. Top with the dressed vegetables. Spoon the remaining dressing over the pears and serve.

◀ Melon salad with ginger sauce

CRÊPE AND PASTA DISHES

Tasty and filling, pasta is a much-loved favorite, from the youngest to the most sophisticated diner. Available in myriad shapes and sizes, it is exceptionally versatile and does service as first course, luncheon special, main dish or party piece. Crêpes may be a little less universally popular but they are every bit as delectable.

Vegetarian bolognese

Asparagus Crêpes

INGREDIENTS *serves 2*
1 small clove garlic, crushed
2 tbsp chopped fresh basil leaves
1 tbsp pine nuts
3 tbsp grated Parmesan cheese
2 tbsp olive oil
salt and freshly ground black pepper
6 tbsp whole-wheat flour
2 tbsp buckwheat flour
1 egg, lightly beaten
$^2/_3$ cup skim milk
7oz frozen asparagus spears
3 tomatoes, peeled, seeded and
    chopped

METHOD
Place the garlic, basil, pine nuts and 2 tbsp
Parmesan cheese in a food processor or
blender and purée. With the motor running,
gradually add the oil and blend to a smooth
sauce. Season to taste.

Place the flours in a bowl, gradually add
the egg and milk, beating well to form a
smooth batter. Leave to stand for 30
minutes.

Heat a lightly oiled 7 in heavy bottomed
skillet. Pour in sufficient batter to thinly
coat the base.

Cook for 1-2 minutes, loosen the edge,
turn or toss and cook the second side.
Transfer to a plate and keep hot. Repeat
with the remaining batter to make 4 crêpes.
Stack the crêpes with waxed paper between
them and keep warm.

Place the asparagus in a saucepan, pour
over just sufficient boiling water to cover
and simmer for 6 minutes.

Divide the asparagus between the crêpes,
top with sauce and fold up. Place in a
shallow baking dish, sprinkle with
tomatoes and remaining cheese.

Place under a broiler until browned.

Basic Crêpes

INGREDIENTS *Makes 5 cups batter*
2$^1/_2$ cups milk
2$^1/_4$ cups all-purpose flour
pinch salt
2 eggs
butter or oil for frying

METHOD
Mix the milk and flour together until
smooth. Add the salt and eggs and beat in
well. Leave to stand at least 30 minutes.

Heat a little butter or oil in a heavy-
bottomed skillet (preferably one used only
for crêpes). Tip out excess butter.

Pour in just enough batter to coat the
bottom of the pan. Fry on one side only if the
crêpes are to be filled.

Mushroom Crêpes

INGREDIENTS *serves 4*
1 recipe crêpes (page 68)
2 tbsp butter
1 large onion, finely chopped
4 cups chopped mushrooms
2 tbsp finely chopped canned red
    pimentos
$^2/_3$ cup sour cream
salt and freshly ground black pepper
melted butter

METHOD
Make the crêpes and keep warm.

Melt the butter, add the onion and cook
until it has softened but not browned. Add
the mushrooms and cook until soft. Drain
off excess liquid. Mix in the pimentos, sour
cream, salt and pepper.

Put a spoonful of the mixture onto each
crêpe on the cooked side. Roll up the crêpes,
tucking in the edges.

Place the rolled crêpes in a buttered
baking dish, drizzle a little melted butter
over the top. Warm through in the oven at
350°F for 25 minutes.

Serve with more sour cream, if desired.

▲ Asparagus crêpes
▶ Mushroom crêpes

Stuffed Cheese Crêpes

INGREDIENTS *serves 3-4*
$\frac{3}{8}$ cup unbleached all-purpose flour
$\frac{3}{8}$ cup whole-wheat flour
pinch salt
1 egg
$\frac{2}{3}$ cup milk
1 tbsp melted butter

CHEESE AND HERB FILLING
2 cups cottage cheese
2 tbsp heavy cream
1 fat clove garlic, crushed
2 tbsp finely chopped fresh herbs
1 tbsp chopped scallion

METHOD
To make the crêpe batter, sift the flour and salt into a bowl. Make a well in the middle of it and add the egg. Gradually beat in the milk. When half of the milk has been added, beat in the melted butter. Continue beating in the milk until you have a thin batter. Allow the batter to stand for at least 30 minutes.

Meanwhile, prepare the filling. Combine the cottage cheese with the rest of the ingredients and mix well.

To make the crêpes, oil a heavy-bottomed frying pan 7 in in diameter. Place it on the heat and when it is very hot, add 2 tbsp of the batter. Tilt the pan so that the batter covers the bottom. Cook until the pancake is beginning to brown on the underside and then turn over and cook the top. You may have to throw the first crêpe away, as it will absorb the excess oil in the pan.

Continue making crêpes, keeping them warm, until all the batter is used up. Divide the filling between them, rolling the crêpe around into cigar shapes. Arrange the stuffed crêpes in a baking dish and heat 350°F for about 1½ minutes.

Genoese Pasta with Pesto Sauce

INGREDIENTS *serves 4-6*
2 tbsp fresh basil leaves
2 cloves garlic
pinch salt
½ cup pine nuts
½ cup grated Parmesan cheese
½ cup olive oil
1lb spaghetti, cooked and drained
2 tbsp butter

METHOD
Blend the basil leaves in a blender or food processor. Add the crushed cloves of garlic and olive oil. Process for a few seconds.

Gradually add the pine nuts, Parmesan cheese and season, remembering that Parmesan has a salty taste. The consistency should be thick and creamy.

Melt the butter in a saucepan and re-heat the cooked pasta. Remove from the heat and mix 2 tbsp pesto with the pasta. Serve on individual plates with a spoonful of pesto on each helping. Parmesan can be added last.

NOTE
The pesto is never heated. It can be served at the table but make sure the pasta is hot.

Fettucini Romana

INGREDIENTS *serves 4*
1lb fettucini
¼ cup butter
½ tsp grated nutmeg
⅔ cup heavy cream
salt and freshly ground black pepper
1 cup Parmesan cheese

METHOD
Bring a well-filled saucepan of salted water to the boil, add a few drops of oil and salt. Feed in the fettucini and cook until al dente - fresh pasta will only take about 2 minutes. Drain in a colander.

Melt the butter in the saucepan, add grated nutmeg. Pour in half the cream and stir until shiny and bubbles start to appear.

Add the fettucini and stir around in the pan. Pour in the remaining cream and cheese alternately, forking the pasta as it is mixed. Serve immediately with Parmesan cheese.

NOTE
This is a real pasta-lovers' dish. To obtain best results, use freshly grated Parmesan cheese rather than the commercially grated variety.

◄ Stuffed cheese crêpes
► Genoese pasta with pesto sauce

71

Eggplant and Apple Pasta

INGREDIENTS *serves 2-3*
1 large eggplant
1 large cooking apple
1 egg, beaten
seasoned unbleached all-purpose flour
¼ cup walnut oil
2 cloves garlic, crushed
1 cup whole-wheat or spinach pasta
   shapes
salt and freshly ground black pepper

METHOD
Slice the eggplant, sprinkle liberally with salt and leave in a colander for 30 minutes. Rinse and dry on paper towels and cut into strips. Peel, core and dice the apple.

Toss the eggplant and apple in the beaten egg, and then in the seasoned flour to give a light coating. Heat some oil in a pan and fry the eggplant, apple and garlic, stirring, until crisp.

Meanwhile, cook pasta shapes in plenty of salted water at a full rolling boil, until al dente. Add a few drops of oil to the water to prevent the pasta from sticking. Drain well, season with black pepper and toss in a little walnut oil. Stir in the eggplant mixture and serve with Parmesan cheese.

Spinach Tagliatelle with Asparagus

INGREDIENTS *serves 2*
6-7 spears asparagus
2 tbsp butter
4 tbsp light cream
salt and freshly ground black pepper
1 cup green tagliatelle
2 tsp oil
grated Parmesan cheese

METHOD
If you are using fresh asparagus, clean it under cold running water, tie it in a bundle and stand upright in a tall saucepan containing about 3 in boiling salted water. Cover with foil so that the asparagus tips cook by steaming. Alternatively, use a double boiler, inverting the inner saucepan over the bottom one. The asparagus will take 10-20 minutes to cook, depending on

its thickness. (Test by piercing half way up the stem with a sharp knife - if you can insert the knife easily, the asparagus is done.) Drain it. Cut off and discard the woody lower pieces. Cut the asparagus into bite-sized pieces.

Melt the butter in a saucepan and toss the asparagus in it. Add half the cream, season and leave for a few minutes over a very low heat to thicken.

Meanwhile, cook the pasta until al dente in plenty of boiling salted water to which you have added 2 tsp oil.

Drain the pasta, toss in the remaining cream and pour over the asparagus sauce. Serve and offer a generous amount of Parmesan cheese.

Spinach and Ricotta Pasta

INGREDIENTS *serves 6-8*
1¼ cups Béchamel Sauce (page 126)
½ cup cooked fresh or frozen spinach
⅔ cup ricotta cheese
½ tsp nutmeg
salt and freshly ground pepper
3-4 cups cooked pasta

METHOD
Make up the Béchamel sauce.

Cook the spinach for a few minutes and then drain well. Squeeze against the colander to remove the liquid.

You will need to cook approx 1½lb fresh spinach to be left with the amount required by the recipe. Chop or purée.

Mix the ricotta with the spinach and season well, add the nutmeg. Gradually stir into the Béchamel sauce and reheat carefully over a low heat.

Serve in spoonfuls over portions of the cooked pasta.

VARIATION
This sauce is also delicious used in a vegetable lasagne.

◄▲ Eggplant and apple pasta
► Spinach and ricotta pasta

Tagliatelle with Sweet Pepper Sauce

INGREDIENTS *serves 4*
12oz spinach tagliatelle noodles
2 tsp oil
½ tsp salt

THE SAUCE
1 small firm red bell pepper
1 small green bell pepper
1 small yellow bell pepper
1-2 tbsp olive oil
1 onion, chopped
2 cloves garlic, chopped
1½ cups canned tomatoes
1 tbsp tomato paste
fresh basil leaves, snipped
salt and freshly ground black pepper

METHOD
Trim and deseed the peppers and cut into narrow strips. You can make the sauce with green peppers alone if you wish, but the red and yellow varieties are sweeter and make the dish look more colorful. Blanch the peppers for a minute in boiling salted water, refresh in cold water, then drain.

Heat the olive oil in a pan, add the garlic and onions and cook gently, stirring, until soft. Add the tomatoes, tomato paste and basil. Break up the tomatoes with a wooden spoon and simmer for about 5 minutes. Season to taste and blend the sauce in a blender. Return to the pan over a very low heat and add the peppers.

Cook the pasta in a large pan with plenty of water to which you have added a little oil and the salt. The water should be at a full rolling boil. The pasta will be ready in about 9 minutes. Drain and divide between individual warmed serving bowls.

Spoon the sauce over each helping of pasta and serve at once with Parmesan cheese.

▲ Spaghetti with Mascarpone
◀ Tagliatelle with sweet pepper sauce

Spaghetti Putanesca

INGREDIENTS *serves 4-6*
1 onion, peeled and diced
2 tbsp oil
2 cloves garlic, crushed
1 carrot, scraped and chopped
1½ cups canned tomatoes
2 tomatoes, peeled and chopped
4 tbsp white wine
1 bay leaf
3-4 fresh basil leaves or 1 tsp dried basil
salt and freshly ground pepper
1 tbsp capers, chopped
1 small can anchovies
½ cup pitted ripe olives
3 drops Tabasco sauce
1 tbsp chopped fresh parsley
1lb cooked spaghetti
grated Parmesan cheese to serve

only fish

METHOD
Put the onion into the oil in a skillet over a low heat. Allow to cook gently for 4 minutes, add the crushed garlic and carrots. Turn in the oil twice more.

Add the tomatoes, the white wine, bay leaf, basil, some seasoning and 4 anchovy fillets. Bring to a boil and simmer for 30 minutes. Strain or purée and return the sauce to the saucepan. Add the chopped capers, the remainder of the anchovies chopped into small pieces, chopped olives and the spicy Tabasco sauce. Reheat and serve over the pasta, with Parmesan cheese.

Spaghetti with Mascarpone

INGREDIENTS *serves 4*
12oz whole-wheat spaghetti
a little oil
4oz Mascarpone or cream cheese
2 egg yolks
salt and freshly ground black pepper
grated Parmesan cheese to serve

METHOD
Cook the pasta in boiling salted water, to which you have added a few drops of oil, until al dente.

While you are draining the spaghetti, stir the egg yolks and Mascarpone together in a large pan over a low heat.

When the sauce begins to set, toss in the spaghetti. Serve at once with plenty of black pepper and Parmesan. This dish should be accompanied by a crunchy salad.

Pasta with Mushroom Sauce

INGREDIENTS *serves 1-2*
2-4 handfuls green pasta spirals
1 tsp oil
1 cup mushrooms
milk
salt and freshly ground black pepper
1 egg yolk
1 tbsp heavy cream
as much parsley as you like, chopped
grated Parmesan cheese

METHOD
Cook the pasta in plenty of boiling salted water with 1 tsp oil, until al dente.

Meanwhile, wipe and slice the mushrooms. Place in a pan with a little milk, season well and poach gently, stirring, until soft and very black and the liquid has almost evaporated.

Beat the egg yolk with the cream and stir in the mushrooms.

Drain the pasta and stir in the mushroom mixture with plenty of parsley. Serve at once with Parmesan and a tender lettuce salad.

Spaghetti with Fresh Tomato and Basil Sauce

INGREDIENTS *serves 4*
2 tsp olive oil
1 onion, chopped
4 stalks celery, chopped
1 green chili, seeded and finely chopped
2 cloves garlic, crushed
2¼ cups peeled and roughly chopped
   tomatoes
3 tbsp tomato paste
1 tbsp chopped basil leaves
1 tbsp chopped majoram
12oz whole-wheat spaghetti, or
   6oz whole-wheat spaghetti and
   6oz spaghetti verdi
⅔ cup pitted ripe olives
3 tbsp grated Parmesan cheese
3 tbsp pine nuts
basil sprigs

METHOD
Heat the oil in a saucepan, add the onion, celery, chili and garlic and fry until soft. Add the tomatoes and tomato paste, 4 tbsp water, half the basil and marjoram. Bring to a boil and simmer for 10 minutes.

Place the whole-wheat spaghetti in a large saucepan of boiling lightly salted water and cook for 12 minutes, or until just tender. Add the spaghetti verdi, if using, 2 minutes after the whole-wheat spaghetti.

Drain the pasta and divide between 4 individual warmed plates. Stir the olives and remaining basil into the sauce and place on top of the spaghetti.

Sprinkle with cheese and pine nuts, garnish with basil sprigs and serve.

Vegetarian Bolonese Sauce

INGREDIENTS *serves 4-6*
1¼ cups brown lentils
salt and freshly ground black pepper
1 bay leaf
1-2 tbsp olive oil
2 cloves garlic, chopped
1 onion, chopped
1 carrot, chopped
1 stick celery, chopped
1½ cups can red tomatoes, mashed
1 tbsp tomato paste
½ tsp Italian seasoning
2 tbsp red wine
12oz whole-wheat or spinach pasta

METHOD
Soak the lentils overnight and simmer in salted water with a bay leaf until they can be mashed with a fork. Drain and discard the bayleaf.

Heat the oil in a pan and fry the onions and garlic until translucent. Add the carrot and celery and cook for a further 2 minutes.

Add the tomatoes and a little juice. Add the remaining ingredients and the lentils. Simmer until the sauce is quite thick. Blend or part-blend in a blender.

Serve the sauce in healthy spoonfuls over the warmed cooked pasta.

Hot Pasta Salad

INGREDIENTS *serves 4*
2 cloves garlic
3 tbsp olive oil
handful fresh basil leaves
1 tbsp grated Parmesan cheese

THE SALAD
4oz Mozzarella cheese
1lb Mediterranean tomatoes
1 cupripe olives
salt and freshly ground black pepper

THE PASTA
12oz spinach pasta twists
1 tsp olive oil

METHOD
Chop the garlic and put it in a mortar. Pour in a little of the olive oil and pound it to a pulp. Gradually add the basil leaves and cheese with the rest of the oil, pounding all the time. You should have a thick paste.

Dice the Mozzarella. Peel the tomatoes by immersing them in boiling water until their skins burst. Chop them roughly. Mix the cheese, tomatoes and olives together and season.

Cook the pasta in boiling salted water, to which you have added a little olive oil, until al dente. Drain. Toss the pasta in the dressing. Pile it into 4 warmed serving bowls and top with the salad.

▲ ◄ Spaghetti with fresh tomato and basil Sauce

MAIN COURSE DISHES

Our vegetarian main courses should appeal as much to everyday meat-eaters as to herbivore gourmets. These cosmopolitan combinations of vegetables, cheeses, herbs and spices result in dishes as full in flavor and varied in texture as any meat-, poultry- or fish-based dishes.

Potato-topped vegetable pie

Belgian Endive Soufflé

INGREDIENTS *serves 4-6*
3 heads Belgian endive
salt
juice 1 lemon
3 tbsp butter
³⁄₈ cup all-purpose flour
1¼ cups milk
½ cup grated cheese
4 eggs, separated
1 tbsp dry whole-wheat bread crumbs

METHOD
Heat the oven to 400°F. Trim the Belgian endive and cook in salted water to which you have added the lemon juice. This will stop it discoloring.

When the Belgian endive is tender, drain and set aside. When it is cool, press the water out from between the leaves with your fingers. Chop very finely.

Meanwhile, melt the butter in a heavy-bottomed pan. Stir in the flour. Remove from the heat and stir in the milk. Return from the heat and stir until the sauce has thickened. Add the cheese and cook for a further minute. Allow to cool.

When the sauce has cooled, mix in the endive, then the egg yolks.

Beat the whites until they form soft peaks and fold into the endive mixture. Spoon into a greased soufflé dish and sprinkle the top with bread crumbs.

Bake in the oven for 20-25 minutes until lightly set, well risen and golden on top. Serve this soufflé with a strongly flavored salad, such as watercress garnished with slivers of orange.

Savory Pumpkin Tart

INGREDIENTS *serves 4-6*
1 recipe Whole-wheat Pastry (page 158)
1lb pumpkin flesh
4 eggs
²⁄₃ cup heavy cream
²⁄₃ cup milk
2 large tomatoes, peeled and chopped
1 tbsp chopped fresh basil leaves
freshly ground black pepper

METHOD
Make the dough as directed on page 158. Roll out and line a greased 8 in quiche pan.

Preheat the oven to 375°F.

Remove rind and seeds from pumpkin and cut into slivers. Pack into a pan with very little water and cook over a low heat, covered. Check the pan occasionally to make sure the pumpkin hasn't dried out. After about 20 minutes you should be able to mash it into a purée.

Beat the eggs with the cream and milk. Mix in the pumpkin, tomato and basil and pour into the crust. Bake for 45 minutes until set and golden.

Spinach and Cheese Soufflé

INGREDIENTS *serves 4*
2 cups washed and picked over spinach
4 tbsp butter or margarine
½ cup all-purpose flour
2 cups milk
6 eggs
1¹⁄₃ cups cottage cheese
grated nutmeg
salt and freshly ground black pepper
grated Parmesan cheese (optional)

METHOD
Cook the spinach without any excess water. Drain it very well (between 2 plates is the most effective way).

While the spinach is cooking, melt the butter and stir in the flour off the heat. Slowly add the milk and return the pan to the heat. Stir to thicken the sauce. Remove the pan from the heat.

Separate the eggs and add the yolks, 1 at a time, mixing after each one. Add the cooked and drained spinach, cottage cheese, nutmeg, salt and pepper to taste. Mix everything together well.

Beat the whites until they are very stiff. Take a scoop of the whites and fold it gently into the spinach mixture to lighten it a little and then incorporate the rest of the whites into it, folding it in lightly. Turn the soufflé mixture into a greased soufflé dish measuring about 8¹⁄₄×3¹⁄₂in. Bake at 375°F for 30 minutes. Test with a clean knife to see if it is ready. If the mixture is still very runny, return the dish to the oven for a further 5 minutes or so. If you like, sprinkle some grated Parmesan on the top 10 minutes before the end of cooking.

◀ ▲ Belgian endive soufflé
▶ Savory pumpkin tart

79

Flageolet and Sage Quiche

INGREDIENTS *serves 4-6*
6oz piecrust dough (enough for a single-crust pie)
4 large tomatoes
4oz Vermont Sage cheese
3 eggs
²/₃ cup milk
salt and freshly ground black pepper
1 cup cooked flageolet beans

METHOD
Preheat the oven to 400°F. Pour boiling water over the tomatoes. After a minute the skins will begin to split. Refresh with cold water. Peel the tomatoes and slice them thickly.

Line an 8 in quiche pan with the piecrust dough and crumble the cheese into it. Arrange the tomato slices to cover the cheese.

Break the eggs into a bowl and lightly beat with the milk and seasoning. Pour the egg mixture into the pie crust, gently pressing down the tomatoes with a fork.

Bake in the center of the oven for 15-20 minutes, until set and golden.

Onion Tart

INGREDIENTS *serves 4-6*
6oz piecrust dough (enough for a single-crust pie) (see page 158)
1 tbsp butter
1 tbsp oil
2½ cups finely chopped onions
2 eggs plus 1 yolk
2 cups light cream
1-2 heaped tbsp grated Cheddar cheese
1-2 heaped tbsp chopped fresh parsley
salt and freshly ground black pepper
pinch of cayenne pepper

METHOD
Preheat the oven to 375°F and line a 8 in quiche pan with the piecrust dough.

Heat the butter and olive oil in a pan. Stir in the onions. Cover the pan, turn down the heat and sweat for about 5 minutes, stirring occasionally until soft and transparent.

Beat the eggs, cream and cheese together and add the onions and parsley. Season with salt, pepper and cayenne to taste, pour into the piecrust case and bake in the middle of the oven for 30-40 minutes until golden and set.

VARIATION
To make an onion and blue cheese tart, combine 1-2 tbsp crumbled blue cheese with the cream before beating it with the eggs. Omit the cheddar, parsley and cayenne pepper.

◄◄ Flageolet and Sage quiche
◄ Onion tart

Leek Quiche

INGREDIENTS *serves 4-6*
8-in pie plate lined with piecrust dough
butter
3 cups trimmed and chopped leeks
1 large onion, chopped
1⅓ cups cottage cheese
3 eggs
salt and freshly ground pepper
a pinch of ground allspice

METHOD
Bake the piecrust case for 10 minutes at 350°F.

Melt the butter and soften the leeks and onion in it for 5 minutes. Mix the cottage cheese with the remaining ingredients.

Cover the bottom of the lined pie plate with the cooked leeks and onions. Spoon over the cottage cheese mixture. Bake at 350°F for 35 minutes. Serve hot or at room temperature.

Green Pea Tartlets with Poached Eggs

INGREDIENTS *makes 8 tartlets*
8oz piecrust dough (enough for a single-
    crust pie)
2lb dried marrowfat peas, pre-soaked
    and cooked
4 tbsp butter
salt and freshly ground black pepper
8 eggs

THE TOMATO SAUCE
1-2 tbsp olive oil
1 onion, chopped
2 cloves garlic, chopped
1¾ cups canned tomatoes
1 tbsp tomato paste
2 tsp dried oregano
salt and freshly ground black pepper

METHOD
Preheat the oven to 400°F. Roll out the dough and line 8 greased fluted tartlet pans. Prick with a fork and bake blind for 20 minutes until golden. Remove tart crusts from the oven and turn the heat down to 350°F/180°C/Gas 4.

Meanwhile, make the tomato sauce. Heat the oil in a pan and add the onion and garlic. Cook until soft. Add the tomatoes, tomato paste, oregano and seasoning. Simmer for 5 minutes, then purée in a blender and keep hot.

Cook the peas until mushy, then drain and purée them in a blender. Heat the butter in a pan and stir in the pea purée. Season well with salt and plenty of black pepper. Divide the pea purée among the tartlet cases.

Poach the eggs until just set. Lift them carefully into the tartlet crusts and return to the oven for 2-3 minutes. Don't let the eggs harden. Serve each tartlet with a spoonful of tomato sauce. Serve 2 tartlets per serving for a main course or individually for an appetizer.

◀ Green pea tarts with poached eggs
▶ Spinach roulade

Nut Loaf

INGREDIENTS *serves 4*
1 small eggplant
1 cup chopped mixed nuts
olive oil
1 large onion, finely chopped
2 cloves garlic, chopped
¾ cup brown rice, cooked
¾ cup can tomatoes, drained and
    mashed
salt and freshly ground black pepper
2 eggs, beaten

METHOD
Preheat the oven to 375°F.

Slice the eggplant, sprinkle with salt and leave for 20 minutes. Rinse off the salt, pat dry and dice.

Put the nuts on a cookie sheet and toest them at the top of theoven for 10 minutes.

Heat 1-2 tbsp oil in a pan. Add the onion and garlic and fry until translucent. Add the egplant and cook, stirring occasionally, for about 10 minutes. Add more oil as necessary.

Transfer the eggplant mixture to a large bowl and stir in the nuts, brown rice and tomatoes. Mix well and season to taste. Stir in the beaten egg.

Pour into a greased small loaf pan and smooth the top. Bake in the center of the oven for 35 minutes until firm. Turn out of the pan and cut into slices to serve.

Spinach Roulade

INGREDIENTS *serves 6-8*
3 cups fresh spinach, washed and picked
    over
1 tbsp butter
4 eggs, separated
grated nutmeg
salt and freshly ground black pepper
¾ cup farmer's cheese
⅔ cup sour cream
4 scallions, finely chopped

METHOD
Cook the spinach without any excess water. Drain the spinach very well (press it between 2 plates for most effective drainage) and when all the liquid has been removed, either chop the spinach very finely or blend it just enough to chop it.

Add the butter, egg yolks, grated nutmeg and salt and pepper to taste. Mix together very well.

Beat the egg whites until they are stiff. Fold a spoonful of the beaten whites into the spinach mixture to lighten it and then fold in the remaining whites. Mix through carefully.

Turn the mixture onto a 15-x10-in jelly roll pan which has been lined with waxed paper or foil. Bake at 400°F for 10 minutes only.

While the spinach is cooking, mix the farmer's cheese with the sour cream and scallions. Season to taste. Have a clean dish towel spread on a board and when the spinach mixture is cooked, turn it upside down on to the dish towel. Carefully peel off the lining paper. Spread the cheese and sour cream mixture over the spinach base, taking care not to tear the surface. Using the dish towel to help you, roll the spinach up into a roll and onto a serving plate. Serve immediately.

NOTE
Although this is usually served hot, in fact, it is very good cold, as well.

Mushroom and Broccoli Nut Loaf

INGREDIENTS *serves 6*
1 cup sliced button mushrooms
2 tbsp polyunsaturated margarine
2 stalks celery, chopped
1 clove garlic, crushed
1 onion, grated
1 tbsp whole-wheat flour
1½ cups canned chopped tomatoes
2 cups fresh whole-wheat bread crumbs
1 cup ground walnuts
1 egg
1 tsp chopped fresh basil
1 tsp chopped fresh oregano
1 tbsp chopped fresh parsley
salt and freshly ground black pepper
4oz broccoli spears, cooked

SAUCE
1 cup chopped mushrooms
3 tbsp whole-wheat flour
½ cup vegetable stock
½ cup skim milk
celery leaves

METHOD
Sauté the mushroom slices in a skillet with 1 tbsp margarine, drain and place in a line down the center of a lightly greased 5 cup loaf pan.

Cook the celery, garlic and onion in the pan until softened.

Stir in the flour and tomatoes and stir until thickened.

Add the bread crumbs, nuts, egg, herbs and seasoning. Place half in the pan. Add the broccoli spears and top with the remaining mixture.

Cover with foil, place in a roasting pan filled with boiling water and cook at 350°F for 1¼-1½ hours.

Melt the remaining margarine, add the chopped mushrooms and cook for 2-3 minutes. Stir in the flour, and cook for 1 minute.

Add the stock, milk and seasoning and stir until boiled.

Turn out the loaf, garnish with celery leaves and serve with the sauce separately.

Summer Vegetable Pasties

INGREDIENTS *makes 4*
1 recipe Whole-wheat Pastry dough
  (page 158)
beaten egg to glaze

FILLING
1 cup diced potatoes
4 baby carrots, sliced
¼ cup garden peas
2 baby zucchinis, sliced
2 stalks celery, sliced
½ green bell pepper, diced

CHEESE SAUCE
2 tbsp butter
4 tbsp unbleached all-purpose flour
up to 1¼ cups milk
½ cup grated Cheddar cheese
salt and freshly ground black pepper

METHOD
Make the pastry dough. Preheat the oven to 350°F.

Boil the potatoes and carrots in salted water until just tender. In another pan, boil the remaining vegetables for about 2 minutes. Drain.

To make the cheese sauce, melt the butter in a heavy-bottomed pan, stir in the flour and gradually add half the milk, stirring. Add the cheese. Stir until melted. Add a little more milk and season to taste. Don't make the sauce too thin or it will pour out of the pastry cases. Mix sauce into vegetables to coat them generously.

Divide the dough into 4 balls and roll out. Share the filling mixture between the dough circles. Crimp together to form pasties and brush with beaten egg. Put the pasties on a cookie sheet and bake in the oven for 30 minutes or until the pastry is cooked.

Lentil and Vegetable Patties or Balls

INGREDIENTS *serves 4*
1 cup lentils
2½-4 cups vegetable stock
1-1½ tbsp oil
1 small onion, chopped
1 clove garlic, chopped
2oz potato
1¼ cup peas
½ tbsp fresh thyme leaves
salt and freshly ground black pepper
beaten egg for binding
whole-wheat flour for coating
parsley to garnish

METHOD

Soak the lentils for 4 hours then drain and simmer in vegetable stock, until they can be mashed with a fork. If you use a mild stock, add a little yeast extract to give a sharper taste. Drain the lentils.

Heat the oil and fry the onion and garlic until transparent. Boil the potatoes in salted water until cooked, adding the peas just before the end of cooking time. Drain.

Put all the vegetables through a food mill or grinder. Mix in the thyme and season to taste. Stir in enough egg to make a sticky dough. Form dough into small patties or balls about 1½in in diameter.

Roll the balls in whole-wheat flour and shallow fry in hot oil until crispy on all sides. Garnish with parsley and serve with Hot Tomato Sauce (see page 127) and puréed spinach or squash in a cheese sauce.

◀▲ Mushroom and broccoli nut loaf
◀ Summer vegetable pasties
▶ Lentil and vegetable patties

Sabzi Vegetable Cutlets

INGREDIENTS *serves 4-6*
1 cup diced beets
1 cup diced carrots
2 cups diced potatoes
1½ cups shredded cabbage
½ tsp chili powder
½ tsp ground roasted cumin
salt and freshly ground black pepper
large pinch sugar
1 tbsp raisins (optional)
½ cup flour
½ cup milk
bread crumbs
oil for deep frying

METHOD
Boil the beet, carrots, potatoes and cabbage together until tender. Drain.

Mash the boiled vegetables with the chili, roasted cumin, black pepper, salt, sugar and raisins. Divide into 12 balls and flatten. Chill for 1 hour.

Make a batter with the flour and milk and dip a cutlet in it. Then roll it in bread crumbs until well coated.

Heat the oil in a large skillet and fry the cutlets for 2-3 minutes turning once, until crisp and golden. Serve with Cilantro Chutney (see page 134).

Adzuki Bean Burgers

INGREDIENTS *serves 4*
1 cup dried adzuki beans
1 bay leaf
2 onions, chopped
3 cloves garlic, chopped
1-2 tbsp oil
4 carrots, peeled and grated
juice of 1 lemon
4 tbsp chopped fresh parsley
salt and freshly ground black pepper
soy sauce to taste
beaten egg for binding
whole-wheat flour for coating

METHOD
Soak the adzuki beans overnight. Drain, then cook until tender in fresh water with a bay leaf added. Drain, reserving the liquid.

Fry the onion and garlic in oil until transparent. Add the carrot and lemon juice and sweat, covered, until soft.

Add the beans, mix well and purée in a blender, adding a little of the bean cooking liquid if necessary to form a malleable consistency. Stir in the parsley, season and add soy sauce to taste. Stir in enough beaten egg to bind.

Form into burgers or balls, coat with flour and shallow fry until brown and crispy on the outside. Serve with homemade Marinara Sauce (page 127).

▶ Adzuki bean burgers
▼ Sabzi vegetable cutlets

Spinach Ring

INGREDIENTS *serves 4*
2lb spinach
6 tbsp butter
$\frac{1}{2}$ cup unbleached all-purpose flour
$1\frac{1}{4}$ cups milk
$\frac{1}{3}$ cup Parmesan cheese
salt and freshly ground black pepper
3 eggs

TOMATO SAUCE
1-2 tbsp oil
1 onion, finely chopped
2 cloves garlic, crushed
$1\frac{3}{4}$ cups canned tomatoes, mashed
1 tbsp tomato paste
salt and freshly ground black pepper

METHOD
Pre-heat the oven to 375°F. Grease a $7\frac{1}{2}$ cup ring mold.

Wash the spinach and discard tough stems. Pack spinach into a large pan with 2 tbsp butter and seasoning and cover tightly. Cook over a low heat for about 5 minutes, stirring occasionally, until spinach is soft. Drain and purée in a blender.

Now make the cheese sauce. Melt the rest of the butter in a heavy-bottomed pan and add the flour, stirring. Gradually add the milk, stirring continuously. Stir in the cheese and season. Stir until sauce bubbles and thickens, then turn down heat and cook for a further minute. Mix thoroughly with the spinach.

Separate the eggs. Beat the yolks into the spinach mixture. Beat the whites until soft peaks have formed and fold into mixture. Pour mixture into ring mold and bake for 30-40 minutes until risen and lightly set.

Meanwhile, make the tomato sauce. Heat the oil in a skillet and add the onion and garlic. Fry, stirring, until transparent. Add the tomatoes, reserving the juice. Add the tomato paste and season. Simmer for 5 minutes, adding more juice and adjusting seasoning as necessary.

To turn out the spinach ring, dip mold into ice-cold water for a few seconds. Run a knife blade around edges of mold. Invert onto a warmed plate. Spoon over the tomato sauce and serve with whole-wheat bread.

Chinese Eight Treasures

INGREDIENTS *serves 4*
$\frac{1}{2}$oz dried bean curd skin sticks
$\frac{1}{3}$ cup dried tiger lily buds
3-4 tbsp dried wood ears
$\frac{1}{3}$oz dried black moss
2oz bamboo shoots
2oz lotus root
2oz straw mushrooms
2oz cashews or almonds
4 tbsp oil
$1\frac{1}{2}$ tsp salt
1 tsp sugar
1 tbsp light soy sauce
1 tsp cornstarch mixed with 1 tbsp cold water
2 tsp sesame seed oil

▼ Spinach ring

METHOD
Soak the dried vegetables separately in cold water overnight or in warm water for at least 1 hour. Cut the bean curd sticks into short pieces.

Cut the bamboo shoots and lotus root into small slices. The straw mushrooms and white nuts can be left whole.

Heat a wok or large skillet. When it is hot, put in about half of the oil and wait until it smokes. Stir-fry all the dried vegetables together with a little salt for about 1 minute. Remove and set aside.

Add and heat the remaining oil and stir-fry the rest of the vegetables and the remaining salt for about 1 minute. Add the partly cooked dried vegetables, the sugar and soy sauce, stirring constantly. If the contents start to dry out, pour in a little water. When the vegetables are cooked, add the cornstarch and water mixture to thicken the gravy. Garnish with the sesame seed oil just before serving. This dish can be served hot or cold.

▶ Chinese eight treasures

Stir-Fried Mixed Vegetables

INGREDIENTS *serves 4*
5-6 dried Chinese mushrooms
4oz snow peas
4oz Chinese cabbage
4oz carrot
3 tbsp oil
1 tsp salt
1 tsp sugar
1 tsp water

METHOD
Soak the dried mushrooms in warm water for 25-30 minutes. Squeeze them dry, discard the hard stems and cut into thin slices. Trim the snow peas and cut the Chinese cabbage and carrots into slices.

Heat the oil in a preheated wok. Add the Chinese cabbage, carrots, snow peas and dried mushroom and stir-fry for about 1 minute. Add the salt and sugar and stir for another minute or so with a little more water if necessary. Do not overcook or the vegetables will lose their crunchiness. Serve hot.

Chinese Mixed Vegetable Casserole

INGREDIENTS *serves 4-6*
2 tbsp dried wood ears
1 cake tofu
4oz thin green beans or snow peas
4oz cabbage or broccoli
4oz baby corn or bamboo shoots
4oz carrots
3-4 tbsp oil
1 tsp salt
1 tsp sugar
1 tbsp light soy sauce
1 tsp cornstarch
1 tbsp cold water

METHOD
Soak the wood ears in water for 20-25 minutes, rinse and discard the hard stems.

Cut the tofu into about 12 small pieces and harden the pieces in a pot of lightly salted boiling water for 2-3 minutes. Remove and drain.

Trim the green beans or snow peas.

Cut the vegetables into thin slices or chunks.

Heat about half of the oil in a flameproof casserole or saucepan. When hot, lightly brown the tofu on both sides. Remove with a slotted spoon and set aside.

Heat the remaining oil and stir-fry the rest of the vegetables for about 1½ minutes. Add the tofu pieces, salt, sugar and soy sauce and continue stirring to blend everything well. Cover, reduce the heat and simmer for 2-3 minutes.

Mix the cornstarch with the water to make a smooth paste, pour it over the vegetables and stir. Increase the heat to high just long enough to thicken the sauce. Serve hot.

Vegetarian Chop Suey

INGREDIENTS *serves 4-6*
2 cakes tofu
2 tbsp dried wood ears
6oz broccoli or snow peas
6oz bamboo shoots
4oz mushrooms
4-5 tbsp oil
1½ tsp salt
1 tsp sugar
1-2 scallions, finely chopped
1 tbsp light soy sauce
2 tbsp rice wine or dry sherry
1 tsp cornstarch mixed with 1 tbsp cold water

METHOD
Cut the tofu into about 24 small pieces. Soak the wood ears in water for about 20-25 minutes, rinse them clean and discard any hard stems.

Cut the broccoli and bamboo shoots into uniformly small pieces.

Heat a wok over a high heat, add about half of the oil and wait for it to smoke. Swirl the pan so that its surface is well greased. Add the tofu pieces and shallow-fry them on both sides until golden, then scoop them out with a slotted spoon and set them aside.

Heat the remaining oil and add the broccoli. Stir for about 30 seconds and then add the wood ears, bamboo shoots and the partly cooked tofu. Continue stirring for 1 minute and then add the salt, sugar, scallions, soy sauce and wine. Blend well and when the sauce starts to boil, thicken it with the cornstarch and water mixture. Serve hot.

◄▲ Stir-fried mixed vegetables
◄ Chinese mixed vegetable casserole
▲ Vegetarian chop suey

Chinese Three Precious Jewels

INGREDIENTS *serves 4*
2 cakes tofu
8oz broccoli or snow peas
8oz carrots
4 tbsp oil
1 tsp salt
1 tsp sugar
1 tbsp light soy sauce
1 tbsp rice wine or dry sherry

METHOD

Cut the tofu into small pieces. Cut the broccoli into flowerets. Peel the stems and cut diagonally into small pieces. Peel the carrots and cut diagonally into small chunks.

Heat about half of the oil in a hot wok or frying-pan. Add the tofu pieces and shallow-fry on both sides until golden. Remove and keep aside.

Heat the rest of the oil. When very hot, stir-fry the broccoli and carrots for about 1-1½ minutes. Add the tofu, salt, sugar, wine and soy sauce and continue stirring, adding a little water if necessary. Cook for 2-3 minutes if you like the broccoli and carrots to be crunchy. If not, cook another minute or two. This dish is best served hot.

Sichuan Tofu Casserole

INGREDIENTS *serves 4*
2 tbsp dried wood ears, or dried Chinese mushrooms
3 cakes tofu
1-2 leeks or 2-3 scallions
3 tbsp
1 tsp salted black beans
1 tbsp chili bean paste
2 tbsp rice wine or dry sherry
1 tbsp light soy sauce
1 tsp cornstarch mixed with 1 tbsp cold water
freshly ground Sichuan pepper to garnish

METHOD

Soak the wood ears in water for 20-25 minutes, rinse them clean, discard any hard stems and then drain. If you use dried mushrooms, they should be soaked in hot or warm water for at least 30-35 minutes. Squeeze them dry, throw out the hard stems and cut into small pieces, retaining the water for later use.

Cut the tofu into ½-in square cubes. Blanch them in a pan of boiling water for 2-3 minutes, remove and drain.

Cut the leeks or scallions into short pieces.

Heat the oil in a hot wok until it smokes and stir-fry the leeks or scallions and the wood ears or mushrooms for about 1 minute. Add the salted black beans, crush them with the scooper or spatula and blend well.

Now add the tofu, the chili bean paste, rice wine or sherry and soy sauce and continue stirring to blend. Add a little water and cook for 3-4 minutes more. Finally add the cornstarch and water mixture to thicken the sauce.

Serve hot with freshly ground Sichuan pepper as garnish.

▲ Sichuan tofu casserole
▶ Chinese three precious jewels

Kidney Bean, Artichoke and Mushroom Casserole

INGREDIENTS *serves 4*
1 cup dried red kidney beans
1-2 tbsp oil
1 large onion, chopped
1-2 cloves garlic, chopped
3 cups sliced mushrooms
4oz thin green beans, trimmed, cut in
   thirds and parboiled
1¾ cups canned artichoke hearts,
   drained
1¾ cups canned tomatoes, mashed
salt and freshly ground black pepper
chopped fresh parsley

METHOD
Soak the kidney beans overnight and cook until tender.

Preheat the oven to 350°F. Heat oil and fry onion and garlic until translucent. Add the mushrooms and stir-fry for 1-2 minutes until just soft.

Transfer all the ingredients to a casserole. Season well. Cover and bake for 30-40 minutes. Sprinkle with parsley and serve.

Bean Moussaka

INGREDIENTS *serves 4*
1 cup dried rose cocoa beans
1 large eggplant, thinly sliced
oil
1 large onion, chopped
2 cloves garlic, chopped
1¾ cups canned tomatoes, mashed
1 tbsp tomato paste
2 tsp chopped fresh thyme
salt and freshly ground black pepper

CHEESE SAUCE
2 tbsp butter
4 tbsp all-purpose flour
1¼ cups milk
½ cup grated Cheddar cheese
grated nutmeg to taste
salt and freshly ground black pepper

METHOD
Soak the beans overnight and cook until you can mash them with a fork. Drain.

Preheat the oven to 350°F. Sprinkle the eggplant slices with salt and allow to stand in a colander for 30 minutes. Rinse and pat dry with paper towels. Heat some oil in a pan and fry eggplants gently until cooked. Set aside.

Add some more oil to the pan and fry the onion and garlic until translucent. Add the tomatoes, tomato paste, thyme and seasoning, and heat through, stirring. Mix in the beans. Set aside.

To make the cheese sauce, melt the butter in a thick-bottomed saucepan. Stir in the flour, then gradually add the milk, stirring all the time, until the sauce bubbles and thickens. Turn down the heat, add the cheese and stir until melted. Season with nutmeg and add salt and pepper to taste.

To assemble the dish, spread a layer of the bean mixture in the bottom of a casserole and top with eggplant slices. Spread thinly with cheese sauce. Continue to layer the ingredients until they are all used up, ending with a thick layer of the sauce. Bake in the oven to heat right through for 30-40 minutes and serve with a crisp green salad.

▶ Vegetable couscous
▼ Kidney bean, artichoke and mushroom casserole

Vegetable Couscous

INGREDIENTS *serves 4-6*
¾-1 cup couscous
1 tsp salt
1¼ cups boiling water
3 tbsp butter

VEGETABLE TOPPING
1 tbsp oil
2 large onions, chopped
2 leeks, sliced
4 carrots, sliced
5 cups vegetable stock
salt and freshly ground black pepper
4 zucchini, sliced
6 tomatoes, sliced
½ cup peas
¾ cup dried kidney beans, pre-soaked
    and cooked
¾ cup dried garbanzo beans, pre-soaked
    and cooked
a few strands of saffron

HOT TOMATO SAUCE
Make this in advance (see page 127).

METHOD
Put the couscous in a bowl, add the salt and
pour over the boiling water. Let it soak for
20 minutes until the water has been
absorbed. Break up any grain that is sticking
together.

Meanwhile, make the vegetable topping.
Heat the oil in a large saucepan and stir-fry
the onions and leeks. Add the carrots and
stock and season well. Bring to a boil.

Place the couscous in a vegetable steamer
(or a strainer or colander) lined with
cheesecloth, and put this over the saucepan.
Put on the lid and simmer for 30 minutes.

Remove the steamer and add the
remaining vegetables and the saffron to the
stock. Stir the couscous with a fork to break
up any lumps. Replace steamer, cover, and
continue cooking for 10 minutes.

Turn couscous into a bowl and stir in the
butter. Serve vegetables separately in a
tureen. Set the table with soup plates,
knives, forks and spoons and offer Hot
Tomato Sauce and pita bread (page 151).

Curried Vegetables

INGREDIENTS *serves 4*
2 cups chopped eggplant
2 tbsp oil
¼ cup cashew nuts
1 medium onion, chopped
1 clove garlic, crushed
2 tsp curry powder
1 large potato, peeled and half cooked
4oz green beans, trimmed
⅔ cup water
1 cup quatered tomatoes
1 tbsp curry powder
⅔ cup yogurt
2 tsp cornstarch
1 tbsp water
salt

METHOD
Salt the eggplant and leave for 30 minutes.
Rinse and pat dry.

Heat the oil and fry the cashews to a
golden brown. Remove them from the pan
and put them to one side.

Stir the onions and garlic into the pan and
cook until they begin to soften. Add the
curry powder and stir in. Add the eggplant
and cook on a low heat for about 5 minutes,
stirring from time to time. Add a little more
oil if necessary.

Add the half cooked potato, cut into
large chunks, together with the green beans.
Pour on the water, cover and leave to cook
until the potatoes are tender.

Add the tomatoes and the remaining
curry powder, stir round carefully and
continue cooking for a few more minutes.

Mix the cornstarch with the water to a
smooth paste, stir into the contents of the
pan and warm through for 3 minutes.

Serve hot, with the browned cashew nuts
sprinkled on top.

Paprika Mushrooms

INGREDIENTS *serves 4*
butter or margarine
1 medium onion, finely chopped
$\frac{1}{2}$ green bell pepper, finely chopped
1 tbsp paprika
6 cups sliced mushrooms
$\frac{2}{3}$ cup sour cream
salt and freshly ground black pepper
chopped parsley

METHOD
Heat the butter, add the onion and cook until it has just softened but not browned.

Add the green bell pepper and paprika and cook on a low heat for 3 minutes. Add the mushrooms, stir well and cook for a further 5 minutes until they are soft.

Stir in the sour cream, season to taste and warm through gently.

Serve, sprinkled with parsley. As an appetizer, serve on circles of fried bread with a crisp salad.

▲ ▶ Savory stuffed grape leaves
▶ Bulgur wheat stuffed peppers
◀ Paprika mushrooms

Bulgur Wheat Stuffed Peppers

INGREDIENTS *serves 4*

1 cup bulgur wheat
2 red bell peppers, cut in half lengthwise
   and deseeded
2 yellow bell peppers, cut in half
   lengthwise and deseeded
1 tbsp sunflower oil
1 onion, chopped
$\frac{1}{2}$ cup chopped hazelnuts
$\frac{2}{3}$ cup chopped dried apricots
$\frac{1}{2}$ tsp powdered ginger
1 tsp ground cardamom seeds
2 tbsp finely chopped cilantro leaves
3 tbsp natural yogurt
fresh cilantro leaves

METHOD

Place the bulgur wheat in a bowl, pour over $1\frac{1}{4}$ cups boiling water and leave to stand for 15 minutes.

Place the peppers in a shallow, lightly oiled baking dish.

Place the remaining oil in a saucepan, add the onion and gently fry until softened.

Stir in the bulgur wheat, hazelnuts, apricots, ginger and cardamom. Cook for 1 minute, stirring continuously.

Add the cilantro and yogurt, mix together and use to fill the pepper shells. Cover the dish tightly with aluminum foil and bake in a preheated oven at 375°F for 30-35 minutes.

Serve immediately, garnished with cilantro leaves.

Savory Stuffed Grape Leaves

INGREDIENTS *serves 4*

1 cup brown rice
olive oil
1 small onion, chopped
2 cloves garlic, chopped
salt and freshly ground black pepper
8oz peeled bottled or canned chestnuts
1-2 tbsp butter
2 cups mushrooms
2 tomatoes, peeled and chopped
1 tsp Italian seasoning
20 grape leaves

METHOD

Wash the rice in several changes of cold water. Heat 1 tbsp oil in a heavy-bottomed pan and fry the onion and garlic until translucent. Stir in the rice and cook for a few minutes before covering with boiling water. (Use about $\frac{2}{3}$ water to $\frac{1}{3}$ rice by volume.) Bring back to a boil, then cover the pan and turn the heat down very low. The rice should be cooked in about 40 minutes.

Meanwhile, drain the chestnuts and chop them finely. Melt the butter in a pan and add the mushrooms. When they are tender, add the tomatoes, chestnuts and herbs. Stir once or twice and remove from the heat.

When the rice is cooked, mix it thoroughly with the nut stuffing and check the seasoning. Use it, by the spoonful, to stuff the grape leaves. Pack them into an baking dish, brush with olive oil and cover the dish with foil. Heat through in the oven. Stuffed grape leaves are best eaten hot, but they're good cold too, if you have any left over.

97

Potato Topped Vegetable Pie

INGREDIENTS *serves 4-6*
½ cup green lentils
¼ cup pot barley
1 onion, chopped
1¾ cups canned chopped tomatoes
6oz cauliflower flowerets
2 stalks celery, sliced
1 leek, thickly sliced
1 turnip, sliced
2 carrots, diced
2 tbsp chopped fresh mixed herbs
1½lb potatoes, scrubbed
3 tbsp low-fat milk
salt and freshly ground black pepper
2 tbsp grated reduced-fat medium-hard
 cheese

METHOD
Place the lentils, barley, onion, tomatoes, cauliflower, celery, leek, turnip, carrots and herbs in a large saucepan with 1¼ cups water.

Bring to a boil, cover and simmer for 40-45 minutes or until everything is soft.

Cover potatoes with boiling water and cook for about 15 minutes, or until soft.

Drain, peel and mash the potatoes with the milk and season to taste.

Place the lentil mix in a pie dish an oval baking dish and either pipe or fork the potatoes on top.

Sprinkle with cheese and place in a pre-heated oven at 400°F for 30-35 minutes.

Omelet Archie Williams

INGREDIENTS *serves 2*
½ cup smoked cod or haddock
⅔ cup milk
2 tbsp butter
4 tbsp all-purpose flour
⅓ cup grated cheddar cheese
3 eggs
salt and freshly ground black pepper

METHOD
Poach the fish in a little of the milk until cooked through. Drain and reserve milk. Skin and flake fish.

Melt the butter in a pan and stir in the flour. Gradually stir in the milk, including the milk from the fish, until you have a smooth sauce. Add the cheese and stir until melted.

Beat the eggs and season well.

Put the fish in a shallow baking dish about 8in across. Cover with cheese sauce, then pour the beaten egg over. Cook under a pre-heated broiler set at high for about 7 minutes until the egg is nearly set and the omelet is beginning to brown on top. Serve with salad. This omelet will make a light lunch for 2 people.

Avocado Soufflé Omelet

INGREDIENTS *serves 2*
1 green bell pepper
3 tbsp butter
1 ripe avocado
dash lemon juice
4 eggs, separated
salt and freshly ground black pepper

METHOD
Seed and slice the green bell pepper. Heat a little of the butter in a pan and fry gently until soft. Set aside.

Cut the avocado in half. Remove the seed and remove the flesh from the shell in one careful movement with a paring knife. Slice the avocado and sprinkle with lemon juice.

Beat the egg yolks and season with salt and pepper. Beat the whites and fold the two together.

Heat half the remaining butter in a pan and pour in half the omelette mixture. Arrange half the avocado and green bell pepper on one side of it. When lightly set, fold the omelet in half, slide out of the pan and keep hot until you have made the second omelet in the same way.

◄▲ Omelet Archie Williams
▲ Avocado soufflé omelet
► Mushroom omelet surprise

Mushroom Omelet Surprise

INGREDIENTS *serves 2*
2 cups mushrooms
about ⅔ cup milk
1 tbsp butter
1 tbsp all-purpose flour
1 tbsp grated Parmesan cheese
salt and freshly ground black pepper
4 eggs, separated

METHOD

Peel or wipe the mushrooms and slice. Put them in a small, heavy-bottomed pan with a little of the milk and poach gently until very black and juicy. Remove the mushrooms with a slotted spoon and arrange them in the bottom of a shallow greased baking dish about 7 in in diameter.

Make a cheese sauce. Heat the butter in a pan and when it has melted, add the flour. Stir well and remove from the heat. Add the milk that the mushrooms have been cooked in and stir in enough extra milk (you may need a little more than ⅔ cup) to make a thick sauce. Stir in the cheese and season well.

Beat the yolks into the cheese sauce. Beat the whites until they form soft peaks and fold into the sauce.

Pour the mixture over the mushrooms and cook under a preheated broiler until the omelet is nearly set and golden on top.

Fried "Pocketed Eggs"

INGREDIENTS *serves 4*
4 eggs
2-3 tbsp oil
1 tbsp light soy sauce
1 scallion, finely chopped

METHOD
Heat the oil in a hot wok or skillet and fry the eggs on both sides. Add the soy sauce and a little water and braise for 1-2 minutes. Ganish with scallion and serve hot.

Taking a bite of the egg and finding the yolk inside the white is rather like finding something in a pocket - hence the name of this dish.

Chinese Scrambled Eggs and Tomatoes

INGREDIENTS *serves 4*
2 large firm tomatoes
5 eggs
1½ tsp salt
2 scallions, finely chopped
1 tsp finely chopped ginger root (optional)
4 tbsp oil

METHOD
Scald the tomatoes in a bowl of boiling water and peel off the skins. Cut each tomato in half lengthwise and then crosscut each half into wedges.

Beat the eggs with a pinch of salt and about a third of the finely chopped scallions.

Heat about half the oil in a hot wok or skillet and lightly scramble the eggs over a moderate heat until set. Remove the eggs from the wok.

Heat the wok again over high heat and add the remaining oil. When the oil is hot, add the rest of the finely chopped scallions, the ginger root (if used) and the tomatoes. Stir a few times and then add the scrambled eggs with the remaining salt. Stir for 1 minute more and serve hot.

NOTE
Other vegetables such as cucumber, green peppers or green peas can be substituted for the tomatoes.

Fu-Yung Tofu

INGREDIENTS *serves 4*
1 cake tofu
4 egg whites
1 romaine lettuce heart
⅓ cup shelled green peas
1 scallion, finely chopped
½ tsp grated ginger root
1 tsp salt
1 tbsp cornstarch mixed with 2 tbsp water
⅓ cup milk
oil for deep-frying
1 tsp sesame seed oil

METHOD
Cut the tofu into long, thin strips and blanch in a pan of salted boiling water to harden. Remove and drain.

Lightly beat the egg whites. Add the cornstarch mixture and milk.

Wash and separate the lettuce heart. If you use frozen peas, make sure they are thoroughly defrosted.

Wait for the tofu to cook and then coat with the egg whites, cornstarch and milk mixture.

Heat the oil in a wok or deep-fryer until it is very hot. Turn off the heat and let the oil cool a bit before adding the tofu coated with the egg whites and cornstarch mixture. Cook for about 1-1½ minutes and then scoop out with a slotted spoon and drain.

Pour off the excess oil leaving about 1 tbsp in the wok. Increase the heat and stir-fry the lettuce heart with a pinch of salt. Remove and set aside on a serving dish.

Heat another tbsp of oil in the wok and add the finely chopped scallion and ginger root followed by the peas, salt and a little water. When the mixture starts to boil, add the tofu strips. Blend well, add the sesame oil, and serve on the lettuce heart.

▲ Fu-yung tofu

▶ Chinese scrambled eggs and tomatoes

Broccoli and Tomato Cheesecake

INGREDIENTS *serves 4-6*
1 cup whole-wheat cracker crumbs
4 tbsp butter, softened

THE FILLING
8oz broccoli flowerets
1 large tomato
1½ cups farmer's cheese
salt and freshly ground white pepper
pinch nutmeg
2 eggs, separated

THE TOPPING
broccoli flowerets
a little dissolved gelatin, if liked

METHOD
Pre-heat the oven to 350°F. Combine the crumbs and the butter and press down well into a greased 8-in quiche pan with a loose bottom.

Steam the broccoli flowerets over boiling salted water until tender. Carefully slice some of the flowerets for decorating and reserve the rest. Immerse the tomato in boiling water for a minute, refresh in cold water, peel and seed.

Mash the farmer's cheese with the broccoli and tomato and season well with salt, pepper and a good pinch of nutmeg. Beat in the egg yolks.

Beat the whites until they form soft peaks and fold into the mixture. Pour the filling over the crumb base and bake for 20-25 minutes until slightly risen and just set.

Allow to cool. When cold, remove the sides of the pan and garnish the top with the remaining broccoli flowerets. Brush with gelatin if you like and chill before serving.

Leek and Blue Cheese Bake

INGREDIENTS *serves 4*
1lb small leeks
6 eggs
1 slice whole-wheat bread, crumbed
2 tbsp cider vinegar
4oz blue cheese

METHOD
Preheat the oven to 400°F. Trim and wash the leeks. Steam for 10-15 minutes. Lay them in a greased baking dish.

Beat the eggs with the vinegar and bread crumbs and crumble in the cheese. Pour over the leeks and bake for 30 minutes until risen and golden.

Eggs with Curly Kale

INGREDIENTS *serves 2-4*
1lb curly kale
4 eggs
2 tbsp butter
¼ cup unbleached all-purpose flour
1¼ cups milk
½ cup grated cheddar cheese
salt and freshly ground black pepper

METHOD
Wash the kale and discard the stems. Pack into a saucepan with a very little water, cover and cook slowly for about 20 minutes until tender. Drain and cut up roughly with a knife and fork. Put the kale in the bottom of a flameproof serving dish and keep warm.

Soft-boil the eggs.

Meanwhile, make the cheese sauce. Melt the butter in a pan and stir in the flour. Cook, stirring for a few minutes. Gradually add the milk. Continue to stir until the sauce has thickened. Add the cheese. When it melts, season.

Plunge the eggs in cold water, then remove the shells. Lay them on the bed of kale and cover with the sauce. Heat the dish through in the oven or under the broiler.

Cheese Strudel

INGREDIENTS *serves 4*
12oz puff pastry dough, thawed
1½ cups grated cheddar cheese
⅔ cup cream cheese
⅔ cup farmer's cheese
1 egg
chopped fresh parsley or mint
salt and freshly ground black pepper
egg white for glazing

METHOD
Roll the dough out as thinly as possible.

Mix the remaining ingredients except the egg white until smooth. Spread the mixture over the dough.

Fold over to make a flattish strip, sealing the edges well. Brush with the egg white. Place on a moistened cookie sheet and bake at 400°F for 20 minutes.

Serve hot, with sour cream if liked.

◀▲ Leek and blue cheese bake
▶ Cheese strudel

Savory Cheesecake

INGREDIENTS *serves 4-6*
either a crumb base or an 8-in pie shell
butter
1 large onion, sliced
4 eggs
1$\frac{1}{3}$ cups farmer's cheese
1$\frac{1}{3}$ cups cream cheese
chopped fresh chives
salt and freshly ground black pepper

METHOD
Put the dough into the springform pan.
Heat the butter, add the onion and cook
until it has just softened but not browned.

Beat the eggs until they are very light and
fluffy. Mix the cheeses with the cooked
onion, chives, salt and pepper. Carefully
fold the cheese mixture into the beaten eggs
and spoon this into the prepared pie shell.

Bake at 350°F for 40 minutes.

Serve cold (preferably the next day) with
a crisp salad. This freezes very well. Leeks
make a tasty addition with the onions,
softened in a little butter.

Vegetable and Rice Hotch Potch

INGREDIENTS *serves 6*
oil
3 cups sliced onions
1 cup rice
1 large green or red bell pepper,
    chopped
salt and freshly ground black pepper
1 tsp paprika
1$\frac{3}{4}$ cups canned tomatoes
$\frac{2}{3}$ cup water
2$\frac{1}{2}$ cups yogurt
4 eggs

METHOD
Heat the oil, add the onions and cook until
they have just softened but not browned.
Add the rice and peppers and stir them
around to color them a little. Season well
with salt, pepper and paprika.

Layer the rice mixture with the tomatoes
in a baking dish. Pour a mixture of 4 tbsp oil
and the water over.

Cover and cook at 375°F for 30 minutes
(or on top of a medium heat).

Mix the yogurt with the eggs. Pour over
the vegetables and return the dish,
uncovered, to the oven for a further 20
minutes.

VARIATION
This Bulgarian dish adapts to endless
variations - add some more vegetables,
such as eggplant, zucchini, mushrooms,
fennel. Salami, sausages or cooked meat
can also be added before the yogurt
topping.

▲ Vegetable and rice hotch potch

VEGETABLE AND RICE
SIDE DISHES

*Just as in non-vegetarian cookery, there are some dishes that
satisfy as main courses and others which serve best as
complements. They round out our enjoyment of a meal and
fulfill nutritive requirements. Potatoes, rice and bean recipes, and
a wide selection of green and root vegetables take to the table in
styles European, Indian and Oriental.*

Three peppers in tomato and garlic

Zucchini with Almonds

INGREDIENTS *serves 4*
6 large zucchini, sliced lengthwise
1 medium onion, finely chopped
1 tbsp olive oil
salt and freshly ground black pepper
$\frac{1}{3}$ cup flaked almonds
1 tsp cornstarch
1 tbsp water
1 cup yogurt

METHOD
Place the zucchini in a shallow baking dish. Mix the onions, oil, salt and pepper and spoon the mixture over the zucchini. Bake, uncovered, at 350°F for 40 minutes, or until tender.

Meanwhile toast the almonds: put them into a heavy skillet over a high heat and shake the pan frequently; don't burn.

Mix the cornstarch with the water and add it to the yogurt with seasoning to taste. Warm the mixture over a gentle heat, stirring constantly, for 3 minutes.

Spoon the sauce over the zucchini and scatter the almonds on top.

Zucchini Gratin

INGREDIENTS *serves 4*
oil
4 large zucchini, sliced
1 large onion, chopped
$1\frac{3}{4}$ cups canned tomatoes
chopped fresh basil, thyme or marjoram
sliver lemon peel
salt and freshly ground black pepper
1 cup macaroni
2 eggs
$\frac{2}{3}$ cup yogurt
$\frac{3}{4}$ cup grated cheddar cheese

METHOD
Heat the oil and fry the zucchini until they are lightly colored. Remove them from the pan and reserve. Add the onion and fry until golden, adding more oil if necessary. Add the tomatoes, herbs, lemon peel, salt and pepper and simmer for 10 minutes, breaking up the tomatoes and stirring from time to time.

Meanwhile, cook the macaroni and drain it well. Put it into an baking dish.

Pour the sauce over the macaroni and mix it through well. Lay the cooked zucchini on top. Mix the eggs, yogurt and half the cheese and pour the mixture over the zucchini. Scatter the remaining cheese on top.

Bake the dish at 375°F for 30 minutes.

VARIATION
You could use eggplants instead of zucchini, in which case slice and salt them, leave them to drain for 30 minutes, rinse and dry them and proceed as above.

▼ Zucchini gratin

Chili Beans

INGREDIENTS *serves 4*
1 cup rose cocoa beans
2 tbsp olive oil
$\frac{1}{2}$ tsp fennel seeds
$\frac{1}{2}$ tsp mustard seeds
1 onion, chopped
2 cloves garlic, chopped
1$\frac{3}{4}$ cup sliced mushrooms
$\frac{1}{2}$ fresh green chili, deseeded and
    chopped
1$\frac{3}{4}$ cups canned tomatoes, mashed
2 tbsp chopped fresh cilantro or parsley
salt and freshly ground black pepper

METHOD
Soak the beans overnight then cook them in salted water until tender. Cooking time will vary depending on the age of the beans. They could be ready in 20 minutes, or they may take an hour, so keep testing.

Meanwhile, heat the oil in a pan and, when hot, add the seeds. As soon as the mustard seeds begin to pop, add the onion and garlic. Cook gently until translucent.

Stir in the mushrooms. When they are tender, add the chili and tomatoes, cilantro and seasoning. If you can't get cilantro, use parsley instead, but the dish will certainly lose some of its character.

Add the beans, heat through for 10 minutes and serve with toasted rarebit or an omelet for a warming winter supper.

Zucchini with Dill

INGREDIENTS *serves 4*
$\frac{1}{4}$ cup olive oil
2 tbsp butter
1 onion, chopped
1 garlic, crushed
1lb zucchini topped, tailed and sliced in
    thickish slices
salt and freshly ground black pepper
2 tsp paprika
1 tbsp dill, chopped (not the stems)
1 small tub sour cream

METHOD
Heat oil and butter in a large skillet. Cook the onion and garlic gently until soft. Turn up the heat.

Add the zucchini, garlic and black pepper and toss.

Cook for 5-10 minutes, stirring to cook both sides of the zucchini slices.

When browning, add the paprika, dill and sour cream. Season and serve.

Magyar Squash

INGREDIENTS *serves 4*
1 medium to large squash
2 tbsp butter
2 tsp cornstarch
1 tbsp water
1 tbsp dried dill weed
salt and freshly ground black pepper
$\frac{2}{3}$ cup sour cream

METHOD
Peel the squash and either finely chop or grate it. Cook the squash with the butter, stirring from time to time, just until it begins to soften. Mix the cornstarch with the water until smooth and add it to the squash. Stir and cook for a further 3 minutes. Add the dill, salt and pepper and finally stir in the sour cream. Warm it through gently and serve the squash hot.

▲ Zucchini with dill
▶ Chili beans

Stuffed Squash

INGREDIENTS *serves 4-6*
1 squash
salt and freshly ground black pepper
1/3 cup brown rice
2 small carrots, diced
1/4 cup shelled peas
1-2 tbsp oil
1 onion, chopped
1 clove garlic, chopped
1 stalk celery, chopped
1 handful chopped fresh parsley
2 tbsp chopped hazelnuts

TOMATO SAUCE
1-2 tbsp oil
1 onion, chopped
2 cloves garlic, chopped
1¾ cups canned tomatoes, mashed
1 tbsp tomato paste
salt and freshly ground black pepper

METHOD
Preheat the oven to 350°F. Cut the squash in half lengthwise and scoop out the pith and seeds. Sprinkle the flesh with salt and leave the halves upside down to drain.

Meanwhile, make the filling. Simmer the rice in a covered pan of salted water until just tender (about 30 minutes). Drain.

Parboil carrots and peas and drain. Heat oil in a pan and fry onion and garlic until translucent. Add celery, carrots and peas. Stir in the rice, parsley and hazelnuts and season well. Dry the squash and pile filling into one half of it. Top with second half.

Make the tomato sauce. Heat oil in a pan and add onion and garlic. Fry, stirring, until soft. Add tomatoes and tomato paste. Simmer for 5 minutes, stirring occasionally, and season well.

Place squash in a baking dish with a lid, if you have one big enough, otherwise use foil to cover. Surround it with the sauce. Cover and cook for 45 minutes until squash is tender. Serve hot or cold with a crisp green salad.

Creamed Spinach

INGREDIENTS *serves 4*
3 cups washed and picked over fresh
 spinach
1 egg yolk
grated nutmeg
salt and freshly ground black pepper
2/3 cup yogurt

METHOD
Cook the spinach without any excess water (the water adhering to it is sufficient) and a little salt. Drain the cooked spinach very well (press it between 2 plates for most effective drainage).

Beat together the egg yolk, nutmeg and seasoning to taste, and yogurt. Mix into the spinach. Warm through gently.

NOTE
If you prefer to use frozen spinach, use leaf, not chopped spinach.

Roasted Eggplant

INGREDIENTS *serves 4*
1 large eggplant
1 small onion, finely chopped
1-2 green chilis, finely chopped
1/2 tsp salt
2-3 tbsp mustard oil

METHOD
Place the eggplant under a preheated broiler for about 15 minutes, turning frequently, until the skin becomes black and the flesh soft.

Peel the skin and mash the flesh.

Add the rest of the ingredients to the mashed eggplant and mix thoroughly.

La Lechuga

INGREDIENTS *serves 4*
1 tight head crisp lettuce, iceberg for
    preference
4 tbsp olive oil
4 cloves garlic, finely chopped

METHOD
Discard looser outer leaves of lettuce. With
a very sharp knife, cut lettuce in half from
stem to tip. Cut each half into thirds. Keep
cold.

Heat oil in skillet and when hot, add
garlic. Fry, stirring, until brown. Pour over
the lettuce and serve immediately. This is
best eaten with the fingers if you don't mind
the mess. Offer plenty of paper napkins.
Lettuce served this way also makes an
unusual and appetizing start to a summer
meal.

Spicy Eggplant

INGREDIENTS *serves 4*
1lb eggplant
3 tbsp oil
1 large onion, finely chopped
3 tomatoes, chopped
1 tbsp chopped fresh cilantro
1-2 green chilis, chopped
$\frac{1}{2}$ tsp ground turmeric
$\frac{1}{2}$ tsp chili powder
$\frac{3}{4}$ tsp ground coriander
$\frac{3}{4}$ tsp salt

METHOD
Place the eggplant under a preheated broiler
for about 15 minutes, turning frequently
until the skin turns black and the flesh soft.
Peel off the skin and mash the flesh.

Heat the oil in a karai or wok over
medium heat and fry the onions until soft.
Add the tomatoes, cilantro and green chilis
and fry another 2-3 minutes.

Add the mashed eggplant, turmeric,
chili, coriander and salt and stir.

Fry for another 10-12 minutes and serve
with Naan or Baktora (page 155).

◄▲ Stuffed squash
▲► La lechuga
► Spicy eggplant

109

Caraway Cabbage

INGREDIENTS *serves 4*

2 tbsp butter
9 cups finely sliced white or green
    cabbage
1 tbsp caraway seeds
salt and freshly ground black pepper
2 tsp all-purpose flour
²/₃ cup sour cream

METHOD

Melt the butter and add the cabbage. Stir
well. Add the caraway seeds, salt and
pepper, cover and cook until the cabbage is
cooked but still crisp.

Add the flour and stir it in well. Cook for
a further 2 minutes, stirring constantly. Add
the sour cream and warm it through.

Cabbage with Peas

INGREDIENTS *serves 4*

3 tbsp oil
2 bay leaves
³/₄ tsp whole cumin seeds
9 cups finely shredded cabbage
1 tsp ground turmeric
¹/₂ tsp chili powder
1¹/₂ tsp ground cumin
1 tsp ground coriander
2 tomatoes, chopped
³/₄ tsp salt
¹/₂ tsp sugar
¹/₂ cup peas

METHOD

Heat the oil in a karai or large pan over
medium high heat and add the bay leaves
and the cumin seeds. Let them sizzle for a
few seconds.

Add the cabbage and stir for 2-3 minutes.
Add the turmeric, chili, cumin, coriander,
tomatoes, salt and sugar and mix with the
cabbage.

Lower heat, cover and cook for 15
minutes. Add the peas and cover again.
Continue to cook for a further 15 minutes,
stirring occasionally.

Remove the cover, turn heat up to
medium high and, stirring continuously,
cook until it is dry.

Shredded Carrot and Cabbage

INGREDIENTS *serves 4*

2 tbsp oil
1 tsp mustard seeds
1 tight head scallions, finely shredded
4 cups grated carrots
a little honey
salt and freshly ground black pepper

METHOD

Heat oil in a heavy pan with a lid. When it is
hot, add the mustard seeds.

As soon as the mustard seeds begin to
pop, pile in the shredded vegetables, drizzle
over the honey and stir well. Turn down the
heat, put on the lid and cook for 3 minutes or
until just tender. Season and serve.

▲ ▲ Caraway cabbage
▲ Shredded carrot and cabbage

Brussels Sprouts with Garlic and Mushrooms

INGREDIENTS *serves 4*
2-3 tbsp oil
4 cloves garlic, chopped
4 cups thinly sliced Brussels sprouts
2 cups sliced mushrooms

METHOD

Heat some oil in a wok or deep-sided skillet. Add the garlic and fry quickly, stirring, until crisp and brown.

Add the sprouts and mushrooms and stir until coated with garlic and oil. Stir-fry for 1-2 minutes and eat while crisp and hot. A delicious accompaniment to bean dishes.

Cauliflower with Potatoes and Peas

INGREDIENTS *serves 4-6*
4 tbsp oil
2 medium onions, finely chopped
4 cups diced potatoes in $\frac{3}{4}$-in pieces
1 small cauliflower, cut into $\frac{3}{4}$-in pieces
$\frac{1}{2}$ tsp ground turmeric
$\frac{1}{3}$ tsp chili powder
1 tsp ground cumin
2 tomatoes, chopped
1 tsp salt
$\frac{1}{4}$ tsp sugar
1 cup peas
$\frac{1}{2}$ tsp Garam Masala (see Sauces and Dressings, page 126)

METHOD

Heat the oil in a wok over medium high heat. Add the onions and fry for 3-4 minutes until light brown.

Add the potatoes and cauliflower and stir. Add the spices, tomatoes, salt and sugar. Stir and fry for 2-3 minutes.

Add the peas, cover and lower heat to medium low and cook for about 20 minutes until the potatoes and cauliflower are tender. Stir the vegetables a few times to stop them sticking.

Sprinkle with Garam Masala before serving.

▲ ▶ Carrots with yogurt
◀ Cauliflower with potatoes and peas

Carrots with Yogurt

INGREDIENTS *serves 4-6*
$3\frac{1}{2}$ cups sliced carrots
1 tsp sugar
$\frac{1}{2}$ tsp ground cumin
1 small onion, finely chopped
juice of $\frac{1}{2}$ lemon
$\frac{2}{3}$ cup yogurt
salt and pepper

METHOD

Cook the carrots with the sugar in boiling water just until they are al dente. Drain them and add the cumin and onion. Stir around.

Mix the lemon juice into the yogurt, season to taste and spoon it over the carrots.

Serve immediately or leave it to cool and serve as a salad or an accompaniment to curry.

Beans with Baby Corn

INGREDIENTS *serves 4-6*
8oz thin green beans
8oz baby corn
3-4 tbsp oil
1½ tsp salt
1 tsp sugar
2 tbsp water

METHOD
Wash and trim the beans. Depending on the size of the baby corns, leave them whole if small, or cut them into 2 or 3 diamond-shaped pieces if larger.

Heat a wok or large skillet over a high heat until very hot, add the oil and swirl it so that the cooking surface is well greased. When the oil starts to smoke, add the beans and baby corn and stir-fry for about 1 minute.

Add the salt and sugar and continue stirring for another minute or so. Add the water if the vegetables dry out before they are cooked.

Serve as soon as all the liquid has evaporated. If you prefer your vegetables slightly underdone, serve when there is still a little juice left in the wok.

Stir-fried Asparagus

INGREDIENTS *serves 4*
1lb asparagus
2 tbsp oil
1 tsp salt
1 tsp sugar

METHOD
Wash the asparagus well in cold water and discard the tough ends of the stems. Cut the tender part of the shoots into 1-in pieces, using the roll-cutting method: make a diagonal slice through the stem, then roll it half a turn and slice again, so that you end up with diamond-shaped slices.

Heat the oil in a very hot wok or skillet, swirling it to grease the pan well. Add the asparagus when the oil starts smoking. Stir-fry until each piece is coated with oil.

Add salt and sugar and continue stirring for 1-1½ minutes only. No extra liquid should be added because it would spoil the color and texture.

This dish can be served either hot or cold.

▲ Beans with baby corn
◀ Stir-fried asparagus

113

Hot-and-Sour Cabbage

INGREDIENTS *serves 6*
1½lb white cabbage
10 Sichuan peppercorns
5 small dried red chili peppers
2 tbsp soy sauce
1½ tbsp vinegar
1½ tbsp sugar
1½ tsp salt
3 tbsp sunflower oil
1 tsp sesame seed oil

METHOD

Choose a round, pale green cabbage with a firm heart - never use looseleafed cabbage. Wash in cold water and cut the leaves into small pieces the size of a matchbox.

Cut the chilis into small bits. Mix the soy sauce, vinegar, sugar and salt to make the sauce.

Heat the sunflower oil in a preheated wok until it starts to smoke. Add the peppercorns and the red chilis and a few seconds later the cabbage. Stir for about 1½ minutes until it starts to go limp.

Pour in the prepared sauce and continue stirring for a short while to allow the sauce to blend in. Add the sesame seed oil just before serving.

This dish is delicious both hot and cold.

Stir fried Green and Red Peppers

INGREDIENTS *serves 4*
1 large or 2 small green bell peppers, cored and deseeded
1 large or 2 small red bell peppers, cored and deseeded
3 tbsp oil
1 tsp salt
1 tsp sugar

METHOD

Cut the peppers into small diamond-shaped pieces; if you use 1 or 2 orange peppers, the dish will be even more colorful.

Heat the oil in a hot wok or skillet until it smokes. Spread the oil with a scooper or spatula so that the cooking surface is well greased. Add the peppers and stir-fry until each piece is coated with oil. Add salt and sugar.

Continue stirring for about 1 minute and serve if you like your vegetables crunchy and crisp. If not, you can cook them for another minute or so until the skin of the peppers becomes slightly wrinkled. Add a little water if necessary during the last stage of cooking.

Green Beans in Garlic Sauce

INGREDIENTS *serves 4*
14oz stringless green beans
1 large or 2 small cloves of garlic
3 tbsp oil
1 tsp salt
1 tsp sugar
1 tbsp light soy sauce

METHOD

Trim the beans. Leave them whole if they are young and tender; otherwise, cut them in half.

Crush and finely chop the garlic.

Blanch the beans in a pan of lightly salted boiling water, drain and plunge in cold water to stop the cooking and to preserve the beans' bright green color. Drain.

Heat the oil in a hot wok or skillet. When it starts to smoke, add the crushed garlic to flavor the oil. Before the color of the garlic turns dark brown, add the beans and stir-fry for about 1 minute. Add the salt, sugar and soy sauce and continue stirring for another minute at most. Serve hot or cold.

▶ Green beans in garlic sauce
▼ Hot and sour cabbage

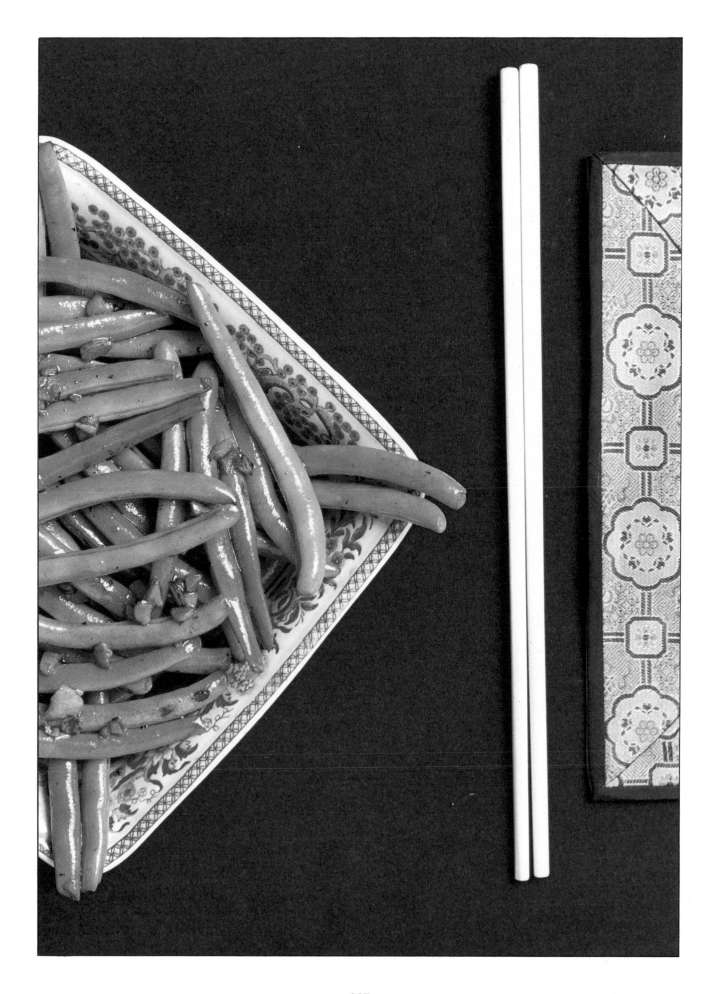

Savory Vegetable Julienne

INGREDIENTS *serves 4*
1 tbsp sunflower oil
1 green chili, deseeded and finely
  chopped
1 clove garlic, crushed
1/2 head fennel, cut into thin strips
1 leek, cut into thin strips
1 green bell pepper, cut into thin strips
1/4 small red cabbage, shredded
1 tbsp lemon juice
salt and freshly ground black pepper

METHOD
Heat the sunflower oil in a large saucepan
and add the chili and garlic. Cook for 1-2
minutes, then add the fennel, leek, pepper
and cabbage.

Stir and cook for 3-4 minutes. Add the
lemon juice and season to taste.

Roasted Cauliflower

INGREDIENTS *serves 4*
4 medium tomatoes
1 large onion
3 cloves garlic
1/2-in ginger root
2 tbsp Ghee (see page 126)
3/4 tsp ground turmeric
1/2 tsp chili powder
1/2 tsp Garam Masala (see page 126)
scant 1 cup shelled peas
1/2 tsp salt
1 medium-sized cauliflower, blanched

Chestnuts and Vegetables

INGREDIENTS *serves 6-8*
1lb chestnuts
4 tbsp olive oil
2 fat cloves garlic, chopped
3 cups sliced mushrooms
12oz Brussels sprouts
2 cups shredded red cabbage
salt and freshly ground black pepper
small glass red wine

▲▲ Savory vegetable julienne
▲ Roasted cauliflower
◄ Chestnuts and vegetables

METHOD
Preheat the oven to 400°F. Make a nick in
the top of the chestnuts with a sharp knife
and boil them for 10 minutes. Plunge them
in cold water and peel.

Heat the olive oil in a flameproof
casserole and fry the garlic. Add the
mushrooms, sprouts and red cabbage and
season. Cook, stirring occasionally, for
about 5 minutes until coated with oil and
beginning to soften.

Stir in the chestnuts and red wine. Cover
and bake in the oven for 40 minutes. Serve
with baked potatoes or a Purée of Root
Vegetables (see page 118).

METHOD
Blend the tomatoes, onion, garlic and
ginger in a blender until you have a paste.

Heat the Ghee in a skillet over medium
heat and add the paste, turmeric, chili and
Garam Masala and stir-fry until the Ghee
and spices separate, about 5-6 minutes.

Add the peas and salt and cook a further
5 minutes, stirring constantly. Remove from
the heat.

Place the cauliflower in a large baking
dish and pour the spices over it. Place in a
preheated oven at 375°F for 30-35 minutes.
Serve on a flat plate with the peas and spices
poured over the top.

Purée of Root Vegetables

INGREDIENTS *serves 4*
6oz carrots
6oz rutabaga
1 turnip
1 parsnip
butter
salt and freshly ground black pepper

METHOD
Trim and peel the vegetables and simmer in salted water until tender.

Drain and mash to a fluffy purée with butter. Season with salt and plenty of black pepper. Serve with a dish that has a crunchy texture, such as Chestnuts and Vegetables (see page 117) or Nut Loaf (see page 84).

Corn Croquettes

INGREDIENTS *serves 4*
3 tbsp butter
3 tbsp all-purpose flour
1¼ cups milk
salt and freshly ground black pepper
1-2 tbsp finely chopped parsley
2⅓ cups whole corn kernels, cooked
2 egg yolks

THE COATING
2 eggs, beaten
seasoned flour
fine stale bread crumbs
oil for frying

METHOD
To make the sauce, cut the butter into small pieces and melt in a heavy-bottomed pan. Stir in the flour and cook for a few minutes until the mixture is a pale gold.

Remove from the heat and pour in the milk. Stir well, return to the heat and stir until the sauce has thickened. Season with salt and plenty of pepper.

Stir the parsley, corn kernels and egg yolks into the mixture. Chill.

The mixture should have a heavy dropping consistency. Form it into croquettes. Dip each in the beaten egg, then roll in the flour and bread crumbs.

Fry the croquettes in oil until crisp.

Fennel Mornay

INGREDIENTS *serves 4*
3 bulbs fennel
bay leaf

THE SAUCE
2 tbsp butter
¼ cup unbleached all-purpose flour
1¼ cups milk
⅔ cup light cream
1 cup grated cheddar cheese
¼-½ cup fresh bread crumbs
salt and freshly ground black pepper

METHOD
Trim the fennel and simmer in salted water with a bay leaf for about 30 minutes until tender.

Meanwhile, make the sauce. Melt the butter in a pan and stir in the flour. Cook, stirring, for a couple of minutes and then gradually stir in the milk. Add the cream and most of the cheese and cook gently until the cheese has melted. Season well and keep warm.

Drain the fennel and cut each bulb in half. Lay the halves in a flameproof dish and pour the sauce over them. Sprinkle with the remaining cheese and the bread crumbs. Put under a hot broiler to brown and melt the cheese.

NOTE
For a tangier sauce, add a little powdered English mustard to taste.

Corn-on-the-Cob with Garlic Butter

INGREDIENTS *serves 4-6*
corn on the cob
butter
garlic paste

METHOD
Remove the outer green leaves from the fresh corn. Place in boiling salted water with a drop of olive oil.

Simmer for 20 minutes, or until the corn is cooked and tender.

Remove from the heat and drain.

Smother liberally with butter and garlic paste.

Cheese and Potato Croquettes

INGREDIENTS *serves 6-8*
2lb potatoes
2 egg yolks
4 tbsp butter
salt and freshly ground black pepper
pinch nutmeg
dash sherry
¹/₂ cup grated Parmesan cheese
pinch mustard
2 tbsp chopped parsley
seasoned flour
egg wash (egg beaten with a little milk)
bread crumbs

METHOD

Wash and peel the potatoes, and cut to an even size. Cook in salted water until soft; then drain.

Put a lid on the pan of the potatoes and place over a low heat to dry out, stirring occasionally to prevent burning.

Place the potatoes in a food processor with the yolks, butter and seasoning.

Mix in the nutmeg, sherry, Parmesan cheese, mustard and parsley. The potatoes should be like a very firm mash. Overmixing will make them gluey, in which case some flour will have to be worked in by hand.

Check that the mix is seasoned well and mold into cylinder shapes (5×2in).

Roll in seasoned flour; dip in eggwash and coat with bread crumbs.

Deep-fry in hot fat, 365°F. When golden, drain well and serve.

NOTE

If you want to keep the croquettes for cooking later, or the next day, place them carefully on a tray, cover with plastic wrap and refrigerate.

◄▲ Corn croquettes
◄ Purée of root vegetables
►▲ Split peas with vegetables
► Corn-on-the-cob with garlic butter

Split Peas with Vegetables

INGREDIENTS *serves 4-6*
scant 1 cup split peas, washed
3 cups water
2 tbsp Ghee (see page 126)
¹/₂ tsp whole cumin seeds
2 bay leaves
2-3 green chilis, cut lengthwise
2¹/₂ cups diced potatoes, cut into 1-in pieces
¹/₃ cup shelled peas
3 cups cauliflower flowerets
¹/₂ tsp ground turmeric
1 tsp salt

METHOD

In a large saucepan, bring the split peas and water to a boil. Cover and simmer for 30 minutes. Remove from heat.

Heat the ghee in a large saucepan over medium-high heat. Add the cumin seeds, bay leaves and green chilis and let them sizzle for a few seconds.

Add the potatoes, peas, cauliflower and fry for 1-2 minutes.

Add the boiled split peas with the water, turmeric and salt. Mix thoroughly, lower heat and cook until the vegetables are tender. (If the mixture gets too thick add a little more water.)

Egg-baked Potatoes

INGREDIENTS *serves 6-8*
3 cups sliced peeled potatoes
salt
2 tsp paprika
4 eggs, hard-boiled and sliced
$2/3$ cup sour cream
2 tbsp milk
butter

METHOD
Boil the potatoes until they are cooked but still firm. Drain off the water and slice them.

Put a layer of potatoes in the bottom of a greased baking dish. Season with salt and paprika. Lay the sliced eggs over the potatoes. Mix the sour cream with the milk until smooth. Spoon over the eggs. Season again. Add the remaining potatoes.

Dot with butter and bake at 350°F for 25 minutes, until golden.

VARIATION
To make this more substsantial you could add slices of cheese over the sliced eggs.

Russian Potatoes

INGREDIENTS *serves 6-8*
2lb potatoes
salt and freshly ground black pepper
4 tbsp butter
1 large onion, sliced
2 cups sliced mushrooms
$3/4$ cup sour cream
3 tbsp chopped chives

METHOD
Scrub the potatoes and cook in salted water until barely tender. Drain, peel and slice.

Melt some of the butter in a flameproof casserole and fry the onion until translucent. Add the mushrooms and cook gently until the juices run. Add the rest of the butter as necessary and stir in the potatoes. Let them gently brown on one side, season, turn over and add the cream.

When most of the cream has been absorbed, sprinkle over the chopped chives and a little more pepper and serve.

▼ Russian potatoes

Swiss Potato Cakes

INGREDIENTS *serves 4*
1lb waxy potatoes
2 eggs
1 tbsp potato flour
salt and freshly ground black pepper
4 tbsp oil

METHOD
Peel the potatoes and grate them into a bowl of cold water. Drain. Squeeze the potato shreds dry in a cloth. Mix the potato with the eggs, flour and seasoning.

Heat 1 tbsp of the oil in a skillet and make your first potato cake using a quarter of the mixture. Spread it out in the pan and flatten it. When the underside is crisp and golden, turn it over and brown the top. Keep it warm while you make the rest.

Patatas Bravas

INGREDIENTS *serves 2-3*
1 onion, chopped
2 tbsp olive oil
1 bay leaf
2 red chilies
2 tsp finely chopped garlic
1 tbsp tomato paste
$1/2$ tbsp sugar (up to 1 tbsp, if the sauce
    is too tart for your liking)
1 tbsp soy sauce
1lb canned plum tomatoes, chopped
1 glass white wine
salt and freshly ground black pepper
3 medium potatoes

METHOD
Sweat the onions in the oil with the bay leaf.

When soft, add the chilies, garlic, tomato paste, sugar and soy sauce. Sweat for a further 5 minutes on a low heat.

Add the chopped tomatoes and white wine. Stir and bring to a boil. Simmer for 10 minutes. Taste and season. (This sauce should be slightly sweet; the flavor of the tomatoes should not dominate it.)

Cut the potatoes like small roast potatoes. Grease a cookie sheet. Season the potatoes well and brush with melted butter.

Roast in a hot oven, 450°F, until golden. Pour the tomato sauce over and serve.

Black-eyed Peas with Onions

INGREDIENTS *serves 4-6*
1 cup black-eyed peas, washed
5 cups water
2 tbsp oil
1 large onion, finely chopped
2 cloves garlic, crushed
¼-in piece ginger root grated
1-2 green chilis, finely chopped
½ tsp salt
1 tsp molasses

METHOD
Soak the beans in the water overnight.

Boil the beans in the water and then cover and simmer for 1 hour until tender. Drain.

Heat the oil in a large saucepan and fry the onion, garlic, ginger and chili until the onions are soft. Add the beans, salt and molasses and cook until all the moisture is absorbed, about 15 minutes. Serve with Baktoras (page 155).

Three Peppers in Tomato and Garlic

INGREDIENTS *serves 6*
¾ cup olive oil
2 yellow bell peppers, deseeded and cut
    into thin strips
2 red bell peppers, deseeded and cut
    into thin strips
2 green bell peppers, deseeded and cut
    into thin strips
1 tbsp chopped fresh parsley
2 tsp finely chopped garlic
8oz fresh or canned tomatoes
salt and freshly ground black pepper

METHOD
Heat the oil in a large skillet and cook the peppers gently for 2-3 minutes, stirring frequently. Add the parsley and garlic and cook for another couple of minutes.

Add the chopped tomatoes and their juice to the pan. Stir and season.

Cover and simmer gently for about 20 minutes, until the peppers are tender.

The sauce should be quite thick - if necessary, remove the peppers and boil rapidly to reduce the liquid. Season.

▲ ▲ Black-eyed peas with onions   ▲ Patatas bravas

◀ Egg-fried rice
▶ Perfect boiled rice

Egg-*fried* Rice

INGREDIENTS *serves 6-8*
3 eggs
2 scallions, finely chopped
1 tsp salt
4 tbsp oil
²⁄₃ cup shelled green peas
4 cups cooked rice
1 tbsp light soy sauce (optional)

METHOD
Lightly beat the eggs with about half of the finely chopped scallions and a pinch of salt.

Heat about half of the oil in a hot wok or skillet, pour in the beaten eggs and lightly scramble until set. Remove.

Heat the remaining oil and when hot, add the remaining scallions followed by the green peas and stir-fry for about 30 seconds. Add the cooked rice and stir to separate each grain. Add the salt and soy sauce together with the eggs and stir to break the eggs into small pieces. Serve as soon as everything is well blended.

Perfect Boiled Rice

INGREDIENTS *serves 4*
1¼ cups long grain rice
2½ cups water

METHOD
Wash and rinse the rice in cold water until clean.

Bring the water to a boil in a saucepan over high heat. Add the washed rice and bring back to a boil. Stir the rice with a spoon to prevent it sticking to the bottom of the pan and then cover the pan tightly with a lid and reduce the heat to very low. Cook gently for 15-20 minutes.

NOTE
It is best not to serve the rice immediately. Fluff it up with a fork or spoon and leave it under cover in the pan for 10 minutes or so before serving.

Chow Mein-Fried Noodles

INGREDIENTS *serves 4*
1oz dried tofu skin sticks
²/₃ cup dried tiger lily buds
2oz bamboo shoots
4oz spinach or any other greens
8oz dried egg noodles
2 scallions, thinly shredded
3-4 tbsp oil
1 tsp salt
2 tbsp light soy sauce
2 tsp sesame seed oil

METHOD
Soak the dried vegetables overnight in cold water or in hot water for at least 1 hour. When soft, thinly shred both the tofu skins and tiger lily buds.

Shred the bamboo shoots and spinach leaves into thin strips.

Cook the noodles in a pan of boiling water according to the directions on the package. Depending on the thickness of the noodles, this should take 5 minutes or so. Freshly made noodles will take only about half that time.

Heat about half the oil in a hot wok or skillet. While waiting for it to smoke, drain the noodles in a strainer. Add them with about half the scallions and the soy sauce to the wok and stir-fry. Do not overcook, or the noodles will become soggy. Remove and place them on a serving dish.

Add the rest of the oil to the wok. When hot, add the other scallions and stir a few times. Then add all the vegetables and continue stirring. After 30 seconds or so, add the salt and the remaining soy sauce together with a little water if necessary. As soon as the gravy starts to boil, add the sesame seed oil and blend everything well. Place the mixture on top of the fried noodles as a dressing.

NOTE
Of course you can use substitutes for any of the ingredients in the dressing. For instance, instead of dried tofu skin, you can use dried Chinese mushrooms or fresh mushrooms. Instead of tiger lily buds, why not use fresh bean sprouts or shredded celery? It is the contrast of texture and color that is important.

Vegetarian Special Fried Rice

INGREDIENTS *serves 4*
4-6 dried Chinese mushrooms
1 green bell pepper, cored and deseeded
1 red bell pepper, cored and deseeded
4oz bamboo shoots
2 eggs
2 scallions, finely chopped
2 tsp salt
4-5 tbsp oil
6 cups cooked rice
1 tbsp light soy sauce (optional)

▲ Vegetarian special fried rice

METHOD
Soak the dried mushrooms in warm water for 25-30 minutes, squeeze dry and discard the hard stems. Cut the mushrooms into small cubes.

Cut the green and red bell peppers and the bamboo shoots into small cubes.

Lightly beat the eggs with about half of the scallions and a pinch of the salt.

Heat about 2 tbsp of oil in a hot wok, add the beaten eggs and scramble until set. Remove.

Heat the remaining oil. When hot, add the rest of the scallions followed by all the vegetables and stir-fry until each piece is covered with oil. Add the cooked rice and salt and stir to separate each grain of rice. Finally add the soy sauce, blend everything together and serve.

123

▼ Pilaf rice with coconut and milk

Pilaf with Coconut

INGREDIENTS *serves 4-6*
1½ cups basmati rice, rinsed and drained
2 tbsp shredded coconut
2-3 green chilies
1 tsp salt
½ tsp sugar
2 tbsp raisins
1 tbsp pistachio nuts, skinned and cut
    into thin strips
2 baby leaves
2-in cinnamon stick
4 cardamom pods
3 tbsp Ghee (see page 126)
2½ cups milk
1¼ cups water

METHOD
Mix the rice with all the dry ingredients.

Heat the Ghee in a large saucepan over
medium heat. Add the rice mixture and
sauté for 5 minutes, stirring constantly.

Add the milk and water, increase the heat
to high and bring to a boil. Stir.

Lower heat to very low, cover and cook
for about 20 minutes until all the liquid has
evaporated. Fluff the pillaf with a fork and
serve hot.

Fried Rice

INGREDIENTS *serves 4*
3 tbsp Ghee (see page 126)
2 bay leaves
2-in cinnamon stick
4 cardamom pods
3 large onions, finely sliced
3 green chilies, cut lengthwise
1½ cups basmati rice, cooked and
    cooled
1 tsp salt
½ tsp sugar
2 tbsp raisins (optional)

METHOD
Heat the Ghee in a large skillet over medium
high heat. Add the bay leaves and spices; let
them sizzle a little.

Add the onions and chilies and fry until
the onions are golden brown. Add the rice,
salt, sugar and raisins and continue frying
until the rice is thoroughly heated up.

SAUCES AND DRESSINGS

Sauces and dressings are invaluable to the vegetarian cook, since they can turn a plainly prepared vegetable or salad into something altogether more interesting. They can save time – and vitamins – allowing the vegetables to be lightly cooked or served raw, and then dressed.

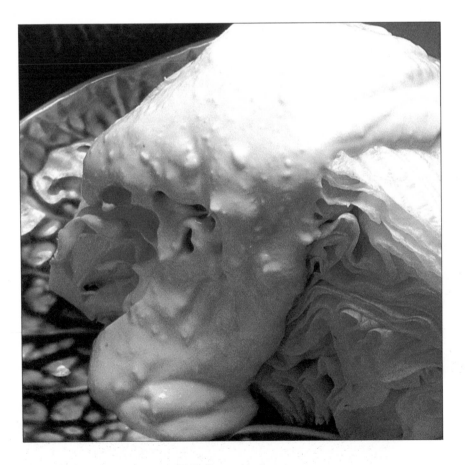

Blue cheese dressing

Yogurt

INGREDIENTS *makes about 5 cups*
5 cups milk
2 tbsp unflavored commercial yogurt at
    room temperature

METHOD

Scald the milk. Heat it until it is ready to
boil. Just before boiling point, remove the
pan from the heat and allow to cool until
lukewarm. Test by dripping a little milk on
your wrist. It should feel warm, not hot.

Put the yogurt in the chosen container
and stir in a little milk until smooth. Now
stir in the remaining milk.

Cover and place container in the
incubator. Be careful not to disturb the
yogurt for about 4 hours. When the
consistency is right, chill in the refrigerator
to set before using.

NOTE

Yogurt can be made in any sterile container
with a tightly fitting lid inside any sort of
incubator, such as an oven with the pilot
light on or a styrofoam box, but because the
secret of successful yogurt making is a
constant lukewarm temperature, it is best to
use a special yogurt maker. Don't put
incubating yogurt near a heat source
regulated by a thermostat that switches on
and off. Use 2 tbsp of the homemade yogurt
to start the next batch. The cost of making
yogurt at home is minimal and the method
is easy.

Ghee-Clarified Butter

INGREDIENTS *makes about 2 cups*
1lb unsalted butter

METHOD

Heat the butter in a saucepan over low heat.
Let it simmer for 15-20 minutes until all the
white residue turns golden and settles at the
bottom.

Remove from the heat, strain and cool.

Pour into an airtight bottle and store in a
cool place.

Homemade Garam Masala

INGREDIENTS *makes about ⅓ cup*
3 tbsp cardamon seeds
3x1-in cinnamon sticks
½ tbsp cumin seeds
½ tsp black peppercorns
½ tsp cloves
¼ nutmeg

METHOD

Grind all the spices together until they are
finely ground. Store in a spice bottle until
required. (The ingredients may be added in
different proportions to suit individual
tastes.)

Béchamel Sauce

INGREDIENTS *makes about 3¼ cups*
2½ cups milk
1 small onion, peeled
1 small carrot, peeled and sliced
1 bay leaf
6 slightly crushed peppercorns
1 blade mace
1 stem parsley
3 tbsp butter
6 tbsp all-purpose flour
salt and white pepper

METHOD

Pour milk into a saucepan. Add the onion
cut into quarters with 2 slices of carrot, bay
leaf, peppercorns, mace and parsley stem.

Cover and allow to heat on a low heat
without boiling for about 10 minutes.
Remove from the heat and allow to infuse
for a further 10 minutes, covered.

Make a roux (a blend of butter and flour)
by melting the butter in a saucepan. Do not
allow the butter to brown. Add the flour and
stir well over a medium heat.

Gradually add the strained milk and stir
briskly or beat until a smooth creamy sauce
is made, season to taste.

Cold Horseradish Sauce

INGREDIENTS *makes about ¼ cup*
2 tbsp prepared horseradish cream
⅔ cup sour cream

METHOD

Stir the horseradish cream into the sour
cream. Refrigerate for an hour before use if
possible.

Use this sauce for potatoes and beet
dishes.

▲ Homemade garam masala

Cucumber Dill Sauce

INGREDIENTS *makes about 2½ cups*
1 medium cucumber, peeled
2 tbsp butter
⅔ cup vegetable stock
⅔ cup dry white wine
2 tbsp chopped fresh dill or
   1 tbsp dried dill
4 tsp cornstarch
2 tbsp water
½ cup sour cream or yogurt
salt and pepper

METHOD
Coarsely grate the cucumber and put it into a saucepan. Add the butter and cook on a gentle heat just to soften the cucumber. Add the stock, wine and dill and simmer for 5 minutes. Mix the cornstarch with the water. Add it to the pan, cook gently until the sauce begins to thicken, stirring constantly. Add the sour cream or yogurt and warm it through. Season to taste.

Serve hot or cold, with salmon or other fish. Also good with poached eggs, boiled potatoes, rice or pasta.

Marinara Sauce

INGREDIENTS *makes about 5 cups*
4 tbsp olive oil
2 cloves garlic, crushed
4½ cups peeled and chopped tomatoes
salt and freshly ground black pepper
6 basil leaves

METHOD
Heat the oil in a saucepan, add the garlic and stir for 1 minute. Add the tomatoes roughly chopped and seasoning and allow to simmer for 6 minutes.

Chop the basil leaves and add to the tomatoes, stir the sauce for a further minute. Serve on freshly cooked pasta. This sauce is a simple accompaniment to pasta which is very good to eat and easy to prepare but the secret is that the tomatoes should be simply heated through, not cooked to a pulp.

Hot Tomato Sauce

INGREDIENTS *makes about 1¼ cups*
1 tbsp oil
1 onion, finely chopped
2-3 cloves garlic, finely chopped
1¾ cups canned tomatoes, mashed,
   with juice
2 tbsp tomato paste
1 tsp ground cumin
1 tsp ground coriander
½ tsp ground chili
salt

METHOD
Heat oil in a pan, add onion and garlic and stir-fry until soft.

Add remaining ingredients, simmer until thickened and check seasoning. Serve with Vegetable Couscous (page 95).

▲ Cucumber dill sauce

Creamy Mustard Vinaigrette

INGREDIENTS *makes about $^2/_3$ cup*
3 tbsp olive oil
2 tbsp heavy cream
2 tbsp red-wine vinegar
1 tbsp Dijon mustard
$^1/_2$ tsp dried thyme
$1^1/_2$ tsp soy sauce
salt and freshly ground black pepper

METHOD
Put the olive oil, cream, vinegar and mustard in a small bowl. Stir with a fork or beat until the mixture is somewhat foamy.

Stir in the thyme, soy sauce, salt and pepper.

Modern Vinaigrette

INGREDIENTS *makes 1 cup*
2 tbsp wine vinegar
1 tbsp lemon juice
1 tsp prepared mustard
salt and freshly ground black pepper
$^3/_4$ cup pure olive oil

METHOD
Put the vinegar, lemon juice, mustard, salt and pepper in a jar with a tightly fitting lid.

Cover the jar tightly and shake until the salt dissolves.

Add the olive oil to the jar and shake until well mixed.

Tofu Dressing

INGREDIENTS *makes about 2 cups*
$1^2/_3$ cups silken tofu
2 tbsp lemon juice
3 tbsp oil
pinch salt
1 tsp soy sauce
1 clove garlic, crushed

METHOD
Blend all the ingredients together in a blender or food processor.

Mayonnaise

INGREDIENTS *makes $1^3/_4$ cups*
2 egg yolks
$^1/_2$ tsp salt
1 tsp Dijon mustard
$1^1/_4$ cups olive oil
2 tsp cider vinegar

METHOD
All the ingredients must be at room temperature. Put the egg yolks in a bowl with the salt and mustard and beat together with a balloon whisk.

Beating constantly and evenly, add the olive oil at a very slow trickle. A bottle with a nick cut in the cork can be used to ensure that only a very little oil dribbles out at a time. The aim is to break up the oil into very small globules so that it can be absorbed by the egg yolks. When all the oil has been added you should have a thick glossy emulsion that will cling to the whisk.

Gradually beat in the cider vinegar. For a thinner mayonnaise, beat in 1 tbsp hot water.

Mayonnaise Maltaise

INGREDIENTS *makes $1^3/_4$ cups*
$1^3/_4$ cups mayonnaise (see above)
grated peel and juice of 2 oranges

METHOD
Combine the ingredients and serve with cooked vegetables such as asparagus and artichokes, or use as a salad dressing.

Blue Cheese Dressing

INGREDIENTS *makes about $1^3/_4$ cups*
1 cup yogurt
$^1/_2$ cup blue cheese
3 tbsp olive oil
salt and freshly ground black pepper

METHOD
Blend all the ingredients together thoroughly.

Tomato Yogurt Dressing

INGREDIENTS *makes $^3/_4$ cup*
$^2/_3$ cup yogurt
4 tsp tomato ketchup
dash Worcestershire sauce
dash Tabasco sauce
salt and freshly ground black pepper

METHOD
Mix all the ingredients together well. Serve on crisp lettuce or as a seafood dressing.

VARIATION
Add finely chopped green or red bell pepper, chopped hard-boiled egg, chopped scallions.

Rich Vinaigrette

INGREDIENTS *makes about $1^3/_4$ cups*
1 egg
$^1/_2$ cup oil
2 tbsp lemon juice
1 clove garlic, crushed
fresh herbs
salt and freshly ground black pepper
1 cup yogurt

METHOD
Blend together the egg, oil, lemon juice, garlic, herbs, salt and pepper. Slowly add the yogurt, with the blender running. Refrigerate until required - it should thicken as it stands.

VARIATION
This makes a delicious salad dressing but if you want to make it thicker, for piping, you can add some gelatin and let it set. Use chives, fennel, parsley, tarragon or any other fresh herb you have on hand - or a mixture.

NOTE
For a less rich dressing omit the egg.

▲▶ Tomato yogurt dressing
▶ Blue cheese dressing

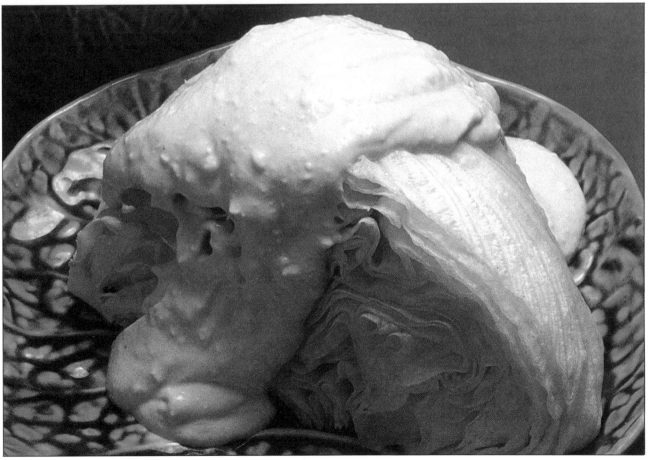

Tomato Dressing

INGREDIENTS *makes ¼ cup*
4 tbsp tomato paste
3 tbsp olive oil
4 tbsp lemon juice
2 cloves garlic, crushed
1 small onion, finely chopped
1 tbsp honey
pinch salt

METHOD
Blend all the ingredients together thoroughly.

Cheese Herb Dressing

INGREDIENTS *makes 2 cups*
1⅓ cups farmer's cheese
¾ cup sour cream
2 scallions, finely chopped
1 tbsp chopped fresh parsley
1 tbsp chopped fresh dill
1 tbsp sugar
1 tbsp chopped onion

METHOD
Combine everything together, mixing well to blend the cheese and sour cream.

Serve over plain poached fish or as a salad dressing.

VARIATION
Use ricotta instead of farmer's cheese, if preferred.

◄ Tomato dressing

Green Mayonnaise

INGREDIENTS *makes about 1½ cups*
3 tbsp chopped fresh spinach
3 tbsp chopped watercress
3 tbsp chopped scallion
3 tbsp chopped fresh parsley
1 cup mayonnaise
½ tsp grated nutmeg
salt to taste

METHOD
Put the spinach, watercress, scallion and parsley in a small saucepan. Add water to cover them.

Quickly bring to a boil. Remove the saucepan from the heat. Let stand for 1 minute.

Drain the greens well. Rub them through a strainer or purée them in a blender. Drain off excess liquid.

Put the mayonnaise in a blender or medium-sized bowl. Add the purée, nutmeg and salt to taste. Blend until evenly mixed.

Touch of Asia Dressing

INGREDIENTS *makes 1 cup*
2 tsp soy sauce
2 tsp water
1 whole scallion, chopped
½ tsp sesame oil
¼ tsp hot pepper chili oil
1 garlic clove, finely chopped
¼ tsp ground black pepper
¾ cup peanut oil
2½ tbsp rice-wine vinegar

METHOD
Put the soy sauce, water, scallion, sesame oil, hot pepper oil, garlic and black pepper in a jar with a tightly fitting lid. Cover and shake until the ingredients are blended.

Add the peanut oil to the jar, cover tightly and shake again. Let the mixture stand for 2 minutes.

Add the vinegar to the jar. Cover tightly and shake well again. Pour over the salad immediately.

Lemon Dressing

INGREDIENTS *makes ¾ cup*
1 tsp water
large pinch salt
large pinch grated lemon peel
2 tsp dried mint
4 tbsp fresh lemon juice
½ cup pure olive oil
large pinch ground black pepper

METHOD
Put the water, salt and lemon peel in a jar with a tightly fitting lid. Let stand for 2 minutes.

Add the mint and lemon juice. Cover the jar tightly and shake.

Add the olive oil and black pepper. Cover the jar tightly, shake again and serve.

Yogurt Mayonnaise

INGREDIENTS *makes 1 cup*
½ cup unflavored yogurt
1 tbsp honey
1 tsp fresh lemon juice
4½ tbsp mayonnaise
¼ tsp salt
1 tsp poppy seeds

METHOD
Combine the yogurt, honey and lemon juice in a bowl. Stir with a wooden spoon until well blended.

Add the mayonnaise, salt and poppy seeds. Stir until thoroughly mixed. Chill for 1 hour and serve.

Basil Dressing

INGREDIENTS *makes 1 cup*
1 cup yogurt
10 basil leaves, finely chopped
1 large clove garlic, crushed
salt and freshly ground black pepper

METHOD
Blend everything together well. Serve over green or mixed salad or tomato and onion salad.

NOTE
This also makes a good sauce for pasta, in which case double the quantity.

Herb Dressing

INGREDIENTS *makes 1½ cups*
½ cup cream cheese
1 cup yogurt or buttermilk
salt and freshly ground black pepper
finely chopped fresh herbs

METHOD
Blend everything together well. Refrigerate until required. Use on salads or fish.

Tahini Dressing

INGREDIENTS *makes 1¾ cups*
1 cup tahini
4 tbsp water
4 tbsp lemon juice
3 cloves garlic, crushed
pinch salt

METHOD
Blend all the ingredients together thoroughly.

Thousand Island Dressing

INGREDIENTS *makes 1¹/₃ cups*
1 cup mayonnaise
4 tbsp Tabasco or chili sauce
2 tbsp finely chopped pimento-stuffed
  green olives
1 hard-boiled egg, finely chopped
1 tbsp heavy cream
¹/₂ tsp fresh lemon juice
1¹/₂ tsp finely chopped scallion
2 tbsp finely chopped sweet green bell
  pepper
2 tbsp finely chopped fresh parsley
¹/₄ tsp paprika
large pinch freshly ground black pepper

METHOD
Put the mayonnaise and Tabasco sauce in a
medium-sized bowl. Stir with a wooden
spoon until well blended.

Add the olives, egg, cream and lemon
juice. Continue stirring.

Add the remaining ingredients. Stir until
well blended. Refrigerate for at least 1 hour
before serving. It goes well on tossed green
salad.

Chutney Dressing

INGREDIENTS *makes about 1¹/₂ cups*
¹/₂ cup sour cream
¹/₂ cup buttermilk
2 tbsp mango chutney
1 tbsp lemon juice
2 tsp oil
2 tsp mustard
salt and freshly ground black pepper

METHOD
Blend everything together well. Refrigerate
until required.

Serve on salad or cold vegetables. Use as
a dressing for hard-boiled eggs, cold fish or
meat.

Fruit Salad Syrup Dressing

INGREDIENTS *makes 1¹/₄ cups*
1 tbsp all-purpose flour
²/₃ cup water
¹/₂ tsp pure vanilla extract
1 egg
5 tbsp sugar
2 tsp butter
large pinch ground nutmeg
3 tbsp heavy cream

METHOD
Put the flour and 2 tbsp water into a
saucepan. Stir to form a thin paste. Add the
vanilla and egg. Beat well until smooth.

Put the sugar, remaining water and butter
in another saucepan. Bring to a boil over a
low heat.

Add the boiling syrup to the vanilla and
egg mixture. Stir well. Cook over low heat,
stirring constantly, until thick and smooth.

Remove the saucepan from the heat.
Allow the dressing to cool.

Stir in the nutmeg and cream. Beat until
well blended and pour over the fruit salad.

Sour Cream Anchovy Dressing

INGREDIENTS *makes about ²/₃ cup*
²/₃ cup sour cream
1 clove garlic, crushed
4 anchovy fillets, finely chopped
3 scallions, finely chopped
chopped fresh dill
juice of 1 lemon
salt and freshly ground black pepper

METHOD
Mix everything together well. Refrigerate
until required.

Serve as a salad dressing or on hot or cold
fish or broiled meats.

▲ Thousand island dressing

DRINKS, PICKLES AND CHUTNEYS

*The emphasis on healthy eating – and less alcohol consumption
– has bought the attractions of fresh fruit drinks to a wide public,
while pickles and chutneys are a much-treasured legacy from
earlier days. The following recipes are the stock of an
international pantry.*

Orange yogurt drink

Mint and Chili Cucumber

INGREDIENTS *makes 1⅓ cups*
1 cucumber, grated, sprinkled with salt
    and placed in a strainer to remove
    excess moisture
1 large tomato, peeled by placing in
    boiling water for 10 seconds and then
    plunged into cold water to remove
    skin
½ tsp garlic, chopped
1 bunch mint, chopped
⅔ cup yogurt
⅔ cup sour cream
1 tsp cumin
2 red chilies, deseeded and chopped
salt and freshly ground black pepper

METHOD
Wash the excess moisture off the cucumber
and drain well, squeezing any moisture out.

Chop the tomato into little cubes;
discard the seeds.

Mix all the ingredients together in a
bowl, season well and chill.

▲ ▲ Mint and chili cucumber
▲ Mint chutney
▲ ▶ Cilantro chutney

Mint Chutney

INGREDIENTS *makes 1 cup*
¼ cup tamarind juice
2oz mint leaves, washed
2 tbsp chopped onions
2 cloves garlic
¾-in piece ginger root
2-3 green chilis
½ tsp salt
½ tsp sugar

METHOD
Make the tamarind juice by soaking 1 dried
tamarind in boiling water for 10 minutes.

Blend all the ingredients together until
you have a smooth paste. Serve with any
fried foods (Can be stored in an airtight jar
in the refrigerator for one week.)

Cilantro Chutney

INGREDIENTS *makes 1¼ cups*
¾ cup cilantro leaves
4 cloves garlic
3 tbsp shredded coconut
2 green chilies
2-3 tbsp lemon juice
½ tsp salt
¼ tsp sugar

METHOD
Chop the sprigs of cilantro and throw away
the roots and lower stems.

Blend the cilantro with all the other
ingredients until you have a smooth paste.
Serve with any fried foods. (Can be stored in
an airtight jar in the refrigerator for one
week.)

Fresh Tomato, Cucumber and Onion Sambal

INGREDIENTS *makes about 3 cups*
3/4 cup tomatoes chopped into 1/4-in pieces
1 cup cucumber, cut into 1/4-in pieces
1/2 cup onions, chopped
2-3 green chilis
1/2 tsp salt
1/4 tsp sugar
3 tbsp lemon juice
2 tbsp chopped fresh cilantro

METHOD
Mix all the ingredients together in a small bowl. Cover and set aside to chill. Serve with any Indian meal.

Pineapple Chutney

INGREDIENTS *makes about 1 cup*
1/2 tbsp oil
1/2 tsp whole mustard seeds
1 cup canned pineapple, crushed and drained
big pinch salt
1 tsp cornstarch mixed with a little milk

METHOD
Heat the oil in a small pan over medium heat. Add the mustard seeds and let them sizzle for a few seconds.

Add the drained pineapple and salt and, stirring occasionally, cook for about 10 minutes.

Thicken with the cornstarch mixture and remove from the heat. Chill.

▲ ▲ Fresh tomato, cucumber and onion sambal

▲ Pineapple chutney

Cucumber Raita

INGREDIENTS *makes about 2 1/2 cups*
1/2 cucumber, peeled and chopped
1 small onion, chopped
2 cups yogurt
squeeze lemon juice
salt and freshly ground black pepper
cilantro leaves

METHOD
Mix all the ingredients together, seasoning to taste, and garnish with the cilantro leaves. Use Italian parsley if cilantro is not available.

Chill well before serving.

Tea Eggs

INGREDIENTS *serves 12*
12 eggs
2 tsp salt
3 tbsp light soy sauce
2 tbsp dark soy sauce
1 tsp five-spice powder
1 tbsp red tea leaves

METHOD

Boil the eggs in water for 5-10 minutes. Remove and gently tap the shell of each egg with a spoon until it is cracked finely all over.

Place the eggs back in the pan and cover with fresh water. Add the salt, soy sauces, five-spice powder and tea leaves (the better the quality of the tea, the better the result). Bring to a boil and simmer for 30-40 minutes. Leave the eggs to cool in the liquid.

Peel off the shells - the eggs will have a beautiful marbled pattern. They can be served either on their own or as part of a mixed hors d'œuvre, whole or cut into halves or quarters.

Pickled Radishes

INGREDIENTS *serves 4-6*
24 radishes
2 tsp sugar
1 tsp salt

METHOD

Choose fairly large radishes that are roughly equal in size, if possible, and cut off and discard the stems and tails. Wash the radishes in cold water and dry them thoroughly. Using a sharp knife, make several cuts from the top about two-thirds of the way down the sides of each radish.

Put the radishes in a large jar. Add the sugar and salt. Cover the jar and shake well so that each radish is coated with the sugar and salt mixture. Leave to marinate for several hours or overnight.

Just before serving, pour off the liquid and spread out each radish like a fan. Serve them on a plate on their own or as a garnish with other cold dishes.

Chinese Pickled Vegetables

INGREDIENTS *use 4 to 6 of the following vegetables or more:*
cucumber
carrot
radish or turnip
cauliflower
broccoli
green cabbage
white cabbage
celery
onion
fresh ginger root
leek
scallion
red bell pepper
green bell pepper
string beans
garlic
5 quarts cold boiled water
$^3/_4$ cup salt
2oz chili peppers
3 tsp Sichuan peppercorns
$^1/_4$ cup Chinese distilled spirit (or white rum, gin or vodka)
4oz fresh ginger root
$^1/_2$ cup brown sugar

METHOD

Put the cold boiled water into a large, clean earthenware or glass jar. Add the salt, chilies, peppercorns, spirit, ginger and sugar.

Wash and trim the vegetables, peel if necessary and drain well. Put them into the jar and seal it, making sure it is airtight. Place the jar in a cool place and leave the vegetables to pickle for at least five days before serving.

Use a pair of clean chopsticks or tongs to pick the vegetables out of the jar. Do not allow any grease to enter the jar. You can replenish the vegetables, adding a little salt each time. If any white scum appears on the surface of the brine, add a little sugar and spirit. The longer the pickling lasts, the better.

◀ Tea eggs with pickled radishes
▶ Pickled vegetables

136

Tomato Cocktail

INGREDIENTS *serves 4*
3-4 medium ripe tomatoes, skinned
1¼ cups yogurt
fresh basil
salt and freshly ground black pepper
pinch sugar
2 ice cubes

METHOD
Squeeze out the seeds of the tomatoes and place the flesh in a blender, together with the remaining ingredients. Blend everything together well. Serve immediately in tall glasses. Garnish with additional basil leaves.

VARIATION
This also makes a good salad dressing, in which case halve the quantity and omit the ice cubes.

Orange Yogurt Drink

INGREDIENTS *serves 2*
¾ cup yogurt
½ cup oz milk
grated peel and juice of 1 orange
grated lemon peel
1 tsp honey
1½ tbsp hazelnuts (optional)

METHOD
Blend all the ingredients together well. Serve immediately or refrigerate until required.

VARIATION
A simpler citrus yogurt drink can be made by blending either the flesh of an orange or that of a small grapefruit together with ⅔ cup yogurt and sugar to taste.

Green Beech Liqueur

INGREDIENTS *makes 1 bottle*
tender young beech leaves
vodka
fruit sugar
brandy

METHOD
Pick young beech leaves in late spring or early summer. Make sure they are tender. (What you don't use in this recipe you can eat in a salad.)

Pack the leaves into a jar and press them well down. Fill the jar with vodka. Seal and leave for 2 weeks in a dark place.

Strain off the vodka, which will now be a bright green in color.

To make the liqueur, prepare a syrup of 1 cup fruit sugar and 1¼ cups boiling water to every 2½ cups of vodka. Stir the sugar into the water until dissolved. When cool, add 1 tbsp brandy for each 1¼ cups of water and sugar and combine with the vodka. Bottle and seal.

Sloe Gin

INGREDIENTS *makes 1 bottle*
ripe sloes
the best Dutch gin

NOTE
Sloes are the blue-black fruit of the blackthorn bush and can be harvested in October. Pick over them and remove the stems.

METHOD
Half fill a bottle with sloes and fill it to the top with gin. Seal the bottle and store in a dark place.

The gin will take on a beautiful pink color and a tangy fruity flavor within about two weeks. You can leave it longer if you want a stronger, fruitier taste, or you can decant the gin and top up the bottle with fresh gin a second time. Sloe gin makes an ideal Christmas drink.

◀ Tomato cocktail

BREADS AND PASTRIES

This is a large section comprising breads of all colors and textures, sweet cookies and savory crackers, rolls and muffins, yeast pastries, tarts and cakes. The home baker and patissiere will find a wealth of inspiration and counsel here.

Fruit tartlets

Quick White Bread

INGREDIENTS *makes 2 large or 4 small loaves*
2oz fresh yeast or 4 tbsp active dry yeast and $\frac{1}{2}$ tsp sugar
3$\frac{3}{4}$ cups warm water
2×25mg tablets vitamin C
12 cups all-purpose flour
2 tsp salt
2 tbsp sugar
$\frac{1}{4}$ cup butter or margarine

METHOD
Oven temperature 450°F.

Grease 2 large (or 4 small) bread pans. Mix the yeast with a few tbsp water adding the 1tsp sugar if active dried yeast is used. Set the dried yeast liquid aside for 10 minutes until frothy. Crush the vitamin C tablets in a little water; add to the yeast liquid.

Mix the flour and salt together in a large warm bowl. Add the sugar and cut in the fat. Stir in the yeast liquid and the rest of the warm water and mix to a soft dough. Turn onto a lightly floured board and knead the dough until it is smooth, elastic and non-sticky. Divide the dough in half, shape into 2 or 4 loaves and put them into the bread pans. Cover the pans with plastic wrap and set aside until doubled in size, about 1 hour.

Preheat the oven. Remove the plasic wrap and bake the loaves for about 45 minutes (30-35 minutes for small loaves). Cool the bread on a wire rack.

White Bread

INGREDIENTS *makes 3 large loaves*
1oz fresh yeast or 2 tbsp active dry yeast and 1 tsp sugar
3$\frac{3}{4}$ cups warm water
12 cups all-purpose flour
2-3 tsp salt
1 tbsp sugar
$\frac{1}{4}$ cup butter or margarine

METHOD
Oven temperature 450°F.

Grease 3 large bread pans. Stir the yeast with a few tbsp water, adding 1tsp sugar if dried yeast is used. Put the bowl of dried yeast liquid aside for 10 minutes until frothy.

Mix the flour and salt together. Add the sugar, cut in the fat, stir in the yeast liquid and the rest of the warm water to make a soft dough. Turn the dough onto a lightly floured board and knead until it becomes smooth, elastic and non-sticky.

Return the dough to the bowl, cover it with plastic wrap and set aside until doubled in size, about 1$\frac{1}{4}$ hours.

Knock back the dough and divide it into 3 portions. Knead and shape into loaves to fit into the 3 bread pans. Cover the bread pans with plastic wrap. Allow to prove until doubled in size, about 45 minutes.

Preheat the oven. Remove the plastic wrap and bake the loaves for 45-50 minutes. Cool on a wire rack.

White and Whole-wheat Rolls

COB LOAF
Shape the dough into a large ball. Flatten it slightly and place on a greased cookie sheet. Slash the top of the dough with a sharp knife to make a cross. Cover and leave to rise for about 45 minutes in a warm place. Bake for 30-40 minutes.

ROLLS
(makes 12) Baking time for rolls is 10-15 minutes after shaping, rising and glazing.

CLOVERLEAF ROLLS
Divide each 2-oz piece of dough into 3 equal parts. Shape into 3 balls. Place on the cookie sheet in the shape of a cloverleaf and press lightly together.

THREE-STRAND BRAIDED ROLLS
Cut off 2-oz pieces of risen dough. Divide and roll each piece into three 4-in strands. Braid.

TWO-STRAND BRAIDED ROLLS
Divide the 2-oz dough pieces in half. Roll each piece into a strand 8in long. Place the strands in the form of a cross on the work surface. Take the 2 ends of the lower strand and cross them over the middle of the upper strand so that they lie side by side. Repeat this with the remaining strand and repeat alternately until all the dough has been used. Pinch the ends firmly together. Place on the cookie sheet, glaze and decorate, cover, leave to rise and bake.

KNOT ROLLS
Roll 2-oz pieces of dough into a thick 6-in strand. Tie into a simple knot.

BRAID
Divide the dough into 3 equal pieces. Roll each piece into a strand 12-14in long. Pinch together one end of the 3 strands and then braid them. Pinch the remaining ends together and lift the braid on to a greased cookie sheet. Cover, leave to rise and glaze. Decorate with poppy seeds, if desired. Bake for 25-30 minutes. Cool on wire rack.

◀ Bread rolls

Whole-wheat Bread

INGREDIENTS *makes 1 loaf*
4$\frac{1}{2}$ cups whole-wheat flour
2 tbsp seeds (sesame, caraway or
   poppy)
1$\frac{1}{2}$ heaped tsp salt
1$\frac{1}{2}$ cups warm water
1oz fresh yeast or 1$\frac{1}{2}$ tsp active dry dried
   yeast
$\frac{1}{2}$ tsp molasses
1 tbsp oil
1 tbsp malt extract
beaten egg to glaze
1 tsp seeds (sesame, caraway or poppy)
   to top the loaf

METHOD

Mix the flour, seeds and salt together in a warm bowl. Pour a little of the water into a small bowl and add the yeast. Put in a warm place for 10 minutes. If using dried yeast, make up according to manufacturer's directions.

Add the oil, the malt extract and the molasses to the rest of the water.

Pour the yeast mixture into the flour and stir. Add enough of the other liquid to make a soft dough, but don't allow it to get too sticky. As different brands of flour absorb different amounts, it may not be necessary to add all this liquid, so don't add it all at once. Gather it with your hands into a ball.

Knead the dough for 20 minutes, then place in a greased plastic bag to rise. Put it in a warm place, such as a sunny windowsill. Leave it there for 1 hour.

Preheat the oven to 400°F. Punch down the dough with the heel of the hand to redistribute the raising agent and knead it for a minute. Put it in an oiled loaf tin 8$\frac{1}{2}$×4$\frac{1}{2}$in/22×12cm. Brush the top with beaten egg and sprinkle over the remaining seeds. Cover the loaf with a clean damp dish towel and leave it to rise on top of the stove.

Bake for 35 minutes. Turn out of the pan and flick the bottom of the loaf with your fingernail. It should sound hollow. The sides of the loaf should spring back when pressed. Allow it to cool on a wire rack.

VARIATION/WALNUT BREAD

For a very good flavorsome loaf with added texture, add $\frac{1}{2}$ cup roughly chopped walnuts to the flour and use walnut oil instead of olive oil. Omit the molasses. This loaf will fill the kitchen with its delicious nutty aroma and taste marvelous with jam for breakfast. Or, try cheddar and watercress sandwiches in walnut bread with tomato soup for supper.

VARIATION/YEAST—EXTRACT BREAD

For a tangy savoury loaf, omit the molasses and replace the malt extract with yeast extract spread. Add 1-2 tbsp caraway seeds to the flour and sprinkle the top of the loaf with the seeds, too. This bread is good with strong cheddar or simply with butter as an accompaniment to a lunchtime bowl of soup.

▲ Wholewheat bread

Milk Bread

INGREDIENTS *makes 2 loaves*
$\frac{1}{2}$oz fresh yeast or 1 envelope active dry
    yeast and $\frac{1}{2}$ tsp sugar
2 cups warm skim milk, or whole milk
    and water mixed
6 cups all-purpose flour
$1\frac{1}{2}$ tsp salt
$1\frac{1}{2}$ tsp sugar
6 tbsp butter or margarine
beaten egg or milk for glazing

METHOD

Oven temperature 400°F.

Grease 1 large and 1 small bread pan. Stir the yeast into the liquid, adding sugar if dried yeast is used. Allow 15 minutes in a warm place for dried yeast to become frothy.

Mix the flour, salt and sugar and cut in the butter or margarine. Stir in the yeast liquid and mix to a soft dough. Turn the dough onto a lightly floured board and knead until it becomes smooth and loses its stickiness. Return the dough to the warm mixing bowl and cover it with oiled plastic wrap. Leave to rise until doubled in size, about $1\frac{1}{2}$ hours.

Knock back the dough, divide it into 1 large and 1 small piece and shape to fit the bread pans. Brush the loaves with beaten egg or milk. Cover the tins with oiled plastic wrap and allow to rise until doubled in size, about 1 hour.

Preheat the oven. Bake for about 50 minutes and cool on a wire rack.

VARIATION/OLIVE BREAD

Omit the $1\frac{1}{2}$ tsp sugar and stir in 5-6 tbsp olive oil instead of cutting in the butter or margarine. Add $1\frac{1}{2}$ cups pitted, sliced ripe olives to the dough with the dough liquid. The olive loaves may be shaped into 2 or 3 rounds and baked on greased cookie sheets instead of being baked in bread pans if preferred.

Potato Bread

INGREDIENTS *makes 3 loaves*
1 (8-9oz) large raw potato
2 cups milk
1oz fresh yeast or 1 envelope active dry
    yeast and 1 tsp sugar
8 cups all-purpose flour
2 tsp salt
1 egg
3 tbsp sour cream

METHOD

Oven temperature 350°F.

Grease three $6\frac{1}{2}$-x$3\frac{1}{2}$-x3-in bread pans. Grate the peeled potato finely. Bring the milk to a boil and pour it over the potato in a bowl. Cool until lukewarm and add the fresh yeast. If dried yeast is used, stir it, with the sugar, into 3 tbsp warm milk or water and leave for 8-10 minutes until frothy. Add the dried yeast mixture to the potato-milk mix.

Beat in half the flour until well mixed. Add the salt, egg, sour cream and the rest of the flour. Beat the mixture thoroughly.

Cover the bowl with plastic wrap and set aside in a warm place for 2-$2\frac{1}{2}$ hours. Knead thoroughly and divide between the 3 bread pans.

Leave to rise once again, covered, for about 40 minutes. Preheat the oven and bake for 45 minutes until cooked.

▶ ▲ Herb bread
▶ Bagels
▲ Milk bread
◀ ▲ Potato bread

142

Herb Bread

INGREDIENTS *makes 2 loaves*
2 cups whole-wheat flour
2 cups all-purpose flour
2 tsp margarine
1 tsp salt
1 tsp sugar
$\frac{1}{2}$ tsp dried dillweed
1 tsp dill seed
1 tsp dried savory
$\frac{1}{2}$oz fresh yeast or 1 envelope active dry
    yeast and $\frac{1}{2}$ tsp sugar
1$\frac{1}{4}$ cups warm water
cracked wheat for decoration

METHOD
Oven temperature 450°F.
    Grease 2 7-in loaf pans. Mix the flours

and cut the fat into them. Add the salt, sugar and dried herbs. Cream the fresh yeast with the water and add to the flour mixture. If dried yeast is used, stir $\frac{1}{2}$ tsp sugar into half the dough liquid, sprinkle the yeast on top and leave for 10 minutes in a warm place until frothy. Add with the rest of the water to the flour mixture.

Mix to a soft dough and knead on a lightly floured board until smooth. Sprinkle the greased pans evenly with cracked wheat. Half-fill each pan with bread dough.

Cover the tins with lightly oiled plastic wrap or plastic bags. Allow the dough to rise in a warm place until doubled in size. Uncover the dough and bake in the preheated oven for about 35 minutes. Remove the loaves from the pans and serve warm.

Bagels

INGREDIENTS *makes 18*
1oz fresh yeast or 2 tbsp active dry yeast
    and $\frac{1}{2}$ tsp brown sugar
2 cups warm milk
1 tsp brown sugar
$\frac{1}{4}$ cup vegetable oil
2 tsp salt
5 cups whole-wheat flour (a little extra
    flour may be needed)
2 quarts water
2 tbsp brown sugar
egg wash for glazing (1 egg yolk plus 1
    tbsp water)
toasted sesame seeds, poppy seeds, or
    sautéed chopped onions for
    decoration

METHOD
Oven temperature 375°F.
    Grease 2 cookie sheets. Dissolve the yeast in the warm milk, adding the sugar if dried yeast is used. Allow about 10 minutes for dried yeast to rehydrate and the liquid to become frothy.

Add the brown sugar, oil and salt to the yeast liquid and work in the flour by degrees, beating at first and then kneading the stiffer dough. When all the flour has been incorporated, knead the dough on a floured board for 10 minutes. Return the dough to the warm bowl, cover with oiled plastic wrap and allow to rise for about 1 hour until doubled in size. Knock back the dough, cover and leave to rise until doubled in size once again.

Knock back the dough and divide it into 18 equal pieces. Roll each piece into a strand 6-in long, 1-in thick, tapering at each end. Shape into rings, pinching the ends firmly together. Cover the shaped bagels and leave to rise for 10-15 minutes. Bring the water to a boil then add the 2 tbsp brown sugar.

Put 2 or 3 bagels at a time into the boiling water and cook until they rise to the surface (takes 1 or 2 minutes). Lift out the bagels with a perforated spoon. Place them on the greased baking sheets.

Glaze the bagels with egg wash and sprinkle with seeds or onions.

Bake until browned, about 20 minutes.

Oatmeal Bread

INGREDIENTS *makes 2 small loaves*
1oz fresh yeast or 1 envelope active dry
    yeast and 1 tsp brown sugar
2¼ cups warm water
4½ cups mixed flour (½ whole-wheat, ½
    all-purpose flour
¼ cup strong (high gluten) flour
2 tbsp brown sugar
2 cups fine oatmeal
4 tbsp wheat germ
4 tbsp soy flour
2 tbsp vegetable oil
1½ tsp salt

METHOD
Oven temperature 350°F.

Grease 2 small bread pans. Put the yeast into a bowl (with the sugar, if dried yeast is used) and stir with ½ cup of the warm water. Set aside for up to 10 minutes until foamy. Add the strong flour, sugar and half the mixed flours to the rest of the water and beat well for 5 minutes. Add the yeast liquid and beat thoroughly. Stir in the rolled oats and set the mixture aside in a warm place for about 30 minutes to make a sponge batter.

Add the wheat germ, soy flour, oil, salt and the rest of the mixed flours to the sponge batter. Turn out onto a floured board and knead well until smooth. Return the dough to the bowl and cover with oiled plastic wrap. Set aside in a warm place until doubled in size, about 30 minutes.

Knock back the dough on a floured board and divide into 2 pieces. Shape into loaves and place them in the bread pans. Cover with oiled plastic wrap and allow to rise until double in size once again. Preheat the oven and bake for about 1 hour. Cool on a wire rack.

Malt Bread

INGREDIENTS *makes 2 small loaves*
½oz fresh yeast or 2 tsp active dry yeast
    and 1 tsp sugar
2½ cups warm water
4 cups whole wheat flour
1 tsp salt
2 tbsp malt
1 tbsp honey
2 tbsp vegetable oil
1 cup golden raisins
honey for glazing

METHOD
Oven temperature 400°F then reduced to 350°F.

Grease 2 6½-x3½-x3-in bread pans. Mix the yeast (and sugar) in the warm water.

Add the malt, honey, oil and golden raisins to the warmed flour. Stir in the yeast liquid and mix thoroughly. Put the mixture into the 2 bread pans.

Set aside for 1 hour in a warm place, covered with plastic wrap. Preheat the oven and bake at the higher temperature for 15 minutes, then reduce to the lower temperature and bake for a further 20 minutes until cooked. A skewer inserted into the center of the loaf should emerge clean. Place the loaves on a wire rack. Warm a little honey and brush the tops of the loaves while they are still hot.

Onion Bread

INGREDIENTS *makes 1 round loaf*
one quarter of the Quick White Bread
    dough (page 140)
2 cups sliced onions
¼ cup butter or margarine
2 tbsp all-purpose flour
⅔ cup milk
¼ tsp salt or garlic salt
pinch freshly ground black pepper
1 tsp poppy or sesame seeds

METHOD
Oven temperature 375°F.

Grease and flour a round cake pan 8in in diameter. Roll out the dough to fit the pan. Put the dough into the pan, cover with plastic wrap and prove until doubled in size, about 30 minutes.

Cook the onions in the fat in a heavy pan until transparent and softened. Stir in the flour and cook for a couple of minutes. Add the milk, stirring constantly. Bring to the boil and simmer for another minute. Add the salt and pepper.

Preheat the oven. Spread the onion mixture over the dough and sprinkle with the seeds. Bake for 30 minutes. Serve hot or cold with soup or salad.

◀▲ Malt bread
▲ Onion bread

Pumpernickel Bread

INGREDIENTS *makes 2 large loaves*
1oz fresh yeast or 2 tbsp active dry yeast
    and 1 tsp brown sugar
5 cups warm water
1 tbsp molasses
6 cups whole-wheat flour
1 cup dark rye flour
²⁄₃ cup buckwheat flour
¹⁄₃ cup cornmeal
2 tsp salt
1 cup mashed potato
1 tsp caraway seeds
1 cup whole-wheat flour (if needed)

METHOD
Oven temperature 375°F.

Grease 2 large bread pans. Stir the yeast into one cup of the warm water, adding the brown sugar in the case of dried yeast. Set the dried yeast liquid aside for 10 minutes until frothy.

Mix the whole-wheat flour, molasses, yeast liquid and the rest of the warm water to make a very wet dough. Beat well, knead in the bowl until it becomes smooth and less sticky. Add the rest of the ingredients and mix well. Turn onto a floured board and knead, working in the last cup of whole-wheat flour, if required. Knead until the dough is smooth and elastic. Return it to the bowl and cover with a sheet of plastic wrap. Prove in a warm place until doubled in size, 1¼-1½ hours.

Knock back the dough, divide it into 2 pieces. Shape into loaves and put the dough into the bread pans. Cover the tins with oiled plastic wrap and leave to rise once again until doubled in size, about 1 hour. Preheat the oven and bake for about 1 hour, remove the loaves from the pans and bake for a further 10-15 minutes. Cool the bread on a wire rack. Keep the bread for 1 or 2 days before slicing.

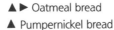
▲ ▶ Oatmeal bread
▲ Pumpernickel bread

Cornbread

INGREDIENTS *makes 16 squares*
1 cup whole-wheat flour
1 cup cornmeal
½ tsp salt
1 tsp baking soda
¾ tsp cream of tartar
1½ cups buttermilk or half yogurt, half
    skim milk
3 tbsp sunflower oil
2 eggs, beaten
1 tbsp brown sugar or honey

METHOD
Oven temperature 425°F.

Grease an 8-in square baking pan. Mix together the flour, cornmeal, salt, soda, and cream of tartar. Stir the buttermilk with the oil, eggs and sugar or honey. Pour the liquid ingredients into the dry mixture and stir together.

Preheat the oven. Put the batter into the baking pan and bake for about 35 minutes. Cut into 2-in squares and serve warm.

145

Cheese Bread

INGREDIENTS *makes 1 large loaf*
$\frac{1}{2}$oz fresh yeast or 1 tbsp active dry
    yeast and $\frac{1}{2}$ tsp sugar
1$\frac{1}{4}$ cups warm water
4 cups all-purpose flour
1 tsp salt
$\frac{1}{4}$ tsp cayenne pepper
$\frac{1}{2}$ tsp dry mustard powder or 2 tsp
    creamed horseradish
2 tbsp chopped fresh chives
1 tbsp butter or margarine
1 cup finely grated cheddar cheese
beaten egg or milk for glazing
1-2 tbsp grated cheese for garnishing
    (optional)

METHOD

Oven temperature 400°F.

Grease 1 large or 2 small bread pans. Stir
the yeast into the warm water, adding sugar
if dried yeast is used. Stand the dried yeast
liquid for 10 minutes to become frothy.

Put the flour, salt, cayenne pepper,
mustard and chives into a bowl and cut in
the fat. Stir in the cheese and then the yeast
liquid (and horseradish if used). Work
together to make a dough. Turn the dough
onto a floured board and knead until
smooth and non-sticky.

Return to the bowl, cover with plastic
wrap and leave to rise for 1 hour until
doubled in size. Knock back the dough and
shape into 1 large or 2 small loaves. Place
the shaped dough in the pan. Brush the
dough with beaten egg or milk. Cover the
pan with clingfilm and prove in a warm
place for about 45 minutes.

Preheat the oven and sprinkle the bread
dough with grated cheese if desired.

Bake for about 40 minutes until brown.
Turn out and cool the bread on a wire rack.

This bread makes delicious toast and
may be used as a quick pizza base.

Swiss Buns

INGREDIENTS *makes 8 buns*
$\frac{1}{2}$oz fresh yeast or 1 tbsp active dry
    yeast and 1 tsp sugar
$\frac{2}{3}$ cup warm milk
2 cups all-purpose flour
2 tsp sugar
$\frac{1}{2}$ tsp salt
2 tbsp butter or margarine

GLACÉ ICING
1$\frac{1}{2}$ cups icing sugar
3 tbsp water
coloring (optional)

METHOD

Oven temperature 425°F.

Grease 1 or 2 baking sheets (according to
size). Stir the yeast with the milk, adding 1
tsp of sugar in the case of the dried yeast. If
the latter, allow the yeast liquid to stand for
10 minutes or so until frothy.

Mix the flour with the sugar and salt and
cut in the fat. Stir in the yeast liquid and mix
to a soft dough. Turn onto a lightly floured
board and knead thoroughly until the
dough loses its stickiness and becomes
smooth. Return the dough to the warm
bowl, cover with oiled plastic wrap and
allow to rise until doubled in size, about 1
hour.

Knock back the dough, divide it into 8
pieces and shape each piece into an oblong
5in long.

Place the buns on the greased cookie
sheet(s). Cover with oiled plastic wrap and
allow to prove in a warm place for about 20
minutes. Preheat the oven, uncover the buns
and bake for about 15 minutes until
browned. Lift on to a wire rack to cool.
Combine the icing ingredients and cover the
buns with it.

◀ ▲ Cheese bread
◀ Swiss buns

146

Braided Bread

INGREDIENTS *makes 2 loaves*
½oz fresh yeast or 1 tbsp active dry
    yeast and ½ tsp sugar
1 cup milk or water
4 cups all-purpose flour
1 tsp salt
¼ cup butter or margarine or 2 tbsp
    vegetable oil
1 tbsp liquid honey
1 egg, beaten, for glazing

METHOD
Oven temperature 400°F.

Grease 2 cookie sheets. Stir the yeast into the milk, adding the sugar in the case of the dried yeast. Set aside the dried yeast liquid for 5-10 minutes to become frothy. Stir in 1 cup of the flour and leave in a warm place to ferment.

Add the salt to the rest of the flour. Cut the fat into the flour or stir the oil into the yeast batter. Add the fat and flour (or flour only, if oil has been used) to the yeast batter and honey. Mix to a soft dough. Turn the mixture onto a floured board and knead vigorously until the dough is smooth, elastic and non-sticky, for about 10 minutes. Put the dough back into the bowl and cover it with a sheet of oiled plastic wrap. Leave to rise in the warm until doubled in size, about 1 hour.

Knock back the dough and knead it thoroughly. Divide the dough into 2 halves and then slice each half into 4 pieces. Allow the 8 pieces of dough to rest for 5 to 10 minutes, covered with oiled plastic wrap. Roll 4 pieces of dough into individual lengths of 15in. Keep the other 4 pieces covered with oiled plastic wrap while the first 4 lengths are braided. Put the bread braid on to a greased cookie sheet, brush with beaten egg and cover with oiled plastic wrap. Braid the other four pieces.

When both braids have rested and risen to double size, preheat the oven and bake them for 30-40 minutes. The loaves should look golden brown and shiny. They keep moist for several days.

Irish Soda Bread

INGREDIENTS *makes 1 loaf*
4 cups all-purpose flour
1 tsp salt
2 tsp baking soda
1½ tsp cream of tartar
2 tbsp shortening
1¼ cups buttermilk

METHOD
Oven temperature 425°F.

Sift the flour, salt, baking soda and cream of tartar into a bowl. Rub in the lard and add enough buttermilk to make a soft dough.

Turn the mixture onto a lightly floured board and knead for a minute. Shape into a round and place on the cookie sheet. Mark with a cross, cutting deep into the dough.

Preheat the oven and bake for 40-50 minutes, until lightly browned and firm when tapped on the base. Cool the bread on a wire rack.

VARIATIONS
You can use plain milk instead of buttermilk, but if you do, double the quantity of cream of tartar. You can also use a mixture of white and whole-wheat flours.

▲ ▲ Braided bread
▲ Irish soda bread

147

Italian Panettone

INGREDIENTS *makes 1 loaf*
1oz fresh yeast or 2 tbsp active dry yeast
   and 1 tsp sugar
$\frac{3}{4}$ cup warm milk
4 cups all-purpose flour
1 tsp salt
5 tbsp sugar
5 tbsp butter
2 eggs plus 2 egg yolks, beaten
2 tsp ground cardamom
finely grated peel of 2 small lemons
$\frac{1}{2}$ cup chopped mixed dried citrus peel
$\frac{3}{4}$ cup raisins, chopped and soaked in 2
   tbsp rum
beaten egg for glazing

METHOD
Oven temperature 425°F for 20
minutes, then reduce to 375°F for 30
minutes.

Grease a deep, round cake pan, 8in in
diameter. Stir the yeast into the milk, adding
1 tsp of sugar if dried yeast is used. Set the
dried yeast liquid aside for about 10 minutes
until frothy. Add a quarter of the flour to the
yeast liquid and set aside in a warm place for
$\frac{1}{2}$ hour. Add to the yeast batter the rest of the
flour, the melted butter, the beaten eggs and
egg yolks, cardamom, lemon peel, mixed
peel and the raisins in rum. Mix thoroughly
to form a heavy dough. Knead well, cover
with oiled plastic wrap and leave to prove
for 1$\frac{1}{2}$-2 hours until risen.

Knock back the dough and knead well.
Put the dough into the greased cake pan.
Brush the top of the loaf with egg wash.
Cover with oiled plastic wrap and leave to
rise for about 40 minutes. Preheat the oven,
remove the covering and bake for 50
minutes (see temperatures above). Turn out
of the pan after 10 minutes and cool on a
wire rack.

Walnut, Apricot and Orange Bread

INGREDIENTS *makes 1 large or 2 small loaves*
$\frac{1}{2}$oz fresh yeast or 1 tbsp active dry
   yeast and 1 tsp honey
1$\frac{1}{4}$ cups warm water
4 cups whole-wheat flour
1 tsp salt
$\frac{1}{4}$ cup sugar
$\frac{1}{4}$ cup butter or margarine
$\frac{1}{2}$ cup chopped walnuts
1$\frac{1}{4}$ cups dried apricots, soaked and
   chopped
2 tbsp grated orange peel

METHOD
Oven temperature 425°F.

Grease 1 large or 2 small bread pans.
Dissolve the yeast (and sugar) in the warm
water leaving the dried yeast to become
frothy (10 to 15 minutes). Mix the flour
with the sugar and salt and cut in the fat. Stir
in the yeast liquid and mix to a dough. Turn
onto a floured board and knead until
smooth. Return the dough to the bowl,
cover it with oiled plastic wrap and let it rise
for about 1 hour until doubled in size.
Knead again, working in the nuts, apricots
and orange peel. Shape into a loaf (or 2
loaves) and place them in the prepared
pan(s). Cover the dough and leave it to rise
once more for 40-50 minutes.

Preheat the oven and bake for about 45-
50 minutes, depending on the size of the loaf
(loaves).

Allow to cool on a wire rack.

▲ Italian panettone
◀ Walnut, apricot and orange bread

148

Sally Lunn

INGREDIENTS *makes 2 cakes*
$^1/_2$oz fresh yeast or 2 tsp active dry yeast
   and 1 tsp sugar
$1^1/_4$ cups warm milk
4 cups all-purpose flour
1 tsp salt
2 eggs, beaten
$^1/_4$ cup butter or margarine, melted and
   cooled

TO GLAZE
2 tbsp water
2 tbsp sugar

METHOD
Oven temperature 425°F.

Grease two 6-in cake pans. Stir the fresh yeast (or dried yeast and sugar) into the warm milk. If dried yeast is used, set the bowl aside for 10 minutes until foamy.

Mix in 1 cup of the flour and leave in a warm place for about 20 minutes until the yeast batter is frothy.

Mix the remaining flour with the salt and stir into the yeast with the eggs and melted butter. Beat well until a smooth batter is produced. Pour the batter into the cake pans, cover them with oiled plastic wrap and leave in a warm place for about $1^1/_2$ hours until doubled in size.

Preheat the oven and bake the cakes for about 20 minutes until nicely browned. Turn the cakes onto a wire rack and brush them with the hot glaze made by boiling the sugar and water together. Allow to cool a little before serving warm with whipped cream or butter.

Swiss Pear Bread

INGREDIENTS *makes 2 small or 1 large loaf*
5 cups dried pears
$1^1/_2$ cup golden raisins
$^3/_4$ cup chopped hazelnuts
6 tbsp finely diced thick candied lemon
   peel
1 cup sugar
7 tbsp rosewater
$^1/_2$ glass kirsch
1 tbsp powdered cinnamon
2lb White Bread dough, see page 140

METHOD
Oven temperature 425°F.

Grease 2 cookie sheets.

Soak the pears overnight in water to cover, then stew them in the water in which they were soaked.

Drain and mash the pears, removing any stems or cores. Mix the mashed pears with the golden raisins, nuts, lemon peel, sugar, rosewater, kirsch and cinnamon. Knead half the bread dough with the pear mixture and shape into 2 oblong loaves.

Preheat the oven. Roll out the other half of the dough on a floured board. Divide it in two and wrap each pear loaf inside a sheet of plain dough. Brush the edges of the dough with milk and seal them. Prick the loaves with a fork. Bake for 50-60 minutes.

◀ ▲ Sally Lunn
▲ Swiss pear bread
▲ ▶ Almond bread

Almond Bread

INGREDIENTS *makes about 45 slices*
3 cups all-purpose flour
2 tsp baking powder
$^1/_4$ tsp salt
2 large eggs
$^1/_2$ cup sunflower oil
5-6 tbsp honey or brown sugar
2 tsp grated orange or tangerine peel
2 tsp almond extract
$^3/_4$ cup chopped almonds

METHOD
Oven temperature 350°F.

Sift together the flour, baking powder and salt. Beat together in an electric blender or a bowl the eggs, oil, honey, citrus peel and almond extract. Transfer the mixture into a large bowl and beat in the flour mixture a little at a time.

Stir the almonds into the stiff dough then divide it into 6 oblong rolls about 2in wide. Place the rolls well apart on a foil covered cookie sheet and bake for 20 minutes.

Lift off the cookie sheet and cut each roll into 7 or 8 slices $^1/_2$in thick. Return the slices to the oven on the baking sheet and bake for a further 15-20 minutes until brown. Cool on a wire rack, then store in a cake pan.

English Muffins

INGREDIENTS *makes 12*
½oz fresh yeast or 1 tbsp active dry
  yeast and 1 tsp honey
1 cup warm water
4 cups all-purpose flour
1 tsp salt
2 tbsp butter, melted
2 small eggs, beaten

METHOD
Oven temperature 450°F for oven-baked muffins.

Grease 2 cookie sheets and dust them well with rolled oats or wheat germ or with cornmeal or semolina. Or, heat a greased and floured griddle (or heavy skillet) if the muffins are to be cooked over heat.

Stir the yeast into the warm milk, adding the honey if dried yeast is used. Set the dried yeast liquid aside for 10 minutes until foamy.

Mix the flour and salt and add the yeast liquid, melted butter and the eggs. Mix to a soft dough in the bowl, then turn it out onto a floured board. Knead the dough until it becomes smooth, non-sticky and elastic. Return the dough to the warm bowl. Cover with oiled plastic wrap and leave to rise for about 1¼ hours, until doubled in size. Turn the dough onto a lightly floured surface, knead and then roll the dough to ½in/1cm thickness. Cover with oiled plastic wrap and rest for 5 minutes. Cut into 3in circles with a plain cutter.

Put the muffins on the cookie sheets and dust the tops with semolina. Cover with oiled plastic wrap and leave to rise for about 40 minutes. Cook the muffins by baking them in the oven for about 10 minutes, turning the muffins over with a spatula after 5 minutes. Or, cook the muffins for 5 minutes on each side on the heated griddle. Stack the muffins on a wire rack.

To serve the muffins, pull them open all around the edges. Leave the halves joined in the center. Toast them slowly on both sides. Pull the muffins fully apart and place a slice of chilled butter inside. Put the muffin halves together again and serve them hot.

Crumpets

INGREDIENTS *makes about 20*
½oz fresh yeast or 1 envelope active dry
  yeast and ½ tsp sugar
1¼ cups warm water
3 cups all-purpose flour
1 tsp salt
½ tsp baking soda
¾ cup warm milk (more, if required, to
  make a pouring batter)

METHOD
Heat a greased griddle or heavy skillet. When ready to cook the batter, grease crumpet rings, egg-poaching rings or plain cookie cutters 3in in diameter. Stir the yeast into the water, adding the sugar if dried yeast is used. Let the dried yeast liquid stand for 5-10 minutes until frothy.

Mix in half the flour and beat well. Set the batter aside in a warm place for about 30 minutes until foamy.

Add the rest of the ingredients to the batter, stirring thoroughly. Beat well, adjusting the milk quantity if necessary.

Place the crumpet rings on the heated griddle and pour 2 tbsp batter into each ring. Cook until set underneath and holes appear on the upper surface. Take away the rings and turn the crumpets with a spatula. Lightly cook the second side. Cool the crumpets stacked on a wire rack. Serve freshly made with butter or toast them on both sides, serving them hot with butter, later on.

▲ Crumpets

▼ English muffins

Oatcakes

INGREDIENTS *makes about 22*
½ cup soft brown sugar
½ cup unbleached all-purpose flour
1 cups wheat flour
1⅓ cups porridge oats
pinch baking soda
pinch salt
8 tbsp butter
1 egg yolk

METHOD
Preheat the oven to 350°F. Mix the dry ingredients together in a bowl. Cut the butter into small pieces in the bowl and cut in with 2 knives.

Mix in the egg yolk and form into a dough. Knead for a few minutes and then roll out thinly on a lightly floured surface and cut into circles with a cookie cutter.

Leaving plenty of space between each one, arrange the circles on a greased cookie sheet and bake for 10-15 minutes until crisp and golden. Allow to cool slightly before transferring to a wire rack. When cool, store in an airtight can. Serve with cheese.

Pita Bread

INGREDIENTS *makes 8*
Use the same ingredients and follow the recipe for Whole-wheat Bread, up to and including paragraph 4 (page 141).

METHOD
Preheat the oven to 450°F. Punch down the dough with the heel of the hand and kneed for a minute. Divide the dough into 8 and roll out into thin ovals. Place on cookie sheets and cover with clean damp cloths. Leave on top of the stove for 20 minutes.

Bake for 5-7 minutes. Allow to cool. These pita breads freeze very successfully.

▲ Pita bread

Bran and Golden Raisin Muffins

INGREDIENTS *makes 12*
2 tbsp oil
2 tbsp honey
1 egg
$\frac{2}{3}$ cup milk
$1\frac{1}{4}$ cups whole-wheat flour
75g bran
2 tsp baking powder
pinch salt
$\frac{1}{3}$ cup golden raisins

METHOD
Preheat the oven to 375°F. Beat together the oil and honey. Beat in the egg. Gradually beat in the milk until smooth.

Combine the dry ingredients and stir these into the liquid ones. When the bran has soaked up the liquid, you should have a soft dough.

Spoon into an oiled muffin pan and bake for about 20 minutes.

Spiced Buttermilk Biscuits

INGREDIENTS *makes 8*
2 cups unbleached all-purpose flour
2 cups whole-wheat flour
2 tsp baking soda
2 tsp cream of tartar
1 tsp fruit sugar
1 tsp ground mixed spice
8 tbsp butter
$1\frac{1}{4}$ cups buttermilk
3 tsp baking powder

METHOD
Preheat the oven to 425°F. Sift the flours together and mix thoroughly with the other dry ingredients. Cut the butter into the flour mix and rub in well.

Stir in the buttermilk and mix to form a soft dough. Knead the dough lightly on a floured board. Divide in half, form each half into a flattened ball and cut each ball into 4 wedges. Place the wedges on a greased cookie sheet, dust with flour and bake for about 12 minutes.

Cool on a wire rack. While still warm, slice in half and fill with butter and jam.

▲ ▲ Bran and golden raisin muffins
▲ Spiced buttermilk biscuits

Sesame Snaps

INGREDIENTS *makes about 20*
1 cup whole-wheat flour
½ cup sesame seeds
1 tsp baking powder
1-2 tsp salt
2 tsp tahini paste
1 tbsp olive oil
3-5 tbsp tepid water

METHOD

Preheat the oven to 425°F. Combine the dry ingredients in a bowl. Add the tahini paste and olive oil and mix with the fingertips until crumbly. Gradually add enough water to form a soft dough.

Knead gently on a floured board and then roll out thinly. Cut out circles with a cookie cutter and arrange on a greased cookie sheet. Bake in the oven for 15 minutes until crisp and golden.

Cool on a wire rack, store in a canister and serve with cheese.

Rye Savory Biscuits

INGREDIENTS *makes about 20*
2 tbsp butter
1 cup rye flour
pinch salt
a little milk, heated

METHOD

Preheat the oven to 350°F. Cut the butter into the flour with a pinch of salt, and bind with a little milk to form a dough. Knead for about 7 minutes.

Form the dough into about 20 small balls and roll flat on a floured surface.

Bake on a cookie sheet for about 10 minutes, until the edges are just beginning to brown. Cool on a wire rack. Store in a canister and serve with butter and cheese.

▶ Sesame snaps

Stuffed Potato Paratha

INGREDIENTS *makes about 20*
5 cups boiled and mashed potatoes
1 small onion, finely chopped
1-2 green chilies, finely chopped
1 tbsp chopped fresh cilantro
¾ tsp salt
¾ tsp ground roasted cumin

DOUGH
2¾ all-purpose flour
½ tsp salt
4 tbsp oil
¾ cup hot water
Ghee (see page 126) for frying

METHOD
Mix all the ingredients of the filling together
and set aside.

To make the dough, sift the flour and salt
together. Stir in the oil. Add enough water to
form a stiff dough. Knead for about 10
minutes until you have a soft smooth
dough. Divide into 20 balls.

Roll out 4 balls into 2-in circles each.
Place about 1½-2 tbsp of the filling on 1 of
the circles and spread it evenly. Place the
other round over the filling, sealing the
edges with a little water.

Roll out gently into 7-in circles, and be
careful that no filling comes out. Roll out all
the parathas in a similar manner.

Heat a skillet over medium heat. Place a
paratha in the skillet and cook for about 1
minute until brown spots appear. Turn and
cook the other side.

Add 2 tsp Ghee and cook for 2-3 minutes
until golden brown. Turn and cook the other
side, adding more Ghee if required. Make
all the parathas in the same way. Serve
warm.

Indian Lucchi Bread

INGREDIENTS *makes about 40*
2¾ cups all-purpose flour
½ tsp salt
2 tbsp oil
¾ cup hot water
oil for deep-frying

METHOD
Sift the flour and salt together. Cut in the oil.
Slowly add enough water to form a stiff
dough. Knead for about 10 minutes until
you have a soft pliable dough.

Divide the dough into about 40 small
balls and flatten each ball.

Roll out a few balls on a slightly oily
surface into circles of 4in across (do not roll
out all the balls at the same time as they tend
to stick).

Heat oil in a karai or cast-iron skillet over
high heat. Put in a lucchi and press the
middle with a slotted spoon as this causes
the lucchi to puff up. Turn and cook the
other side for a few seconds. Drain and serve
hot.

▲ ◄ Stuffed potato paratha
◄ Indian lucchi bread

154

N *aan*

INGREDIENTS *makes 12*
1 tsp active dry yeast
1 tsp sugar
$\frac{3}{8}$ cup lukewarm water
$2\frac{3}{4}$ cups all-purpose flour
$\frac{1}{2}$ tsp salt
$\frac{3}{4}$ tsp baking powder
1 tbsp oil
about 3 tbsp plain yogurt

METHOD

Stir the yeast and sugar into the water and set aside for 15-20 minutes until frothy.

Sift together the flour, salt and baking powder. Make a well in the middle, add the yeast liquid, oil and yogurt and knead for about 10 minutes until soft and not sticky.

Place the dough in an oiled plastic bag and set aside in a warm place for 2-3 hours, until double in size. Knead again for 1-2 minutes and divide into 12 balls. Roll into 7-in circles.

Place as many as possible on a cookie sheet and put in a preheated oven, 400°F for 4-5 minutes each side until brown spots appear. Place them for a few seconds under a hot broiler until slightly browned. Keep warm to serve. Repeat with any remaining dough circles.

▲ Naan   ▼ Baktora yogurt bread

B *aktora* Y *ogurt* B *read*

INGREDIENTS *makes 12-14*
$2\frac{1}{4}$ cups all-purpose flour
$1\frac{1}{2}$ tsp baking powder
$\frac{1}{2}$ tsp salt
1 tsp sugar
1 egg, beaten
about 3 tbsp yogurt
oil for deep-frying

METHOD

Sift the flour, baking powder and salt together. Mix in the sugar.

Add the beaten egg and enough yogurt to form a stiff dough. Knead for 10-15 minutes until you have a soft, smooth dough. Cover with a cloth and let it rest for 3-4 hours.

Knead again on a floured surface for 5 minutes. Divide into 12-14 balls.

Roll out on a floured surface into 5-in circles.

Heat the oil in a karai over high heat. Fry the batora, pressing in the middle with a slotted spoon so that it puffs up. Turn and cook the other side for a few seconds until lightly browned. Drain.

Hazelnut and Apricot Crunch

INGREDIENTS *makes about 16*
8 tbsp butter
⅓ cup soft brown sugar
2 tbsp maple syrup
1⅓ cups rolled oats
½ cup chopped hazelnuts
⅓ cup dried apricots, chopped

METHOD
Preheat the oven to 350°F. Put the butter, sugar and syrup in a heavy pan and stir over a low heat until combined.

Stir in the remaining ingredients. Press into a jelly roll pan lined with waxed paper. Bake for about 45 minutes, until golden. Cut into bars in the pan using an oiled knife. Cool in the pan.

Amaretti Cookies

INGREDIENTS *makes about 20*
2 egg whites
½ cup fruit sugar
⅔ cup blanched almonds, ground
1 tsp kirsch (optional)
few drops vanilla extract
almond slivers for decorating

METHOD
Preheat the oven to 350°F. Beat the egg whites until they form soft peaks. Gradually add the sugar, beating continuously until the mixture is thick and lustrous. Stir in the ground almonds, kirsch and vanilla.

Line cookie sheets with sheets of rice paper. Take a spoonful of mixture about the size of a plum and roll it into a ball in the palms of your hands. With a sticky mixture, you will find it easier if your hands are wet. Flatten the balls and arrange them on the cookie sheets with plenty of space for them to expand during cooking.

Decorate each cookie with a sliver of almond and bake for 20-30 minutes. Allow to cool slightly, then carefully remove cookies with their rice paper bases (which are edible) and cool them completely on a wire rack. Store in an airtight can.

◄ Hazelnut and apricot crunch

Zucchini and Cream Cheese Loaf

INGREDIENTS *makes 1 loaf*
4 baby zucchini
1 egg, beaten
4 tbsp oil
2 tbsp honey
2 tbsp molasses
2 tbsp cream cheese
1½ cups whole-wheat flour
½ cup soy flour
pinch salt
2 tsp baking powder
1 tsp baking soda

METHOD
Preheat the oven to 325°F. Cut the zucchini into thin strips, leaving on the peel, then cut into ½-in pieces.

Put the egg in a bowl and beat in the oil, honey and molasses. Beat in the cream cheese until smooth.

In another bowl, combine the dry ingredients, stirring well. Mix in the zucchini. Gradually stir the dry ingredients into the cream cheese mixture.

Transfer batter to a greased and floured bread pan and bake for 50-60 minutes.

Muesli Biscuits

INGREDIENTS *makes 15-20*
1 cup golden raisins or raisins
⅜ cup finely chopped dried apricots
1 egg, beaten
2 tbsp butter, melted with
   2 tbsp hot water
1½ cups muesli
1 heaped tbsp chopped nuts

METHOD
Preheat the oven to 350°F. Pick over dried fruit and wash in boiling water. Drain. In a bowl, beat the fruit with egg and butter. Stir in muesli and nuts.

Line a cookie sheet with waxed paper and spread the mixture thinly over it. Mark into fingers and bake for 45 minutes.

Cut fingers through and allow to cool for 10 minutes before removing from the cookie sheet. Finish cooling on a wire rack.

◀ Zucchini and cream cheese loaf

Whole-wheat Pastry Dough

INGREDIENTS
¾ cup whole-wheat flour
¾ cup whole-wheat self-rising flour
pinch salt
6 tbsp polyunsaturated margarine
water

METHOD
Mix the flours and salt together in a bowl. Cut the fat into small pieces in the flour, then cut in until the mixture is fine and crumbly. Add enough water to bind together and roll into a smooth ball. Chill in the refrigerator for at least 20 minutes.

To use, roll the pastry out on a floured surface.

▲ Whole-wheat pastry
► Cheese pastries

Piecrust Dough

INGREDIENTS
1 cup all-purpose flour
pinch salt
4 tbsp butter or a mixture of butter and margarine
2 tbsp cold water

METHOD
Sift the flour and salt into a bowl. Cut up the butter and cut it into the flour. Mix in just enough water with a knife to make a firm dough and gather it into a ball. On a floured surface, knead the dough gently until smooth. Wrap it in plastic wrap and refrigerate for a short while to firm.

To line a pie plate, roll out the pastry on a floured surface to a thickness of ⅛-¼in and about 2in bigger than the pie plate. Lay the pastry gently in the pie plate, pressing it down to fit the bottom and sides. Prick the bottom lightly and leave to rest in the refrigerator for at least 30 minutes.

Sour Cream Pastry Dough

INGREDIENTS
14 tbsp butter or margarine.
2¾ cups all-purpose flour
1 egg
1 tbsp rum (optional)
2 tbsp sour cream
⅓ cup superfine sugar

METHOD
Cut the butter into the flour. Mix in the remaining ingredients to make a firm dough. Knead well and let it rest for at least 30 minutes before using.

This is excellent for any pie or tart that requires a sweet pastry. You can make delicious cookies from any trimmings when using the pastry (or make some especially for cookies).

Yogurt Pastry Dough

INGREDIENTS
½ cup butter or margarine, cut into small pieces
1½ cups all-purpose flour
1 tsp baking powder
6 tbsp yogurt

METHOD
Combine the butter, flour and baking powder, cutting them together until the mixture is like fine bread crumbs. Add the yogurt and stir it in well. Gather the dough together and knead it gently. Refrigerate it for at least 1 hour. Use as required. This recipe makes a nice soft piecrust, suitable for sweet or savory pies.

Cheese Pastry Dough

INGREDIENTS
1⅓ cups farmer's cheese
½ cup butter
½ cup margarine
2¼ cups all-purpose flour
1 tsp baking powder

METHOD
Mix the cheese and fats together and cut them into the flour and baking powder. Refrigerate for at least 3 hours.

VARIATION
For a strudel, roll out and spread with chopped apples, jam, raisins, crushed cornflakes and sugar. Roll up and bake.

For individual pastries, cut the dough into 2-in squares. Fill with apricot jam, finely chopped apples with raisins, or cheese filling. Fold over to make a triangle or bring the corners together in the middle. Brush with beaten egg and bake at 350°F for 30 minutes.

CHEESE FILLING
½ cup cream cheese
½ egg, beaten
1 tbsp sugar
grated lemon peel

METHOD
Mix everything together well and use as required.

Apricot Tart

INGREDIENTS *serves 4-6*
2½ cups yoghurt
   piecrust dough to line a pan
   approximately 7½in
1½ cups canned apricots
7 tbsp whipping cream
2 tbsp cornstarch
¼ cup superfine sugar
1 tbsp lemon juice
2 tsp vanilla extract
1 egg, separated

METHOD

Drain the yogurt for 3 hours. Bake the pastry shell for 10 minutes. Drain the fruit (save the juice for use in a fruit salad) and lay the apricot halves on the pastry. When the yogurt has drained, mix it together with the whipped cream and remaining ingredients, except the egg white, beating everything to a smooth mixture.

Beat the egg white until it is stiff and fold it into the other mixture. Spoon it over the apricots and bake at 325° for 50 minutes.

VARIATION

Use farmers' cheese (1⅓ cups) instead of the yogurt if preferred.

▲ Apricot tart
▶ French apple tart

Danish Apple Pie

INGREDIENTS *serves 4-6*
piecrust dough to line a pan
   approximately 7½in
5 medium cooking apples, peeled, cored
   and sliced
¼ cup water
¼ cup sugar
1 tbsp butter
1 tsp ground cinnamon
1 cup sour cream
2 tbsp superfine sugar

METHOD

Bake the pastry for 10 minutes at 350°F. Make a thick apple sauce using the apples, water, sugar, butter and half of the cinnamon. There shouldn't be any excess liquid when the apples are cooked, but if there is, cook for a few minutes more without a lid, stirring to prevent the apples sticking.

Let the apple sauce cool a little before turning into the pie shell. Spoon the sour cream over the apples. Mix the rest of the cinnamon with the sugar and sprinkle this over the sour cream. Bake at 400°F for 30 minutes.

This is best served warm, rather than straight from the oven, but it is also good cold.

French Apple Tart

INGREDIENTS *serves 6*
¾ cup unbleached all-purpose flour
¾ cup whole-wheat flour
⅓ cup blanched almonds, ground
8 tbsp butter softened
1 egg
¼ cup fruit sugar
pinch salt

THE FILLING
6 cooking apples
10 tbsp butter
2-3 tbsp fruit sugar
2 tsp mixed spice

METHOD

Preheat the oven to 400°F. To make the dough, sift the flours and almonds together onto a board and make a well in the middle. Put the remaining ingredients into the well and work in with your fingertips until you have a smooth dough. Knead for a few minutes, then leave for at least 30 minutes in the refrigerator.

Meanwhile, peel, core and slice the apples. Heat the butter in a pan and fry the apples gently until soft and golden.

Add the sugar and spice and cook, stirring, until the apple is coated with syrup.

Line a greased 8-in loose-bottomed quiche pan with the dough and fill with the apple. Bake for 25-30 minutes and serve with whipped cream.

Chocolate Cake

INGREDIENTS *serves 6*
1/2 cup butter or soft margarine
3/4 cup sugar
2 eggs, beaten
2 1/4 cups all-purpose flour
1 tsp baking powder
4 tbsp cocoa powder
1 tsp baking soda
1 cup yogurt
1 tsp vanilla extract

METHOD
Beat the butter and sugar together until light. Add the eggs and continue beating. Sift the flour, baking powder, cocoa and baking soda, and mix it into the butter mixture. Add the yogurt and vanilla extract, mix in thoroughly.

Turn the mixture into a well-greased cake pan, measuring approximately 8in. (Use two sandwich pans or a large ring mold, if preferred.) Bake at 350°F for 25 minutes. Insert a knife to test and cook a little longer if necessary. Timing obviously depends on the type of pan used.

Cool and ice with Cream Cheese Frosting (see page 165) or serve sprinkled with confectioners' sugar.

Fruit Tartlets

INGREDIENTS *serves 6-8*
6-8 small pie shells, baked
1/2 cup cream cheese
1/2 tsp vanilla extract (optional)
1-2 tsp superfine sugar
3-4 cups fresh fruit (raspberries, grapes, strawberries, red currants etc)
apricot jam to glaze

METHOD
Mix the cream cheese with the vanilla and just enough sugar to make a mixture the consistency of thick cream. Spoon into the baked and cooled pie shells. Cover the cream cheese with fresh fruit (pit the grapes). Melt a little apricot jam in a saucepan and brush over the fruit to glaze.

Use a selection of different fruits to make an attractive plate of pastries. You could also make one large pie and fill the pie shell with alternate rings of different fruits.

Buttermilk Spice Cake

INGREDIENTS *serves 6*
2 1/4 cups all-purpose flour
1 cup sugar
1 1/2 tsp baking soda
1 tsp baking powder
pinch salt
1 tsp ground cinnamon
1/2 tsp ground cloves
1/2 cup butter, melted
1 1/2 cups buttermilk
2 eggs

METHOD
Sift the dry ingredients together. Add the eggs, butter and buttermilk and beat the mixture until it is smooth. Pour the batter into a greased and floured cake pan measuring approximately 8in. Bake at 350°F for 40 minutes.

Pumpkin, Sunflower and Raisin Cake

INGREDIENTS *serves 6-8*
12oz pumpkin
2 1/4 cups whole-wheat flour
pinch salt
2 tsp baking powder
1 tsp baking soda
1/3 cup sunflower seeds, chopped
1/3 cup raisins
2 eggs
2 tbsp honey
2 tbsp molasses
1 tbsp warm water

METHOD
Preheat the oven to 375°F. Peel the pumpkin, cut into smallish pieces and boil until tender. Drain and cut up finely.

Combine flour, salt, baking powder, baking soda, sunflower seeds and raisins and mix well.

In another bowl, beat the eggs and stir in the honey and molasses. Add 1 tbsp of warm water with the pumpkin and beat well.

Mix all the ingredients together thoroughly and pour into a greased and floured cake pan. Bake for 50-60 minutes until done. Allow to stand for 10 minutes in the pan, then cool on a wire rack.

Pecan Pie

INGREDIENTS *serves 4-6*
8oz pastry dough (see page 158)
4 tbsp butter, softened
2 tbsp honey
2 tbsp maple syrup
3 eggs
1 tsp vanilla extract
1 cup pecan halves
whipped cream

METHOD
Preheat the oven to 425°F. Line an 8 1/2-in loose bottomed pan with the chosen pastry. Prick and bake blind for 10 minutes.

Meanwhile, make the filling. Beat the butter together with the honey and syrup until smooth. In another bowl, beat the eggs and vanilla essence thoroughly with a wire or rotary whisk. Pour in the syrup, beating constantly with a fork.

Scatter the nuts evenly over the pastry base and pour the custard over. Bake in the middle of the oven for 10 minutes. Reduce the heat to 325°F and bake for a further 25-35 minutes until the filling is set, but not dry. Serve warm (but not hot) or cold with whipped cream.

Yogurt Cake

INGREDIENTS *serves 4*
2/3 cup yogurt
2 1/2 cups all-purpose flour
1 tbsp baking powder
1/4 cup oil
3/4 cup sugar
1 tsp vanilla extract
2 eggs

METHOD
Mix everything together well. Beat until smooth. Turn the mixture into a well-greased cake pan measuring approximately 8in. Bake at 350°F for 45 minutes. Insert a knife to test and cook a little longer if necessary.

This is a good basic recipe with many variations. To make an upside-down fruit cake sprinkle the bottom of the pan with brown sugar and lay sliced apples, pears or canned pineapple on the sugar, cover with the cake mixture and cook as directed.

▲ Pecan pie   ▼ Pumpkin, sunflower and raisin cake

Continental Cheesecake

INGREDIENTS *serves 6-8*
Sour Cream Pastry Dough (see page 158)
6 tbsp butter or margarine
4 tbsp superfine sugar
$\frac{1}{3}$ cup raisins
grated lemon peel
$1\frac{1}{3}$ cups farmers' cheese
2 tbsp sour cream
2 eggs, separated
1 tsp vanilla extract

METHOD

Line a 9-in pie plate with the dough and bake for 5 minutes. Reserve some dough to decorate the top of the cake. Mix the remaining ingredients, except the egg whites, together well. Beat the whites until they are stiff and fold them into the mixture.

Turn it into the prepared pie shell and decorate with the reserved dough in a criss-cross pattern. Bake at 350°F for 30 minutes.

Greek Cheesecake

INGREDIENTS *serves 6*
piecrust pastry dough to line a pan
    approximately $7\frac{1}{2}$-in
$2\frac{2}{3}$ cups farmers' cheese
4 eggs
$\frac{1}{2}$ cup clear honey
1 tsp ground cinnamon

METHOD

Bake the dough for 15 minutes at 350°F. Mix the farmers' cheese, eggs, honey and cinnamon together well (in a blender or food processor is excellent). Fill the partially baked pie shell with the mixture and bake it at 350°F. for 30 minutes.

VARIATION

The Greek name for this cake is siphnopitta (literally cake from the island of Siphnos). It is very easy to make and a nice variation on the cheesecake theme. You can use ricotta cheese, if you prefer.

▲ ▶ Carrot cake
◀ Continental cheesecake

Carrot Cake

INGREDIENTS *serves 6*
6 tbsp butter
generous 1 cup superfine sugar
3 eggs
$2\frac{3}{4}$ cups all-purpose flour
2 tsp baking soda
$\frac{1}{2}$ tsp salt
$\frac{1}{2}$ tsp ground cinnamon
$\frac{2}{3}$ cup yogurt
4 cups finely grated carrots
$\frac{3}{4}$ cup chopped walnuts or mixed nuts

METHOD

Cream the butter and sugar. Add the eggs, 1 at a time. Sift the flour, baking soda, salt and cinnamon, and add this mixture to the creamed mixture alternately with the yogurt. Fold in the carrots and nuts and mix them in thoroughly but gently.

Turn into a greased and floured cake pan measuring approximately 8in. Bake at 350°F for 45 minutes. Insert a knife to test and cook a little longer if necessary.

Frost the cake with the Cream Cheese Frosting (see next column) for the all-American cake. It is very good on its own if you find the frosting too rich.

Cream Cheese Frosting

INGREDIENTS *Frosts an 8-in cake*
2 tbsp unsalted butter
$\frac{2}{3}$ cup confectioners' sugar
grated lemon peel
1 cup cream cheese

METHOD

Mix everything together until smooth - a blender or food processor speeds the work. Refrigerate until required. Spread on top or as a filling for cakes.

This is the classic frosting for carrot cake (preceeding recipe). It is also good with the Chocolate Cake (see page 162) or, indeed, any cake which you want to frost.

VARIATION

To make frosting with different flavors, omit the lemon peel and substitute:
1 tsp vanilla extract;
or 1 tbsp orange juice and grated orange peel;
or $\frac{1}{2}$ tsp ground cinnamon;
or 2 tbsp melted bitter chocolate;
or 2 tbsp very strong coffee.

Apple Cake

INGREDIENTS *serves 6*
3 medium cooking apples, peeled, cored
   and sliced
a little cider
1 clove
2 tbsp butter, softened
2 tbsp honey
2 tbsp molasses
1 egg
1 tsp mixed spice
pinch salt
2 tsp baking powder
1 tsp baking of soda
$\frac{1}{2}$ cup raisins
$1\frac{1}{2}$ cups whole-wheat flour
4 tbsp wheat germ
1 tsp ground mixed spice

METHOD
Pre-heat the oven to 350°F. Poach the apple
slices in a little cider with the clove until soft.
Remove clove. Drain and reserve cider.
Purée apples in a blender.

In a large bowl mix butter, honey,
molasses and 1 tbsp reserved cider. Beat in
the egg. Stir in apples and remaining
ingredients and mix well.

Pour batter into a greased and floured
bread pan, 9×4in, and bake for about 1
hour until firm. Allow to stand for 10
minutes, then turn out of the pan and cool
completely on a wire rack.

Fresh Fruit Dessert Cake

INGREDIENTS *serves 8*
2 eggs
$\frac{1}{3}$ cup milk
2 tbsp honey
2 tbsp molasses
$1\frac{1}{2}$ cups whole-wheat flour
1 ts baking powder
1 tsp baking soda
1 tsp ground cinnamon
pinch salt
1lb peaches
$\frac{1}{2}$lb plums

$\frac{1}{2}$lb cherries
1 cup chopped walnuts
a little butter
fresh fruit to decorate
whipped cream

METHOD
Preheat the oven to 400°F. Beat the eggs with
the milk. Stir in the honey and molasses. Stir
in the rest of the dry ingredients and mix
well.

Pit and chop the fruit. Mix it into the
batter with the nuts. Pour into a greased and
floured 9-in cake pan with a removable
bottom (spring form cake pan) and bake for
50-60 minutes until set in the middle. Dot
with butter toward the end of the cooking
time to prevent the top drying out.

Allow to cool in the pan. Chill in the
refrigerator, decorate with fresh fruit and
serve with whipped cream.

▲ Apple cake

166

DESSERTS AND PUDDINGS

*Fruit fools and trifles, soufflés and mousses, rich ice creams and
low-calorie ices are on the menu. There is something for
everyone here; from the most sweet-toothed to the carefully diet-
and health-conscious.*

Rose petal trifle

167

Blueberry Froth

INGREDIENTS
²⁄₃ cup yogurt
2 eggs, separated
1 tbsp crème de cassis (or black currant
  syrup)
¼ cup superfine sugar
2 cups blueberries

METHOD
Stir the yogurt and egg yolks together with
the crème de cassis and sugar until the sugar
is dissolved.

Just before serving, beat the egg whites
until stiff and fold them into the yolk
mixture. Fold the blueberries in gently.
Spoon into individual dishes.

Serve with sponge fingers or cookies.

VARIATION
Change the flavors by using a different
liqueur: orange liqueur with a little grated
orange peel; chocolate liqueur with some
grated chocolate. If you want to prepare this
some time before serving it, refrigerate the
yolk mixture and add the whites and berries
at the last minute.

▲ Blueberry froth

Orange Chiffon

INGREDIENTS *serves 4-6*
1 tbsp unflavored gelatin
½ cup orange juice
5 tbsp superfine sugar
2 eggs, separated
1 cup buttermilk
grated orange peel

METHOD
Soak the gelatin in orange juice. Heat this
gently until the gelatin is dissolved. Remove
the pan from the heat. Beat 3 tbsp sugar with
the yolks until light and fluffy. Add this to
the gelatin mixture and stir it over a very low
heat until it begins to thicken. Pour the
thickened mixture into a bowl and add the
buttermilk and orange peel. Mix together
and chill until it is beginning to set.

Beat the egg whites until they are stiff.
Fold in the remaining sugar. Combine the
egg whites and the gelatin mixture, stirring
gently.

Turn the chiffon into a serving dish (or use
individual glasses) and refrigerate until
required.

VARIATION
If you prefer you can make a pie by turning
this mixture into a baked pie shell and
refrigerating it in the crust. Decorate the
chiffon with slivers of candied fruit or
chocolate.

Orange Cream

INGREDIENTS *serves 4*
2 eggs, separated
2 tbsp superfine sugar
juice and grated peel of 1 orange
1¹⁄₃ cups cream cheese
2 tbsp orange-flavored liqueur

METHOD
Beat the yolks with the sugar until they are
thick and creamy. Add the orange juice and
peel and mix it in well. Soften the cheese and
add it to the egg mixture. Add the liqueur.

Beat the whites until they are stiff. Fold in
a little of the beaten whites to the cheese
mixture and then gently fold in the rest.
Spoon into 4 glasses and serve immediately.

If you want to prepare this in advance,
leave the egg whites until just before you are
going to serve, then beat the whites and fold
them into the cheese mixture at the very last
minute. If you make it in advance with the
egg whites it may separate - if this happens,
stir through before serving.

VARIATION
Use farmers' cheese for a less rich version.

Rhubarb Cream Jelly

INGREDIENTS *serves 6*
2¹⁄₂ cups yogurt
1lb rhubarb
sugar to taste
1 tsp vanilla extract
½ tsp ground cinnamon or a small piece
  of cinnamon stick
1 cup whipping cream, whipped
2 tbs unflavored gelatin
2 tbsp hot water

METHOD
Drain the yogurt for about 3 hours.

Cook the rhubarb with the sugar, vanilla
extract and cinnamon with just enough
water to stop it from burning. You will need
1¼ cups of cooked rhubarb. Mix the cooked
rhubarb with the drained yogurt and the
whipped cream. Mix gently until
everything is combined.

Dissolve the gelatine in the hot water,
mixing well until smooth. Add to the
rhubarb mixture, stirring the gelatin in
quickly.

Turn the mixture into a moistened small
ring mold and chill until set. Serve with
more whipped cream if desired.

VARIATION
Use 1¹⁄₃ cups fromage blanc or farmers'
cheese, if preferred, instead of the drained
yogurt.

Crème Caramel

INGREDIENTS *serves 6*
4 tbsp fruit sugar
4 tbsp water

THE CUSTARD
2½ cups milk
few drops vanilla extract
4 eggs
3 tbsp fruit sugar

METHOD
Preheat the oven to 350°F. For the caramel, put the sugar and the water in a heavy saucepan and stir over a low heat until the sugar has dissolved. Bring to a boil and boil until the syrup is golden. Pour the caramel into 6 individual molds (or one large one) and swirl it around so that it coats the bottom and sides.

Bring the milk and vanilla essence to a boil in a saucepan. Remove from the heat.

Beat the eggs and sugar together in a bowl. Gradually add the hot milk, stirring all the while.

Strain or ladle the custard into the molds. Stand them in a roasting pan half filled with hot water and bake for 45 minutes until set. Allow to cool and then chill. Don't turn out the crème caramels until you are ready to serve or they will lose gloss.

▼ Crème caramel

Russian Pashka

INGREDIENTS *serves 6*
¾ cup superfine sugar
¾ cup unsalted butter
2 egg yolks
2 cups cottage cheese, drained and
    strained
⅔ cup sour cream or heavy cream
1⅓ cups mixed dried fruit
1 tsp vanilla extract

METHOD
Cream the sugar and butter together until it
is light and fluffy. Beat in the egg yolks, 1 at a
time. Add the drained and strained cottage
cheese to the butter mixture and mix well
together. Add the remaining ingredients,
mixing them all in well.

Turn the mixture into a serving dish and
refrigerate for a minimum of 2 hours.

Damson Mousse

INGREDIENTS
1lb damsons or other plums
sugar to taste
1 cup water
1 tbsp unflavored gelatin
3 tbsp hot water
⅔ cup yogurt
2 egg whites

METHOD
Cook the damsons with sugar and water.
Rub the cooked fruit through a strainer to
make a thick purée. Check the sweetness
and add more sugar if necessary.

Dissolve the gelatin in the hot water and
add it to the purée. Leave the mixture to
cool and when it is beginning to set, fold in
the yogurt. Beat the egg whites until they are
stiff. Add a little of the beaten whites to the
damson mixture to lighten it and then fold
in the rest of the whites.

Refrigerate for a minimum of 6 hours -
overnight if possible. The longer you leave
it, the better the flavor.

VARIATION
Try this with other fruit - well-flavored
plums or other stewed fruit.

Chestnut Whips

INGREDIENTS *serves 4*
1¼ cups canned unsweetened chestnut
    purée
2 tbsp dark rum
1 tbsp dark muscovado sugar
⅔ cup thick yogurt
2 egg whites
chopped chestnuts or pistachio nuts

METHOD
Beat the chestnut purée, rum, sugar and
yogurt together until smooth.

Beat the egg whites until stiff and fold
into the chestnut mixture.

Spoon into 1 large or 4 individual serving
dishes.

Chill for 1 hour, decorate with chopped
nuts and serve.

▲▲ Russian pashka
▲ Chestnut whips
◄ Damson mousse

171

Rose Petal Trifle

INGREDIENTS *serves 6*

2 eggs
4 tbsp dark brown muscovado sugar
$\frac{1}{2}$ tsp ground cinnamon
4 tbsp whole-wheat flour
4 tbsp all-purpose flour
1 tbsp polyunsaturated margarine,
    melted
2 egg yolks
2 tbsp cornstarch
2 tbsp light muscovado sugar
$1\frac{1}{4}$ cups skim milk
1 tbsp triple-strength rosewater
4 passion fruit, halved
6oz raspberries
2 tbsp whipping cream, whipped
rose petals

METHOD

Line and lightly grease a 7-in cake pan. Beat the eggs and dark muscovado sugar together, until thick and creamy.

Fold in the cinnamon, flours and melted margarine. Pour into the pan and bake in a preheated oven at 350°F for 20 minutes, or until risen and firm. Turn out and cool.

Beat the egg yolks, cornstarch and light muscovado sugar together. Heat the milk until boiling and pour onto the egg mix. Return to the saucepan and cook, stirring continuously, over a gentle heat until thickened.

Add the rosewater, cover and set aside until cold.

Cut the cake into cubes and place in the bottom of a serving dish. Scoop the flesh from the passion fruit and spoon over the sponge. Top with raspberries.

Pour the custard over and pipe the cream on top. Garnish with rose petals and serve.

Raspberry and Apple Layer

INGREDIENTS *serves 6*

1lb dessert apples, peeled, cored and
    chopped
8oz ripe raspberries, puréed
1 tbsp light muscovado sugar
2 tbsp polyunsaturated margarine
1 cup fresh whole-wheat bread crumbs
1 cup crushed muesli cookies
1 tsp ground mixed spice
raspberries
green apple slices

METHOD

Place the apples in a saucepan with 1 tbsp water, cover and gently cook until tender. Beat or process in a blender or food processor to a purée.

Mix with the raspberry purée and sugar. Leave to cool.

Melt the margarine in a saucepan, add the bread crumbs and stir over a low heat until browned. Stir in the muesli cookies and mixed spice. Place the fruit purée and crumb mix in alternate layers in glass bowls. Decorate with fruit and serve.

Banana and Cherry Yogurt

INGREDIENTS *serves 4*

4 very ripe bananas, cut into pieces
2 tsp lemon juice
$1\frac{1}{4}$ cups lowfat yogurt
8oz fresh cherries, pitted
cherry pairs with stems

METHOD

Mash the bananas with the lemon juice. Mix in the yogurt.

Divide the pitted cherries between four tall glasses and top with the banana-flavored yogurt.

Hang a pair of cherries over the edge of each glass to decorate. Serve chilled, alone or with whole-wheat cookies.

Berry Meringue

INGREDIENTS *serves 4-6*

crushed meringues to line a 7-in baking
    dish
$2\frac{1}{2}$ cups blackberries
$\frac{2}{3}$ cup sour cream
2 tsp superfine sugar
$\frac{1}{2}$ tsp vanilla extract

METHOD

Line the baking dish with the crushed meringues. Cover with the blackberries. Mix the sour cream, sugar and vanilla essence together and spoon this over the berries. Bake at 350°F for 20 minutes.

NOTE

If you are a frequent baker of meringues you may well suffer from a surfeit of crushed meringues - here is the answer to the problem. Other berries would do but blackberries have the particular acidity which contrasts with the sweetness of the meringues.

▲ ▲ Banana and cherry yogurt
▲ Raspberry and apple layer
▶ Berry meringue

Cheese Blintzes

INGREDIENTS *makes 8-9 blintzes*
1 recipe Crêpes (see page 68)
2 cups farmers' cheese
1 egg yolk
1 tbsp sugar
butter

METHOD
Make the crêpes. Mix the cheese, egg yolk and sugar together well. Put a spoonful of the mixture onto the cooked side of each pancake and make a square parcel by folding 2 edges to the middle and then folding the remaining two edges over.

Melt a little butter and fry the filled crêpes, folded side down first, turning over to fry the second side until lightly browned. Keep the cooked blintzes hot while frying the remaining ones. Serve hot.

NOTE
Blintzes freeze very well. Cook them and, when cold, wrap in foil and freeze. Cook them from frozen in the oven with a dab of butter on each one, or if defrosted, warm through in a skillet. You can make a less rich filling by using cottage cheese, or a richer one by using cream cheese.

▶ Cheese blintzes

Buckwheat Crêpes with Blueberries

INGREDIENTS *makes 9 small crêpes*
3/8 cup whole-wheat flour
1/8 cup buckwheat flour
pinch salt
1 egg
2/3 cup milk
1 tbsp butter, melted

THE FILLING
1lb bilberries
4tbsp honey
whipped cream to serve

METHOD
To make the crêpe batter, sift the flours and salt into a bowl. Make a well in the middle of it and add the egg.

Gradually beat in the milk. When half of the milk has been added, beat in the melted butter. Continue beating in the milk until you have a thin batter. Allow the batter to stand for at least half an hbil.

Meanwhile, prepare the filling. Wash and pick over the blueberries. Put them in a heavy-bottomed pan over a very low flame. It is best to add no water at all. When the fruit is submerged in its own juice, add the honey and stir until dissolved. The syrup should be thick and fruity.

To make the crêpes, oil a heavy-bottomed pan 7in in diameter. Place it on the flame and when it is very hot, add 2 tbsp of the batter. Tilt the pan so that the batter covers the bottom. Cook until the crêpe is beginning to brown on the underside and then turn over and cook the other side. You may have to throw the first crêpe away, as it will absorb the excess oil in the pan.

Continue making crêpes, keeping them warm, until all the batter has been used up. Divide the filling between them and roll the crêpes into cigar shapes.

Serve each pancake with a dollop of whipped cream.

▶ Buckwheat crêpes with blueberries

Apple Cakes

INGREDIENTS *serves 4-6*
1 1/2 cups all-purpose flour, sifted
5 tbsp brown sugar
1 egg
7/8 cup yogurt
3 medium cooking apples, peeled, cored and grated
1/2 tsp ground cinnamon
butter or margarine for frying

METHOD
Combine the flour, sugar, egg and yogurt and mix together very well until smooth. Fold in the grated apples and the cinnamon and mix well. Heat a skillet or griddle and grease lightly.

Drop spoonfuls of the mixture onto the pan, cooking 3 or 4 at a time, depending on the size of the pan. Flip the apple cakes over when bubbles start to appear. Keep them warm while you cook the rest.

NOTE
Serve with butter or jam if desired, although they are good just on their own.

Sweet Potato and Apricot Crêpes

INGREDIENTS *serves 6-8*
recipe Crêpes (page 68)

FILLING
3/4 cup dried apricots
2 large sweet potatoes
butter
honey
cinnamon
sour cream

METHOD
Soak the apricots overnight. Bring to a boil and simmer until tender. Drain and reserve the liquid. Chop the apricots.

Peel and roughly cut up the sweet potatoes. Put in a saucepan, pour over the apricot liquid and cover with water. Bring to a boil and simmer until cooked.

Mash the sweet potatoes with a little butter. Add honey and cinnamon to flavor. Mix in the apricots.

Place a dollop of mixture onto each crêpe and roll up. Heat through and serve with a drizzle of honey and sour cream.

Toffee Bananas

INGREDIENTS *serves 4*
4 bananas, peeled
1 egg
2 tbsp all-purpose flour
oil for deep-frying
4 tbsp sugar
1 tbsp cold water

METHOD
Cut the bananas in half lengthwse and then cut each half into two crosswise.

Beat the egg, add the flour and mix well to make a smooth batter.

Heat the oil in a wok or deep-fryer. Coat each piece of banana with batter and deep-fry until golden. Remove and drain.

Pour off the excess oil leaving about 1 tbsp oil in the wok. Add the sugar and water and stir over a medium heat to dissolve the sugar. Continue stirring and when the sugar has caramelized, add the hot banana pieces. Coat well and remove. Dip the hot bananas in cold water to harden the toffee and serve immediately.

Red Bean Paste "Pancakes"

INGREDIENTS *makes about 12*
2 cups all-purpose flour
6 tbsp boiling water
1 egg
3 tbsp oil
4-5 tbsp sweetened red bean paste or
    chestnut purée

METHOD
Sift the flour into a mixing bowl and very gently pour in the boiling water. Add about 1 tsp oil and the beaten egg.

Knead the mixture into a firm dough and then divide it into 2 equal portions. Roll out each portion into a long "sausage" on a lightly floured surface and cut it into 4-6 pieces. Using the palm of your hand, press each piece into a flat pancake.

On a lightly floured surface, flatten each pancake into a 6-in circle with a rolling pin and roll gently.

Place an ungreased skillet on a high heat. When hot, reduce the heat to low and place one pancake at a time in the pan. Turn it over when little brown spots appear on the underside. Remove and keep under a damp cloth until you have finished making all the pancakes.

Spread about 2 tbsp red bean paste or chestnut purée over about 80 percent of the pancake surface and roll it over 3 or 4 times to form a flattened roll.

Heat the oil in a skillet and shallow-fry the pancakes until golden brown, turning over once. Cut each pancake into 3-4 pieces and serve hot or cold.

▲ Red bean paste "pancakes"
▶ Toffee banana

Noodle Pudding

INGREDIENTS *serves 6*
1 cup cottage cheese
$\frac{1}{2}$ cup cream cheese
$\frac{2}{3}$ cup sour cream
3 eggs
$\frac{1}{2}$ cup sugar
12oz flat noodles, cooked and drained
$\frac{1}{2}$ cup raisins or golden raisins
4 tbsp butter or margarine, melted
1 tsp ground cinnamon
1 tsp sugar

METHOD
Mix the cottage and cream cheese with the sour cream. Beat the eggs and sugar together and add them to the cheese mixture. Fold in the cooked noodles and raisins.

Turn the mixture into a buttered baking dish. Pour over the melted butter. Mix the cinnamon and sugar together and sprinkle it over the top of the noodle mixture. Bake at 350°F for 1 hour. Serve hot.

VARIATION
This hearty Central European pudding has many variations. Add chopped apples or soaked dried apricots to the mixture before baking. Vary the cheese mixture to include more cottage cheese or use farmers' cheese instead of the cream cheese.

Brown Rice Pudding

INGREDIENTS *serves 4*
$\frac{1}{2}$ cup brown rice
$2\frac{1}{2}$ cups China tea
1 stick cinnamon
$\frac{1}{3}$ cup golden raisins
$\frac{1}{3}$ cup chopped dried apricots
$\frac{1}{4}$ cup almonds
sliced fresh fruit (optional)

METHOD
Wash the rice thoroughly under running water. Put it in a heavy pan with the tea and simmer gently for about 1 hour with the cinnamon.

Preheat the oven to 350°F. Remove the cinnamon and transfer the rice to a baking dish. Stir in the remaining ingredients and bake for about 25 minutes until done. Serve hot or refrigerate and serve cold. Garnish with sliced fresh fruit, if liked.

Apple Pudding

INGREDIENTS *serves 4-6*
$2\frac{1}{2}$ cups yogurt
$\frac{2}{3}$ cup whipping cream
2 eggs
4 tbsp superfine sugar
grated lemon peel
1 large cooking apple, peeled and sliced
$\frac{1}{2}$ tsp ground cinnamon
2 tbsp sugar

METHOD
Drain the yogurt for about 4 hours. Whip the cream and fold it into the drained yogurt. Beat the eggs with the sugar and lemon peel and add to the yogurt mixture.

Turn into a greased shallow baking dish. Lay the apple slices on top of the yogurt mixture. Scatter cinnamon on top and then the sugar.

Bake at 350°F for 50 minutes. Serve warm.

► Baked apple
►► Apple, Strawberry and Blackberry Pudding

Apple, Strawberry and Blackberry Pudding

INGREDIENTS *serves 4*

4 cooking apples
1 tbsp honey
4oz strawberries
4oz blackberries
2¼ cups whole-wheat flour
½ cup butter, chilled
2 tbsp sesame seeds
1 tsp ground mixed spice
pinch salt

METHOD

Preheat the oven to 350°F. Peel and core the apples and cut into slices. Put apples in a shallow baking dish with a little water and the honey and cook, covered, in the oven for 30 minutes.

Meanwhile, hull and slice the strawberries and pick over the blackberries.

Now make the crumble. Place the remaining ingredients in a bowl and cut in the butter until the mixture resembles fine bread crumbs.

When the apples are ready, mix in the strawberries and blackberries, adding a little more honey if liked. Press the crumble mixture gently on top of the fruit and return to the oven for 15 minutes until golden brown. Serve hot or cold with cream.

Baked Apples

INGREDIENTS *serves 4*

4 cooking apples, cored
2 tbsp butter
2 tbsp sugar
⅔ cup yogurt
2 tbsp brown sugar
½ cup chopped nuts

METHOD

Score the apples around the middle. Place them in a shallow baking dish. Mix the butter and sugar together and fill the center of each apple with the mixture.

Bake the apples, uncovered, at 400°F for 20 minutes. Mix the yogurt with the brown sugar and nuts and pour this mixture over the baked apples. Return to the oven for a further 10 minutes. Serve hot.

179

Lemon Soufflé

INGREDIENTS *serves 4-6*
3 eggs, separated
¾ cup superfine sugar
6 tbsp all-purpose flour
4 tbsp lemon juice
grated peel of 1 lemon
1½ cups yogurt
confectioners' sugar

METHOD
Mix the egg yolks with all the remaining
ingredients in a heatproof bowl. Place the
bowl over a pan of simmering water and
cook until you have a mixture the
consistency of thick cream, stirring
constantly. Remove the bowl from the heat.

Beat the egg whites until stiff. Fold them
into the cooled mixture.

Turn it into a buttered soufflé dish,
measuring 7×3in, and bake at 325°F for 40
minutes. Sprinkle with confectioners' sugar
before serving.

Pear Soufflé

INGREDIENTS *serves 4-6*
1lb pears
1-2 tbsp butter
a little honey
pinch cinnamon
3 large eggs, separated

METHOD
Preheat the oven to 400°F. Peel, halve and
core the pears. Cut them into slices.

Heat the butter in a pan and add the pear
slices. When the fruit has softened, raise the
heat a little, break up the fruit with a
wooden spoon and cook until mushy.

Put the contents of the pan into a blender.
Blend until smooth and add a little honey
and cinnamon to taste. Pour into a bowl and
beat in the egg yolks.

Butter a 7½ cups soufflé dish. Beat the egg
whites until they form soft peaks and fold
into the mixture. Pour into the soufflé dish
and bake in the oven for 20-25 minutes until
just golden brown and nearly set.

▶ Lemon soufflé

Clementine Cups

INGREDIENTS *serves 4*

4 clementines
juice 1 orange
¾ envelope powdered gelatin
1 tsp clear honey
6 tbsp thick yogurt
1 egg white
1 clementine, peel and pith removed,
    segmented
evergreen leaves
grated plain carob bar

METHOD

Using a zig-zag cut, remove the tops from the clementines. Carefully scoop out all the flesh and reserve the shells.

Press the fruit through a strainer to extract the juice. Mix with the orange juice.

Sprinkle the gelatin over 3 tbsp juice in a small saucepan and heat gently to dissolve. Stir in the honey and place in the bowl.

Add the remaining juice and leave until almost setting. Fold in the yogurt. Whip the egg white until stiff and fold in.

Refrigerate until the mixture holds its shape, place in shells and chill until set. Sprinkle with grated carob, decorate with clementine segments and serve on a bed of green leaves.

Cœur à La Creme

INGREDIENTS *serves 4*

1⅓ cups cream cheese
½ cup yogurt
8oz strawberries
⅔ cup heavy cream
1-2 tbsp honey

METHOD

Blend the cream cheese with the yogurt and pack into the small heart-shaped molds traditional with this dessert. Chill.

Make a strawberry sauce by blending half the strawberries with the cream and honey. Unmold the cheeses onto individual plates, surround with the sauce and decorate with the remaining strawberries.

Ricotta al Cafe

INGREDIENTS *serves 4*

1 cup ricotta cheese
2 tbsp fruit sugar
4 tbsp finely ground fresh coffee
2 tbsp brandy

METHOD

Choose really moist ricotta cheese, or use cottage cheese as a substitute. Press the cheese with half the sugar through a strainer to make it light and fluffy. Form into mounds on 4 individual dessert plates.

Sprinkle half the coffee over the cheese mounds. Spoon the remaining coffee and sugar onto the plates in two separate heaps at the side of the cheese and pour the brandy over the sweetened cheese. Scoop up some of the cheese and eat with a little of the coffee and sugar with each mouthful.

Fruity Yogurt Cassata

INGREDIENTS *serves 4*

⅓ cups no-need-to-soak apricots
1¼ cups grapefruit juice
2 egg whites
1 cup thick yogurt
⅓ cup golden raisins
¼ cup slivered almonds
mint sprigs

METHOD

Place the apricots and grapefruit juice in a saucepan, bring to a boil, cover and simmer for 10 minutes, until apricots are soft.

Purée in a blender or food processor and leave to cool, and thicken.

Fold the yogurt into the apricot purée and place in a freezerproof container. Freeze for 1½-2 hours or until the edges become softly frozen.

Beat the egg whites until stiff. Mix the yogurt ice together and fold in the golden raisins, almonds and egg whites. Return to the freezer for 3-4 hours or until frozen.

Serve scoops in individual dishes, garnished with mint sprigs.

NOTE

Where possible use freshly squeezed fruit juices, rather than ready prepared ones, to ensure a healthier juice.

▲ ▲ Clementine cups
◀ ▲ Fruity yogurt cassata

Carob Upside-down Pudding

INGREDIENTS *serves 4*
2 small pears, peeled, cored and halved
2 eggs, separated
3 tbsp dark brown muscovado sugar
1½ tbsp carob powder
2 tbsp whole-wheat flour
2 tbsp blanched almonds, ground
1 tbsp clear honey
kumquat slices

METHOD
Arrange the pears in the base of a 7-in round cake tin, which has been lightly greased.

Beat the egg yolks together with the sugar until light and creamy. Beat in 1 tbsp hot water and the carob powder. Fold in the flour and almonds.

Beat the egg whites until stiff and fold into the carob mix. Pour over the pears and cook in a preheated oven at 375°F for 35 minutes.

Turn out onto a warmed serving dish. Brush the pears with honey. Decorate the pudding with kumquat slices and serve.

Carrot Halva

INGREDIENTS *serves 4-6*
4 cups peeled and grated carrots
3¾ cups milk
⅔ cup sugar
3 cardamom pods
4 tbsp Ghee (see page 126)
2 tbsp raisins
2 tbsp skinned and chopped pistachio nuts

METHOD
Place the carrots, milk, sugar and cardamoms in a large saucepan and bring to a boil. Lower heat to medium low and, stirring occasionally, cook until all the liquid has evaporated.

Heat the ghee in a large skillet over medium heat, add the cooked carrots, raisins and pistachios and, stirring constantly, fry for 15-20 minutes until it is dry and turned reddish in color. Serve hot or cold.

▲ ▲ Carrot halva
◀ ▲ Carob upside down pudding
▲ ▶ Pineapple delights
▶ Yoghurt with saffron

182

Pineapple Delights

INGREDIENTS *serves 4-6*
2 small pineapples, trimmed and halved
3 kiwi fruits, sliced
2 peaches, peeled and sliced
2oz black grapes, halved and pitted
2 tbsp orange liqueur
2 tbsp orange juice
1 tbsp clear honey

METHOD
Scoop the flesh out of the pineapple shells, leaving the skins intact. Remove the hard core and cut the flesh into bite-sized pieces.

Add the kiwi fruit, peaches and grapes. Mix the liqueur, orange juice and honey together. Warm gently in a saucepan to dissolve the honey, if necessary.

Pour over the fruit and leave to marinate until ready to serve. Pile the fruit into the pineapple shells, pour over the syrup and serve.

Vanilla Soufflé

INGREDIENTS *serves 4-6*
2½ cups yogurt
6 tbsp butter, softened
3 eggs, separated
⅔ cup superfine sugar
1 tsp vanilla extract

METHOD
Drain the yogurt for about 4 hours. Mix the drained yogurt with the butter, egg yolks and vanilla extract. Beat the egg whites until they are stiff and fold in the sugar. Fold a little of the white mixture into the yogurt mixture to lighten it and then carefully fold in the rest.

Butter and lightly flour a small soufflé dish, measuring 7×3in. Turn the mixture into the dish and bake at 375°F for 30 minutes.

VARIATION
Use 1⅓ cups fromage blanc or farmers' cheese instead of yogurt if preferred.

Yogurt with Saffron

INGREDIENTS *serves 4*
2½ cups yogurt
¼ saffron
1 tbsp warm milk
½ cup superfine sugar
2 tbsp skinned and chopped pistachio
    nuts

METHOD
Put the yogurt in a cheesecloth bag and hang it up for 4-5 hours to get rid of the excess water.

Soak the saffron in the milk for 30 minutes.

Beat together the drained yogurt, sugar and saffron milk until smooth and creamy.

Put in a dish and garnish with the nuts. Chill until set.

Chocolate Yogurt Ice Cream

INGREDIENTS *serves 4-6*
4 tbsp cocoa powder
$\frac{1}{2}$ cup sugar
$\frac{2}{3}$ cup boiling water
2 tsp vanilla extract
2$\frac{1}{2}$ cups yogurt
$\frac{1}{2}$ cup whipping cream
2 egg whites

METHOD
Make a syrup by combining the cocoa powder and sugar with the boiling water. Mix until it is smooth and add the vanilla extract. Leave to cool.

Whip the cream and mix the chocolate syrup with the yogurt and whipped cream.

Pour the mixture into a shallow tray and place it in the freezer. Stir it from time to time while it is freezing.

When it has frozen, after about 6 hours, remove from the freezer and mix in a blender or food processor until it is mushy. Add the egg whites to the mixture and blend them in to make the mixture light.

Return the mixture to the freezer for a minimum of 12 hours.

Rich Honey and Plum Ice Cream

INGREDIENTS *serves 4*
4-5 plums
1 tbsp milk powder
6 tbsp honey
2 tbsp yogurt
few drops vanilla extract
$\frac{2}{3}$ cup whipping cream

METHOD
Put plums in a bowl and pour over boiling water. After 1 minute, the skins will split. Drain and pour over cold water. Peel the fruit, discard the pits and chop finely.

Purée the fruit with the milk powder and honey in a blender until smooth. Stir in the yogurt and vanilla extract. Freeze the mixture.

When the mixture is almost frozen, remove it from the freezer and beat it. Whisk the cream and stir the two together. Return to the freezer.

Orange Buttermilk Ice

INGREDIENTS *serves 4*
2 eggs
$\frac{1}{4}$ cup superfine sugar
$\frac{3}{4}$ cup light corn syrup
2 cups buttermilk
$\frac{2}{3}$ cup orange juice
grated peel of 1 orange

▲ ▲ Orange buttermilk ice
▲ Grapefruit sorbet

METHOD
Blend everything together well. Freeze for a minimum of 3 hours. Blend again until smooth and return to the freezer. Freeze overnight or longer. (This ice stays remarkably soft even when frozen for some weeks.)

Grapefruit Sorbet

INGREDIENTS *serves 4*
1$\frac{3}{4}$ cups grapefruit juice
3 tbsp granulated sugar
2 egg whites
1 pink grapefruit, peel and pith
   removed, segmented
4 tsp Grenadine (optional)

METHOD
Mix the grapefruit juice and sugar together and freeze in a shallow freezer container until slushy, about 1-1$\frac{1}{2}$ hours.

Beat the egg whites until stiff, beat the grapefruit mixture to break up the ice crystals and fold in the egg whites.

Freeze until firm. Place the grapefruit segments in the base of chilled glasses and top with scoops of sorbet.

Pour 1 tsp Grenadine over the top of each sorbet, just before serving, if wished.

QUICK MICROWAVE DISHES

The microwave and vegetables were made for each other. Little or no water is needed for cooking, keeping the goodness in the food, and crispness, flavor and color intact. Since the microwave has become a fact of life in many homes, this section is a valuable extra for the modern vegetarian cook.

Cannelloni

185

Mushroom Soup

INGREDIENTS *serves 4*
2 tbsp butter
1 onion, peeled and chopped
1 garlic clove, crushed
6 cups mushrooms, washed
¼ cup all-purpose flour
2½ cups vegetable stock
½ tsp thyme
1 bay leaf
2 sprigs of parsley
¼ cup half-and-half cream

METHOD
Melt the butter in a large casserole or bowl
for 2 minutes.

Add the onion and garlic and cook on full
power for 2 minutes.

Slice the mushrooms finely and chop the
stems separately. Add to the onion, cook on
full power for 3 minutes. Stir and cook for a
further 2 minutes.

Remove from the microwave oven and
stir in the flour until it has mixed well with
any remaining butter. Add half the
vegetable stock, stir well and cook for 5
minutes at full power.

Mix the thyme, bay leaf and parsley with
the remaining stock and pour the mixture
over the mushrooms. Season well and cook
on full power for a further 10 minutes.
Allow to stand for 5 minutes and remove the
herbs.

Stir in the cream. The soup can be puréed
if you prefer a smoother texture.

Parsnip and Apple Soup

INGREDIENTS *serves 4*
2 tbsp butter
1 onion, diced
4 cups diced peeled parsnips
8oz cooking apples
1 tsp Italian seasoning
4 cups vegetable stock
1 cup light cream
1 tbsp chopped fresh parsley

METHOD
Melt the butter in a browning dish for 2
minutes. Add the onion to the melted butter
and cook on full power for 2 minutes.

Add the parsnips to the onion and cook
on full power for 3 minutes. Add the sliced
apple and herbs and cook for a further 2
minutes.

Pour on the stock and cook, covered, for
10 minutes on full power. Allow to stand for
a few minutes.

Put the soup in a blender or food
processor, add the cream and re-heat for 5
minutes.

Sprinkle with chopped parsley and serve
with whole-wheat bread.

French Onion Soup

INGREDIENTS *serves 4*
2 tbsp butter
8½ cups sliced onions
¼ cup all-purpose flour
1 tsp mixed chopped herbs, preferably
    fresh
4 cups vegetable stock
salt and freshly ground black pepper
1 small French loaf (bread)
4oz Mozzarella cheese, sliced
1 tbsp chopped fresh parsley

METHOD
Melt the butter in the browning dish,
remove from the oven and stir in the onions.
Return to the microwave and cook on high
power for 6 minutes, stirring once.

Sprinkle the flour over the onions and
return for a further 1 minute on full power.

Add the herbs, vegetable stock and
seasoning, stir well and cook, covered, on
full power for 10 minutes.

Toast the French bread, cover it with
slices of Mozzarella and melt under the
broiler or in the microwave for a few
seconds.

Arrange the bread and cheese in the soup
bowl, pour over the onion soup and sprinkle
generously with chopped parsley.

◀▲ Parsnip and apple soup
▶ Mushroom soup

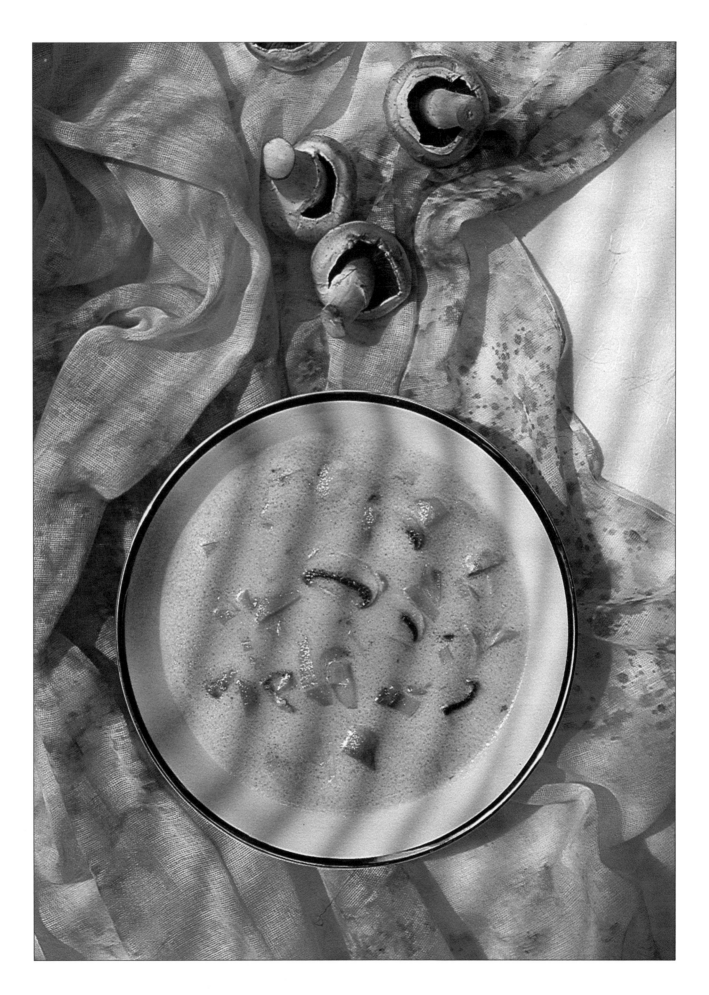

Vegetable Soup with Spicy Sauce

INGREDIENTS *serves 6*

3½ cups dried navy beans, soaked
   overnight
12oz ripe tomatoes
1 onion, peeled and diced
¼ cup vegetable oil
salt and freshly ground black pepper
1 tsp Worcestershire sauce
1 tsp Italian seasoning
4 cups vegetable stock
2 carrots, sliced
2¼ cups shelled peas
2 potatoes, peeled and sliced
1 leek, trimmed and sliced
¼ cup butter
½ cup all-purpose flour
1 tbsp chopped fresh parsley

METHOD

Put the beans into a bowl, cover them with
water and microwave on full power for 10
minutes. Allow to stand for 2 minutes, then
cook for a further 5 minutes.

Place the tomatoes in a bowl with water
and scald for 2 minutes at full power. Peel
and slice the tomatoes. Add to the onion in a
dish with the oil. Season with salt and
pepper and cook for 2 minutes on full
power.

Add the Worcestershire sauce, mixed
herbs and half of the stock. Cook on full
power for 5 minutes.

Clean and prepare the rest of the
vegetables. Just cover with the remaining
vegetable stock and cook, with the beans,
on full power for 15 minutes.

Strain the tomato mixture, collecting the
purée in a bowl.

Melt the butter for 1 minute on full
power. Remove from the oven, add the flour
and stir carefully. Mix until smooth with the
tomato mixture and then cook for 5 minutes
at full power, stirring well.

Mix the tomato purée into the vegetable
soup. Cook on full power for 10 minutes.

Sprinkle with chopped fresh parsley.

▲▲ Vegetable soup with spicy sauce
▲▶ Tomato and carrot soup
▶ Lettuce soup

Leek and Potato Soup

INGREDIENTS *serves 4*
2 potatoes, peeled and diced
4 cups vegetable stock
2 tbsp butter
1 onion, peeled and diced
2 leeks, washed and sliced
2 tsp chopped fresh chives
salt and freshly ground black pepper
1 bouquet garni
1 tbsp chopped fresh parsley
whole-wheat bread

METHOD
Place the potatoes in a large microwave dish and pour the vegetable stock over the potatoes. Cook on full power for 10 minutes.

Melt the butter in a browning dish, add the onion and leeks and cook on full power for 5 minutes.

Add the leeks and onion to the potato stock with the chives, seasoning and bouquet garni. Cook at full power for 10 minutes. Taste for seasoning, checking that the potatoes are cooked. If not, cook for a further 2 minutes on full power.

Sprinkle with chopped parsley and serve with slices of whole-wheat bread.

VARIATION
Purée or put through a vegetable mill or food processor.

Add $\frac{1}{4}$ cup cream and serve hot or cold.

Tomato and Carrot Soup

INGREDIENTS *serves 4*
2 cups vegetable stock
3 cups thinly sliced carrots
1 onion, thinly sliced
$2\frac{1}{2}$ cups canned plum tomatoes, or 2lb
    tomatoes, peeled
$\frac{1}{4}$ tsp basil
salt and freshly ground black pepper
2 drops soy sauce
4 tsp cream (optional)

METHOD
Add the cold stock to the carrots and blanch for 5 minutes at full power.

Add the onion to the carrots with all the other ingredients, except the cream. Cook on full power for 10 minutes, reduce to half power and cook for a further 20 minutes. Test the carrots; if they are not soft enough cook for a further 5 minutes on full.

Allow to cool slightly and then blend, sieve or purée in a blender or food processor. Taste for seasoning.

Reheat in individual bowls or in a large bowl as required, sprinkle a swirl of cream on top of each portion, if liked, and garnish with a few slivers of raw carrot.

Lettuce Soup

INGREDIENTS *serves 4*
2 tbsp butter
1 onion, peeled
1 potato, peeled
$2\frac{1}{2}$ cups vegetable stock
2 lettuces
1 tsp chopped fresh chervil or chives
salt and freshly ground black pepper
$\frac{1}{2}$ cup light cream
1 scallion

METHOD
Melt the butter in a large casserole on full power for 1 minute. Slice the onion and potato finely.

Stir the onion and potato into the butter and cook on full power for 5 minutes; allow to stand for 2 minutes.

Add the vegetable stock and cook for a further 5 minutes. Remove from the microwave and stir in the lettuce, chervil or chives and seasoning. Cook on full power for a further 10 minutes. Allow to stand until slightly cool.

Put the mixture through a coarse strainer, food mill or blender. Reheat as required.

Add swirls of light cream before serving and garnish with finely chopped scallion. Serve hot or cold.

▲ Leek and potato soup

Vegetable Loaf

INGREDIENTS *serves 6*
8oz broccoli spears
2 carrots, grated
3 stalks celery, tops discarded
2 tbsp butter
2 tbsp all-purpose flour
3 eggs
salt and freshly ground black pepper
$\frac{1}{4}$ tsp paprika
$\frac{1}{4}$ tsp mustard powder
$\frac{1}{2}$ cup cottage cheese
1 cup grated cheddar cheese
2 tomatoes, peeled
2 scallions, washed and trimmed

METHOD
Arrange the broccoli spears in a ring on a shallow dish with heads to the center of the dish. Sprinkle with 2-3 tbsp water, cover and cook for 8 minutes at full power.

Remove the dish, arrange the grated carrot in heaps and the celery in 1-in pieces between the broccoli. Cover and cook for 5 minutes at full power, drain.

Melt the butter for 1 minute in a bowl at full power, then stir in the flour. Gradually beat in the eggs and season them well with salt, pepper, paprika and mustard. Beat in the cottage cheese and then the grated cheese.

Mix the cheese mixture with broccoli, celery and carrot. Cook on full power for 3 minutes, stir well.

Butter a glass loaf pan or a rectangular china terrine dish. Cover the bottom of the dish with the sliced tomatoes and chopped scallions, then arrange half the cooked mixture in the dish. Pour on the remaining mixture, cover and cook on full for 3 minutes. Turn power to half, or defrost, cook for a further 6 minutes. Allow to stand for 3 minutes.

Test to make sure the mixture is cooked. Unmold the dish onto a heated plate and test the bottom with a fork. Cut into slices and serve with Tomato Sauce (see page 219) and new potatoes, if desired.

Stuffed Artichokes

INGREDIENTS *serves 4*
4 globe artichokes
grated peel and juice of 1 lemon
$\frac{1}{2}$ cup soft bread crumbs
2 cups mushrooms
salt and freshly ground black pepper
1 scallion chopped
$\frac{1}{4}$ cup heavy cream
4 slices Gruyère cheese
2 tbsp butter

METHOD
Prepare the artichokes: cut off the stems and remove the two rows of outer leaves with a sharp knife or scissors. The shaped artichokes should then stand on a plate evenly. Cut across the top of each artichoke about 1in from the top, giving a flat top.

Put the prepared artichokes in a covered casserole dish with water and half the lemon juice. Cook on full power for 20 minutes.

Remove and drain upside down on a wire rack.

Push down with three fingers into the middle section of the leaves and pull these out, leaving the choke visible. Remove it with a teaspoon, making sure that you do not scrape away the heart.

Mix the bread crumbs in a bowl with the finely grated lemon peel. Chop the mushrooms and tip into the bread crumbs, season well with salt and pepper. Add the chopped scallion and mix in the cream.

Stuff the artichoke hearts with the mixture and lay a slice of cheese on top of the stuffing.

Lay the artichokes on a flat plate, cover with plastic wrap and cook on full power for 5 minutes. Allow to stand for 2 minutes.

Melt the butter and mix it with the remaining lemon juice. Pour a little butter and lemon juice over each artichoke.

Crudités with Hot Anchovy Dip

INGREDIENTS *serves 6 - 8*
½ cup butter, diced
2 cloves garlic, crushed
8 anchovy fillets, pounded
1¼ cups heavy cream

METHOD
To make the dip, put the butter in a bowl and microwave on full for 1 minute until melted. Add the garlic and cook for a further 30 seconds.

Put the anchovy fillets with the cream in a blender and blend until smooth.

Pour the anchovy cream onto the garlic butter, stir well and cook on full for 1-2 minutes, until hot.

Put the pot with the anchovy dip on a large platter and arrange the crudités around it.

Mushroom Pâté

INGREDIENTS *serves 4*
½ cup butter
2 cloves garlic, crushed
4 cups sliced mushroom caps
3 tbsp chopped fresh parsley
½ cup grated cheese
pinch of grated nutmeg
salt and freshly ground black pepper
juice of 1 lemon
1 tbsp Cognac
2 tbsp heavy cream (or yogurt)
parsley sprig to garnish

METHOD
Place the butter, garlic and mushrooms in a bowl and cook on full power for 6 minutes. Add the parsley, bread crumbs, cheese, nutmeg, seasoning, lemon juice, Cognac and cream (or yogurt) to the mushrooms. Stir well and cook for a further 1 minute on full.

Blend all the ingredients in a blender or food processor and turn into a bowl. Allow to cool before chilling for 1 hour. Garnish with parsley and serve with toast.

◄▲ Vegetable loaf
◄ Stuffed artichokes
► Crudités with hot anchovy dip

191

Marinated Mushrooms

INGREDIENTS *serves 4*
5 cups button mushrooms, wiped
4 tbsp olive oil
4 tbsp lemon juice
1 tbsp coriander seeds
salt and freshly ground black pepper
parsley or cilantro leaves
chopped chives
toast

METHOD
Put the mushrooms in a dish with the oil, lemon juice and coriander seeds. Let them marinate for an hour or two or in the refrigerator overnight.

Remove the mushrooms from the marinade with a slotted spoon and place in a shallow dish. Brush with the marinade and microwave on full for 3 minutes, stirring every minute.

Season to taste, sprinkle with parsley or cilantro and chives, if liked, and serve with triangles of toast.

Artichokes with Hollandaise Sauce

INGREDIENTS *serves 2*
2 artichokes
2 tbsp lemon juice
6 tbsp water

HOLLANDAISE SAUCE
¼ cup chilled butter, diced
1 tbsp lemon juice
2 small egg yolks
salt and white pepper

METHOD
Soak the artichokes for an hour or so in a bowl of water acidulated with half of the lemon juice to loosen any soil or grit that may be stuck between the leaves. Rinse thoroughly in clean water and set upside down to drain. Trim off the stem close to the vegetable so that it stands upright. Remove any damaged outer leaves and rub the cut surfaces with lemon juice. Do not bother to cut the points off the leaves - this is unnecessary and ruins the look of the vegetable.

Put the artichokes upright in a dish, add the water and the remaining lemon juice, cover and cook for 7-8 minutes on full. Tug at one of the lower leaves to see if done. If it promises to come away in your fingers, the artichokes are ready. Leave them to stand for 3 minutes while you make the sauce.

Put the butter in a bowl and cook on medium or defrost for 2 minutes until melted. Add the lemon juice and egg yolks and beat lightly.

Cook on medium or defrost for 1 minute, whisk again and season.

Drain and serve with the sauce.

To eat the artichoke, pull away the leaves and suck off the tender fleshy part, dipped in the sauce. When you come to the "choke," cut it away and discard it. Eat the heart with a knife and fork - and more sauce.

▲ ▶ Sweet pepper hors d'œuvre
◀ Marinated mushrooms

Sweet Pepper Hors D'Oeuvre

INGREDIENTS *serves 4*
4 red, green or yellow bell peppers,
    deseeded
1/2 cup vegetable oil
1 garlic clove, peeled
2 lemons
salt and freshly ground black pepper
1 tsp marjoram

METHOD
Slice the peppers into thin strips.

Place the peppers in a flat dish. Avoid piling the strips on top of each other. Add 1/4 cup water, cook, covered, on full power for 2 minutes, and then drain.

Place the oil and crushed garlic in a microwave serving dish. Cook on full power for 2 minutes. Add the pepper strips and cook, covered, for 5 minutes on full power.

Allow to cool, sprinkle with lemon juice and seasoning.

Chill and serve as an appetizer.

French Bean Salad

INGREDIENTS *serves 4*
4 cups thin green beans, trimmed and
    left whole
4 tbsp water
3-4 cups tomatoes peeled, seeded and
    cut into strips
1 1/2 tbsp olive oil
1 1/2 tbsp lemon juice
salt and freshly ground black pepper
2 hard-boiled eggs
chives (optional)

METHOD
Put the beans in a dish, add the water, cover with vented plastic wrap and cook on full for 6 minutes, rearranging twice. The beans should be done but still crisp. Set aside, covered, while you make the dressing.

Mix the oil, lemon juice and seasoning. (Shake them together in a screw-topped jar if you have one handy.)

Drain the beans, mix them with the tomatoes and toss in the dressing.

Separate the whites from the yolks of the eggs. Chop both. Garnish the salad with the egg.

VARIATION
If you are feeling artistic, tie the beans into bundles with the chives instead of mixing them together with the tomatoes.

Hot Potato Salad

INGREDIENTS *serves 4*
1½lb new potatoes, washed but not
    peeled
4 tbsp water
2 tbsp virgin olive oil
1 tbsp lemon juice or white-wine
    vinegar
salt and freshly ground black pepper
1 tsp dry mustard
1 bunch scallions
1 bunch radishes
about 12 ripe olives, pitted
1 cup canned green beans, drained, or
    fresh beans if in season
chopped chives (optional)

METHOD
Put the potatoes in a dish with the water, cover and cook for about 8 minutes, shaking twice, until done. Do not overcook the potatoes, or they will be spongy.

Drain the potatoes, slice them and return to the dish.

Make a dressing by combining the olive oil, vinegar or lemon juice, salt, pepper and mustard in a screw-topped jar and shaking well. Pour this over the hot potatoes and keep covered.

Trim the scallions and slice down the stem, making 2 cuts at right angles to each other on each stem. Put the onions in iced water for a couple of minutes. The stems will curl up to make tassels.

Trim and slice the radishes.

Mix the scallion tassels, radishes, olives, green beans and chives, if liked, into the salad and serve at once.

Salad Provençale

INGREDIENTS *serves 4*
1lb whole green beans
4 scallions
1 tsp thyme
1 green bell pepper, deseeded
1 red bell pepper, deseeded
4 tomatoes, peeled
4 hard-boiled eggs
½ cup olive oil
1 tsp French mustard
3-4 tbsp wine vinegar
1 garlic clove
20 ripe olives
1 lettuce

METHOD
Trim the beans, arrange in a dish with 2 tbsp water, cover and cook on full power for 10 minutes.

Chop all but 2 of the scallions finely. Add the chopped scallions with the thyme to the beans after 5 minutes of cooking. Mix well and cook for another 5 minutes. Drain and allow to cool.

Slice the peppers into strips and arrange them in a shallow dish. Cover with 3 tbsp water and cook for 5 minutes on full power. Drain and allow to cool.

Cut each tomato into 8 wedges and each egg into 6 wedges lengthwise.

To make the dressing, mix the oil, mustard, vinegar, salt and pepper in a screw-top jar and shake well.

Take a large salad bowl and rub it with a cut clove of garlic. Line with lettuce leaves, and put the beans mixed with half the dressing in the bottom of the bowl. Arrange the peppers, tomatoes and eggs on top with the ripe olives. Chop the reserved scallions and sprinkle them over the dish. Add rest of the dressing just before serving. Serve with slices of whole-wheat or French bread.

▲ Salad provençale
◀ Hot potato salad

195

Eggplant Lasagne

INGREDIENTS *serves 4*
2 medium eggplants
2-3 tbsp water
6 sheets spinach lasagne
salt
oil
Tomato Sauce (see page 127)

CHEESE SAUCE
3 tbsp butter or margarine
6 tbsp all-purpose flour
1¼ cups milk
½ cup grated Edam cheese
salt and freshly ground black pepper

METHOD
Slice the eggplants. Arrange them in a deep
oblong dish, in which you will cook the
finished lasagne. Add the water, cover with
vented plastic wrap and cook on full for 7
minutes, rearranging once, until tender.
Drain and set aside.

Put the lasagne in a large deep pot and
pour over enough boiling water to cover.
Add salt and a few drops of oil to stop the
pieces sticking together. Cover and cook on
full for 12-15 minutes, until done.

Tip the lasagne into a colander and rinse
thoroughly under running cold water. If you
omit this step you are liable to be left with a
soggy mass of unmanageable pasta. Lay the
sheets to dry on a dish towel. (Don't use
paper towels - they will stick.)

To make the cheese sauce, put the butter
or margarine in a bowl and cook on full for 1
minute. Stir in the flour. Pour the milk on.
Cook on full for 3 minutes, beating after
each minute. Stir in the cheese. Cook for a
further minute and beat again. Season to
taste with salt and pepper.

To assemble the dish start with a layer of
eggplants, then cover with Tomato Sauce, a
layer of pasta and a layer of Cheese Sauce.
Continue until all the ingredients are used
up, finishing with a layer of cheese sauce.

Heat through in the microwave, or in a
conventional oven or under the broiler if you
want the top to brown.

Serve hot.

VARIATION
Omit the pasta for an Eggplant Layer Bake.

Pizza

NOTE
Making pizzas using the microwave oven to
prove the dough is even faster than making a
pie or a tart. However, the pizza is better
cooked in a conventional oven for a crisp
crust. A special browning dish is available in
the shape of a pizza which will give a crisp
base if the dish is heated for 5 minutes, then
brushed over with oil. This dish is also
useful for re-heating frozen pizzas. If using
active dry yeast, follow the manufacturer's
directions if they conflict with recipe
directions below.

INGREDIENTS *serves 4*
4 cups all-purpose flour
1 tsp salt
½oz fresh yeast or 1 envelope (active dry
   yeast) and ½ tsp sugar
1 tbsp oil
1¼ cups tepid water

METHOD
Sift the flour into a bowl with the salt. If
using fresh yeast, cream the yeast with a
little of the water. If using dried yeast, mix
the sugar with the water. Beat, and leave for
10-15 minutes to froth.

Add the yeast, oil and water to the flour
and mix to a smooth elastic dough on a
floured board. Knead for 5 minutes, or until
the dough is smooth and elastic. Clean the
bowl, return the dough to it and cover with
plastic wrap. Cook on full power for 15
seconds, then allow to stand for 10 minutes.

Microwave the dough for a further 15
seconds and allow to stand for another 10
minutes. Repeat this 15 second burst once
more leaving to stand as before.

The dough should now have doubled in
size and is ready to be made into pizzas.

NOTE
Dough can also be made with whole-wheat
flour, or half whole-wheat, half white flour.

Pizza Napolitana

INGREDIENTS *serves 4*
4 rounds bread dough, about 8in in
   diameter
¼ cup olive oil
1 garlic clove, peeled
2½ cups canned tomatoes
salt and freshly ground black pepper
2 tsp chopped basil
24 ripe olives
8oz Mozzarella cheese, sliced

METHOD
Preheat a conventional oven to 450°F.

Oil 2 cookie sheets or 4 flan rings. If you
use flan rings you will have a deep dish
pizza. For a thin pizza, roll out the dough
thinly and shape into circles on the cookie
sheets. Brush the dough with olive oil.

Rub the dough with a cut clove of garlic.
If you like a stronger flavor, crush the
remainder into the tomatoes.

Mash the tomatoes with a wooden spoon
and season well with salt and pepper. Add
the chopped basil. Cover the circles of
dough with the tomato mixture. Arrange
the ripe olives and Mozzarella cheese over
the top.

Brush the pizza with oil. Bake thin pizzas
for 12 minutes and for thicker pizzas reduce
the oven temperature to 350°F and bake for
a further 10 minutes.

NOTE
It is possible to cook a quick pizza in the
microwave but it must be eaten quickly or
the dough will become tough. Take a
browning dish or pizza tray and heat for 4-5
minutes at full power. Brush with oil, lay the
dough in the dish, cover it with the filling
and cook on full for 5 minutes. Allow to
stand for 3 minutes. The pizza is tasty but
looks rather pale.

▶ Pizza Napolitana

Mixed Vegetable Lasagne

INGREDIENTS *serves 4*
1 eggplant
2 zucchini
salt and pepper
juice of 1 lemon
2 tbsp butter
1 garlic clove, crushed
2½ cups Tomato Sauce (see page 219)
2½ cups Béchamel Sauce (see page 219)
2 cups mushroom caps
3 tbsp vegetable oil
16 sheets lasagne, pre-cooked
½ cup fresh bread crumbs
¼ cup grated Parmesan cheese

METHOD

Slice the eggplant and zucchini and sprinkle with salt and lemon juice. Allow to stand for 20 minutes.

Rub a large square dish with a little butter mixed with the garlic.

Make up the Tomato and Béchamel Sauces.

Cut the mushrooms into slices including the trimmed stems.

Drain the eggplants and zucchini and pat dry with paper towels. Heat the oil in a flat dish and cook the eggplant and zucchini in batches for 3 minutes, each batch arranged flat on the dish.

Place a little of the Tomato and Béchamel sauces on the serving dish for the lasagne. Cover with the sheets of lasagne. Spread with a little Tomato Sauce and a layer of eggplant, zucchini and mushrooms, finishing with Béchamel Sauce.

Season well and continue layering. Arrange all the vegetables between the first 2 layers of pasta.

Top with the remaining Tomato and Béchamel sauces. Microwave on full power for 10 minutes. Allow to stand for 5 minutes and then cook for a further 5 minutes on full.

Sprinkle with mixed fresh bread crumbs and Parmesan cheese. Cook for a further 5 minutes and then brown under the broiler if required. This makes an ideal main course with green salad.

Artichoke Risotto

INGREDIENTS *serves 4*
3 tbsp butter
1 onion, chopped
1½ cups arborio rice
3 cups boiling water
1 vegetable stock cube
4 very small artichokes
salt and freshly ground black pepper
2 tbsp grated Parmesan cheese

METHOD

Put half the butter in a deep pot and cook on full for 30 seconds. Add the onion, cover and cook for 1 minute.

Stir in the rice. Pour over the boiling water and crumble on the stock cube. Cover and cook on full for 8 minutes.

Meanwhile, prepare the artichokes. Trim off the stems and remove any tough outer leaves. Slice the artichokes vertically. Stir them into the rice and cook on full for a further 4 minutes. Let the pot stand, covered, for 7 minutes.

Stir in the remaining butter, season with salt and pepper and stir in the Parmesan cheese.

Serve at once.

NOTE

To make this risotto you will need very young, very tender artichokes. If these are not available, use canned artichoke hearts.

Cannelloni with Spinach and Ricotta

INGREDIENTS *serves 4*
1½ cups cooked chopped or frozen
   spinach
1 cup ricotta cheese
¼ tsp grated nutmeg
salt and freshly ground black pepper
12 pre-cooked cannelloni tubes
1¾ cups canned sieved tomatoes
1 tsp chopped basil
2 tbsp butter
1 onion, diced
¼ tsp oregano
2½ cups Béchamel Sauce (page 219)
½ cup grated cheese
1 tbsp chopped fresh parsley

METHOD

Mix the cooked or defrosted spinach with the ricotta cheese, nutmeg and seasoning.

Spoon or pipe into the cannelloni tubes.

Season the tomatoes with salt, pepper and basil. Place a layer of them in the bottom of a glass or china dish.

Heat the butter in another small dish for 1 minute. Add the onion and cook on full power for 3 minutes. Stir in the oregano. Pour this over the tomato mixture. Arrange the cannelloni tubes on the tomato and onion.

Cover with the Béchamel Sauce and cook for 5 minutes.

Quickly brown under a hot broiler.

Mix the remaining cheese with the parsley, and sprinkle over the dish.

◄ Mixed vegetable lasagne

Piperade

INGREDIENTS *serves 4*
1/4 cup vegetable oil
1 garlic clove
1 small onion, peeled and diced
2 scallions, sliced
1 sweet red bell pepper, deseeded
1 green bell pepper, deseeded
1 bouquet garni
1 bay leaf
2 large tomatoes, peeled
salt and freshly ground black pepper
8 eggs
2 tbsp butter, cut into pieces

METHOD
Heat the vegetable oil in a browning dish. Slightly crush the garlic clove but leave it whole and add it to the dish. Cook for 30 seconds at full power in the oil.

Add the onions and scallions to the garlic and cook on half power for 6 minutes.

Prepare the peppers by pouring boiling water over them in a bowl and leaving them to stand for 2 minutes. If preferred, prepare them the traditional way by charring under a hot broiler and then removing the skins from the flesh. Chop the peppers very finely by hand or in a food processor, taking care not to purée them completely. Add to the onion and cook on full power for 5 minutes with the bouquet garni and bay leaf.

Remove the seeds from the tomatoes, chop finely and add to the vegetable mixture. Season well and cook on full for a further 5 minutes.

Beat the eggs in a bowl with 1/4 cup water. Add the butter.

Remove the bouquet garni, bay leaf and garlic from the tomato mixture and stir in the eggs. Cook on full power for 4 minutes, remove and mix well.

Return to the microwave oven, cook for a further 4 minutes. Remove and stir again. If the mixture is too liquid, cook for a further 2 minutes and test after stirring.

NOTE
Remember that the mixture thickens very quickly at this stage and the delicious, creamy eggs can toughen if microwaved for a few seconds too long. This dish can also be used to fill savory pastry shells.

Potato Omelet

INGREDIENTS *serves 2*
1 cup sliced cooked potato
a little butter
4 eggs
salt and freshly ground black pepper
freshly chopped herbs or chives
    (optional)

METHOD
Put the potato in 1 or 2 layers in a buttered dish. Use a shallow dish or a pie plate. Cover and cook on full for 45 seconds.

Beat together the eggs, seasoning and chives or herbs if used and pour them over the vegetables. Cook on low power for 8 minutes, or until almost set.

Leave to stand for 1-2 minutes before serving, then cut in two.

Left until cold, then cut into wedges, this makes a good picnic dish, especially if served with salad.

NOTE
Quite often quiches and omelets won't cook in the "cold spot" in the middle of the microwave. To correct this place under a hot broiler for 2-3 minutes.

▼ Potato omelet

Eggs Provençale

INGREDIENTS *serves 4*
8 tomatoes, peeled and sliced
1 tbsp vegetable oil
1 garlic clove, crushed
1 sprig fresh parsley
1 sprig fresh thyme
1 bay leaf
salt and freshly ground black pepper
¼ tsp sugar
4 eggs
2 tsp chopped fresh parsley

METHOD
Place all the ingredients, except the eggs and parsley, in a microwave bowl. Cook on full power for 5 minutes, stir and cook for a further 5 minutes.

Remove the tomato sauce from the microwave oven, take out the sprigs of herbs and the bay leaf. Strain or blend the sauce, taste and correct seasoning.

Butter 4 individual ramekin dishes, and divide the tomato mixture between them.

Break the eggs one at a time into a cup and pour into the center of each dish. Sterilize a skewer or large needle by dipping it in boiling water and use it to prick the yolks.

Season the eggs and place the dishes in the microwave oven. Cook on full power for 1 minute, then reduce to half power and cook for a further 5 minutes. Allow to stand for 1-2 minutes before serving.

Sprinkle with chopped parsley and serve with fingers of toast.

Welsh Rarebit

INGREDIENTS *serves 2*
1 cup grated cheddar cheese
½ cup blue cheese
2 tsp French mustard
pinch salt
freshly ground black pepper
2 tbsp milk or 2 tbsp whiskey or beer
4 slices of toast

METHOD
Place all the ingredients, except the toast, in a medium-sized deep bowl and mix well.

Cook for 2 minutes on full power. Stir well and remove after another 2-3 minutes or when bubbling. Pour over the pieces of toast and brown under a hot broiler.

Eat as a snack or serve with a vegetable casserole. Use milk if serving with vegetables.

◀▲ Eggs provençale
▲▲ Welsh rarebit

Egg, Potato and Mushroom Pie

INGREDIENTS *serves 4*
1lb potatoes, peeled and sliced
2½ cups mushrooms
1 onion
salt and freshly ground black pepper
grated nutmeg
⅔ cup milk
2-3 tbsp heavy cream
4 eggs
¼ cup grated cheese
1 tbsp chopped fresh parsley

METHOD
Arrange a layer of potatoes on a buttered dish of approximately 1qt capacity.

Slice the mushrooms, with trimmed stems still attached, and the onion. Layer the mushrooms and onion with the potatoes, seasoning between layers until all the ingredients are used. Make 4 hollows to hold the eggs. Add the milk and cream and cook on full power for 10 minutes.

Stand for 6 minutes, then microwave for 6 minutes on full power. Stand for another 5 minutes and then test the potatoes. If they are too hard, cook for a further 4 minutes on full power.

Prick the 4 eggs and poach them in a little water in the microwave.

With a slotted spoon, lift the eggs carefully into the spaces on the vegetable casserole. Return to the microwave oven for 30 seconds to re-heat.

Sprinkle with grated cheese and if liked, brown under a very hot broiler for a few seconds. Serve sprinkled with chopped parsley and crisp triangles of brown toast.

Eggs Florentine

INGREDIENTS *serves 4*
half quantity Artichoke Hearts with
    Spinach, omitting pimiento (page 207)
4 eggs
salt and freshly ground black pepper
4 tbsp heavy cream
chopped fresh parsley

METHOD
Prepare the creamed spinach. Butter 4 individual ramekin dishes and divide the spinach between them.

Make a well in the center of each dish with the back of a spoon. Break the eggs into a cup 1 at a time and slide each into a bed of spinach. Prick the yolks with a sterilized needle, season with salt and pepper and carefully pour the cream over the top.

Stand the dishes in a deep glass dish. Pour some boiling water around them. Cook in the microwave oven for 4 minutes at full power. Check to see if the eggs are cooked; if not, cook for a further 1 minute or to taste. Sprinkle with chopped parsley and serve.

NOTE
If cooking the dishes individually, check after 1½ minutes.

◀▲ Egg, potato and mushroom pie
◀ Eggs Florentine

Cheese Soufflé

INGREDIENTS *serves 6*
¼ cup butter
1¼ cups milk
¼ cup all-purpose flour
½ tsp mustard
¼ tsp cayenne pepper
salt and freshly ground black pepper
1 cup grated cheddar cheese
4 eggs
2 tsp Parmesan cheese
1 tbsp chopped fresh parsley

METHOD
Place the butter in a large soufflé dish, cook on full power for 1 minute. Remove from the oven, replace with the milk in a jug. Heat on full power for 2 minutes. Stir the flour into the melted butter to make a smooth paste.

Add the warm milk to the roux of flour and butter, beat well to form a smooth mixture. Add the mustard, cayenne and seasoning. Cook on full power for 2 minutes, beat again and cook for a further 2 minutes until the sauce is thick.

Add the grated cheddar cheese and beat in the egg yolks until the mixture is smooth.

Beat the egg whites just until they form soft peaks. Fold the egg whites into the mixture in the soufflé dish with a plastic spatula.

Cook on low power for 25 minutes.

Sprinkle with Parmesan cheese and parsley. Serve immediately with a salad or crisp green vegetables.

Peppers and Fried Eggs

INGREDIENTS *serves 4*
1 red bell pepper, cut into julienne strips
1 green bell pepper, cut into julienne strips
1 yellow bell pepper, cut into julienne strips
2 large tomatoes, peeled, seeded and cut into strips
1 bunch scallions, trimmed
3 tbsp water
knob of butter
4 eggs
salt and freshly ground black pepper

METHOD
Put the vegetables into a dish with the water, cover with vented plastic wrap and cook on full for 4-5 minutes, stirring once, until tender but not soft. Keep warm.

Heat a browning dish for 3-4 minutes. Add the butter and, using oven mitts, tilt the dish to coat with the hot fat. Break an egg into each corner of the dish and pierce the yolks with a toothpick. Cook until nearly set (about 2½ minutes, but this will depend on the size of the eggs). Allow to stand for 30 seconds.

Divide the vegetables between 4 heated plates and lay an egg on each.

Offer salt and pepper at the table.

VARIATION
You can add garlic to the ingredients if you like and, for a touch of style, make the scallions into tassels.

◄ Peppers and fried eggs

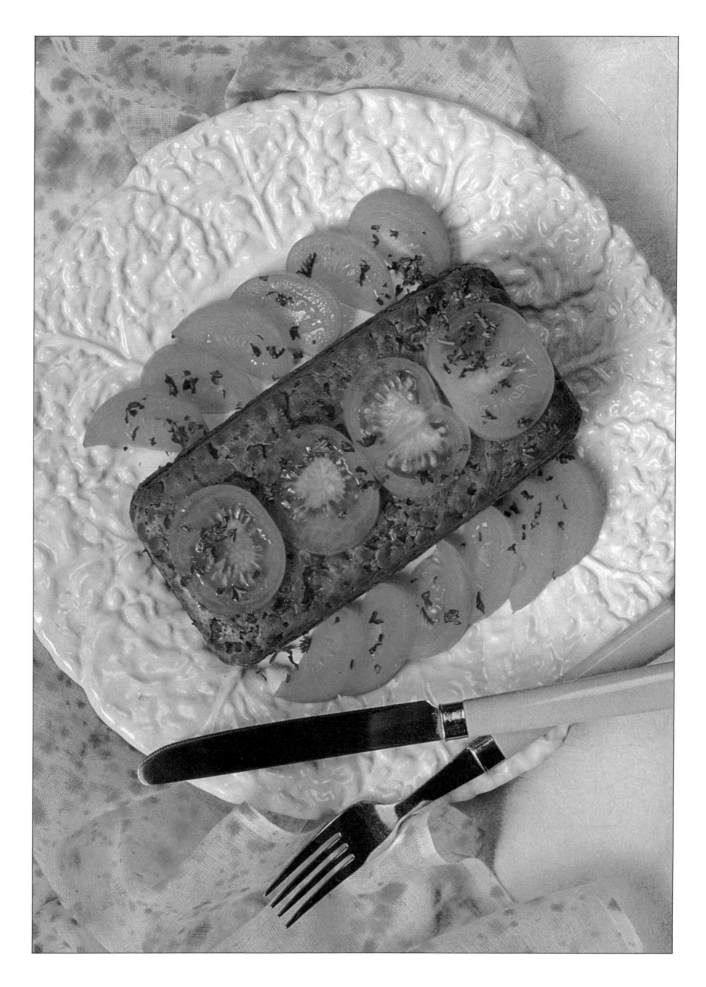

Lentil Loaf

INGREDIENTS *serves 4*
1¼ cups lentils
¼ cup oil
1 onion, diced
4 cups sliced mushrooms
2 tbsp butter
1¼ cups vegetable stock
¼ tsp paprika
salt and freshly ground black pepper
1 tsp chopped fresh herbs
1 egg, beaten
½ cup heavy cream
1 tbsp chopped fresh parsley or 2
    tomatoes, peeled and sliced

METHOD

Wash the lentils under cold running water and remove any discolored seeds. Pour 1¼ cups boiling water over the lentils and allow to stand for 5 minutes before draining.

Heat the oil in a casserole on full power for 1 minute, add the onion and cook on full power for 3 minutes.

Remove the onion from the oil with a slotted spoon and reserve. Cook the mushrooms in the oil and the butter for 3 minutes, covered. Allow to stand for 2 minutes.

In a separate bowl, cook the lentils in the vegetable stock for 7 minutes on full power. Leave to stand for 3 minutes or until most of the liquid is absorbed.

Mix the cooked lentils with the onion, seasonings, herbs, egg and cream.

Spread half the mixture in a microwave bread pan or a 3 cup glass bowl. Arrange the mushrooms over the mixture and add the remaining lentil mixture. Smooth the surface with a spoon, cover and cook for 5 minutes on full power. Allow to stand for 4 minutes before turning out onto a heated serving dish.

Serve sprinkled with chopped parsley or sliced tomatoes. Serve with Tomato Sauce (see page 218) or 1¼ cups Béchamel Sauce (see page 219) with 1½ cups finely chopped mushrooms.

VARIATION

Cheese and Lentil Loaf. Add ½ cup grated cheese to the lentil mixture before cooking.

Winter Chili

INGREDIENTS *serves 4*
¼ cup butter
2 onions, chopped
1 garlic clove, peeled and crushed
2 carrots, diced
2½ cups vegetable stock
6 tomatoes, peeled and chopped
2 red bell peppers, deseeded, sliced
1 chili pepper, deseeded, sliced
¼-½ tsp chili powder
1 eggplant, sliced
2 cups sliced mushrooms
1 tbsp cornstarch
1¼ cups canned kidney beans
1 tbsp tomato paste
2 tbsp whole corn kernels
chopped fresh parsley

METHOD

Melt the butter in the browning dish for 1 minute on full power.

Add the onion and garlic and cook at full power for 1 minute. Add the carrots and vegetable stock and cook at full power for 5 minutes.

Add the tomatoes, peppers, mushrooms, eggplant and chili to the vegetable stock and cook on full power for 2 minutes.

Blend the cornstarch with a little water and the tomato paste and add the chili powder. Remove the casserole from the oven and stir in the tomato mixture until well blended. Return to the microwave and cook at full power for 5 minutes.

Add the canned kidney beans and corn kernels and cook on full power for 10 minutes. Allow to stand for 5 minutes before serving. Serve sprinkled with parsley.

▲ Winter chili
◀ Lentil loaf

205

Nut and Vegetable Cobbler

INGREDIENTS *serves 4*

1lb canned butter beans

1⅓ cups peeled and cubed potatoes

1 small green chili pepper, deseeded and
sliced

1⅓ cups sliced carrots

2 celery stalks, sliced

1 onion, sliced

1 small can tomatoes

2 dessert apples, cored and chopped

1 vegetable stock cube

salt and freshly ground black pepper

TOPPING

1 cup all-purpose flour

1 tsp baking powder

salt and freshly ground black pepper

1 tsp French mustard

½ tsp Italian seasoning

¼ cup butter

¼ cup grated cheese

½ cup finely ground hazelnuts

¼ cup cold water

METHOD

Drain the butter beans, reserving their
liquid, and combine with all the vegetables
and the apples in a large casserole.

Heat the juice from the butter beans for 2
minutes on full power, then dissolve the

stock cube in it.

Pour the stock over the vegetables and
season well. Cover with pierced plastic
wrap, or a plate, and cook on full power for
12 minutes, stirring after 4 and 8 minutes.

Sift the flour, salt and pepper and mustard
into a bowl. Add the herbs.

Cut in the butter until the mixture
resembles fine bread crumbs. Stir in the
cheese and nuts. Add the water and mix to a
soft, elastic dough. Shape into 8 balls and
place them around the outside of the
vegetables. Cover with the lid of pierced
plastic wrap and microwave on full power
for 7 minutes.

Artichoke Heart and Bean Casserole with Vegetable Purée

INGREDIENTS *serves 4*

1 onion, sliced
1 clove garlic, crushed
1 tbsp sunflower oil
4 cups sliced mushrooms
1¾ cups tinned kidney beans
1 generous cup canned artichoke hearts, drained
salt and freshly ground black pepper
fresh cilantro or parsley leaves
¾ cup Purée of Root Vegetables (see page 212)

METHOD

Put the onion and garlic in a casserole with the oil, cover and cook on full power for 3 minutes. Stir in the mushrooms, kidney beans - with a little of the liquid from the can - and artichoke hearts and cook on full power, covered, for about 5 minutes, stirring once, until the mushrooms are done and the beans cooked through.

Season to taste with salt and pepper and sprinkle with cilantro or parsley leaves.

Serve with Purée of Root Vegetables.

Artichoke Hearts with Spinach

INGREDIENTS *serves 4*

2lb fresh spinach
2 tbsp butter
1 large onion, chopped
8 artichoke hearts, fresh or canned
⅓ cup canned pimiento, cut into strips

SAUCE

3 tbsp butter
6 tbsp all-purpose flour
1¼ cups milk
½ cup grated Parmesan cheese
nutmeg
salt and freshly ground black pepper

METHOD

Wash the spinach and discard tough stems and discolored leaves. Put it in a boiling or roasting bag and tie loosely. Cook on full power for about 6 minutes, shaking the bag once, until the spinach has collapsed. Let it stand for a while, then chop coarsely.

Put the butter in a dish and cook on full power for 30 seconds. Add the onion and the artichoke hearts and cook for 3 minutes. (If using canned artichoke hearts, however, arrange them on top of the onion when cooked.)

Lay strips of pimiento in between the artichokes and put the chopped spinach in a layer on top of that.

To make the sauce, put the butter in a bowl and cook on full power for 30 seconds to 1 minute to melt it. Stir in the flour. Pour on the milk and continue to cook for 3 minutes, beating after each minute. Add the cheese. Cook for a further minute and beat again. Season to taste with nutmeg, salt and pepper.

Pour the sauce over the vegetables and heat through in the microwave, or brown in a conventional oven or under the broiler.

◀◀ Nut and vegetable cobbler
◀ Artichoke hearts, kidney beans and mushrooms with vegetable purée

Eggplant with Two Sauces

INGREDIENTS *serves 4*
2 medium eggplants, sliced
4 tbsp water
flour
beaten egg
bread crumbs
a little butter
Tomato Sauce (page 219)
Béchamel Sauce with cheese (page 219)

METHOD
Put the eggplants in a dish, add the water, cover with vented plastic wrap and cook on full power for 7 minutes, rearranging once, until tender. Drain the eggplants.

Dust the eggplants slices with flour, then dip in beaten egg and in bread crumbs. Push the bread crumbs on well with your fingers.

Heat a browning dish to maximum, according to the manufacturer's directions. Add a little butter and, holding the dish with oven mitt, tilt it to cover in the hot fat.

Fry the eggplant slices in batches for 30 seconds on each side, until golden. Keep warm.

Serve with Tomato Sauce and Cheese Sauce.

VARIATION
Omit the cheese sauce.

Ratatouille Alla Mozzarella

INGREDIENTS *serves 4*
1 large eggplant, sliced
3 zucchini, sliced
salt and freshly ground black pepper
4 tbsp olive oil
1 large onion, sliced
2 cloves garlic, chopped
1 small red bell pepper, seeded and chopped
1 small green bell pepper, seeded and chopped
2 cups sliced mushrooms
1¼ cups canned tomatoes, mashed
1 tbsp tomato paste
2 tsp chopped fresh mixed herbs
1 bay leaf
1 cup cubed Mozzarella cheese

METHOD
Place eggplant and zucchini in a colander, sprinkle with salt and allow to stand for 30 minutes. Rinse in cold water and pat dry. Cut the eggplant into bite-sized pieces.

Pour the oil into a casserole and cook on full power for 1 minute. Add onion and garlic and cook on full power for 1 minute. Stir in peppers, eggplant and zucchini and cook on full power for 5 minutes, stirring once.

Stir in remaining ingredients, cover and cook on full power for 15 minutes, stirring twice. Stir in Mozzarella. Cover and continue cooking for 5 minutes until cheese has melted or brown under the broiler if preferred. Serve with crusty French bread to mop up the juices.

▶ Ratatouille alla Mozzarella
◀ Eggplant with two sauces

Rice with Peppers and Cheese

INGREDIENTS *serves 4*

1½ cups rice

3 cups boiling water

1 vegetable stock cube

1 small red bell pepper, deseeded and
   chopped

1 small yellow bell pepper, deseeded
   and chopped

1 small green bell pepper, deseeded and
   chopped

1 cup grated Edam cheese

salt and freshly ground black pepper

1 bunch parsley, chopped

METHOD

Put the rice in a deep pot, pour over the
boiling water and crumble on the stock
cube. Cover and cook on full power for 8
minutes.

Stir in the green, yellow and red peppers.
Cover and cook on full power for 4 minutes.

Stir in the cheese. Check the seasoning
and add salt and pepper if necessary
(depending on the saltiness of the stock
cube). Cover and leave to stand for 5
minutes.

If the cheese has not melted by then, heat
through again for 2 minutes.

Stir in the parsley and serve.

▲ Rice with peppers and cheese

Thai Rice

INGREDIENTS *serves 4*
2⅓ cups long-grain rice
1 tsp salt
1 tsp turmeric
¼ cup vegetable oil
2 garlic cloves, crushed
2 onions, peeled and diced
1 chili pepper, deseeded
1 red bell pepper, deseeded
1 tsp curry powder
2 scallions
2 cups shelled peas
2 eggs
salt and freshly ground black pepper
1 tsp soy sauce
1 tbsp butter

METHOD

Wash the long-grain rice and put in a large casserole with 4 cups boiling water with the salt and turmeric. Cook on full power for 15 minutes and then allow to stand. The rice should be fluffy and separated.

Heat the oil in a dish for 1 minute on full power, add the garlic and cook for a further 1 minute. Add the onion, stir well and cook for 2 minutes.

Dice both the peppers, add them to the garlic and onion and cook for 2 minutes. Stir in the curry powder with half of the chopped scallion, mix with the rice and stir in the peas.

Make up an omelet mixture by beating 2 eggs, 2 tbsp water, seasoning and soy sauce in a bowl. Put the butter into a browning dish and heat on full power for 1 minute. Stir in the eggs and cook on full power for 1 minute and remove.

Mix to allow any uncooked mixture to run under the cooked egg. Cook on full power for another 1 minute, allow to stand for 30 seconds and remove to a chopping board.

Re-heat the rice for 4 minutes on full power.

Cut the omelet into strips and use it to decorate the top of the rice. Sprinkle with chopped scallion and serve.

► Thai rice

Oriental Rice

INGREDIENTS *serves 4*
1 cup long-grain rice
salt
1 cup small mushrooms
2 dessert apples
1 tbsp wine vinegar
1 large onion, finely chopped
1 tbsp vegetable oil
⅓ cup golden raisins
½ cup cashew nuts
½ cup salted peanuts
20 pitted ripe olives
1 tbsp curry powder

METHOD

Wash the rice until the water runs clear. Put it into a very large container with 3¾ cups water and salt. Microwave, uncovered, on full power for 15 minutes. Rinse and leave to drain thoroughly.

Slice the mushrooms, chop the apples leaving the skins on. Put the chopped apple in a bowl with the vinegar.

Put the oil in a large bowl and heat for 2 minutes on full power. Add the onion, stir and cover with a plate or pierced plastic wrap and microwave on full power for 3 minutes.

Combine all the ingredients, season to taste and cook on full power for 4 minutes stirring after 2 minutes. Serve with a salad.

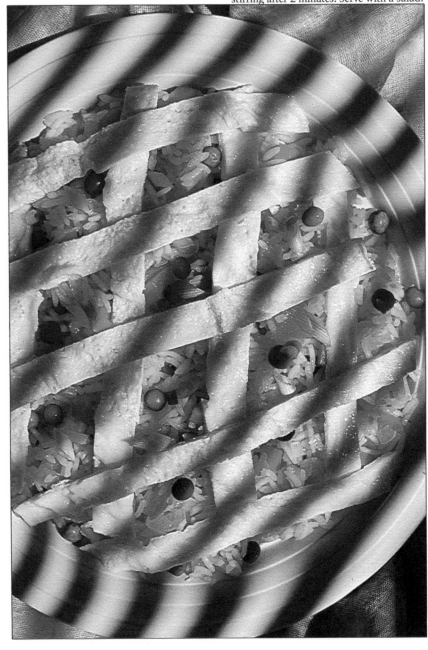

Broccoli with Almonds and Blue Cheese Sauce

INGREDIENTS *serves 4*
1lb broccoli
3 tbsp water
$\frac{2}{3}$ cup heavy cream
6 tbsp crumbled Danish blue cheese
salt and white pepper
scant $\frac{1}{3}$ cup slivered almonds, toasted
diamonds of red bell pepper

METHOD
Wash the broccoli and remove the outer leaves and tough stems. Make slits up the stems to speed up cooking.

Put the broccoli in a dish with the water. Cover with vented plastic wrap and cook on full power for 10 minutes, rearranging once, until tender. Drain and keep hot.

Mash the cream into the cheese until smooth. Cook for 1-2 minutes. Season with salt and pepper and pour over the broccoli.

Serve garnished with slivered almonds, or with the broccoli flowerets in a pool of sauce, as shown, and decorated with diamonds of red pepper.

smooth. Cook for 1-2 minutes. Season with salt and pepper and pour over the broccoli.

Serve garnished with slivered almonds, or with the broccoli florets in a pool of sauce, as shown, and decorate with diamonds of red pepper.

Purée of Root Vegetables

INGREDIENTS *serves 4*
3 cups sliced carrots
$2\frac{1}{4}$ cups sliced rutabaga
3 tbsp water
butter to taste
salt and freshly ground black pepper
$\frac{2}{3}$ cup light cream
snipped fresh chives

METHOD
Reserve some of the carrot slices and cut them into star shapes for the garnish.

Put the vegetables in a dish with the water. Cover with vented plastic wrap and cook on full power for 6-8 minutes, until soft.

Drain the vegetables and purée in the blender with butter to taste. Season the purée and re-heat on full for 1 minute.

To serve, spoon a thin pool of cream onto each of 4 heated plates. Make a small mound of purée on each plate and garnish the surrounding cream with shooting stars made of carrot and snipped chives.

VARIATION
You can make this purée with any of the winter root vegetables, such as turnip, parsnip and sweet potato.

▶ Couscous with vegetables
▼ Broccoli with almonds and blue cheese sauce

Green Bean and Mushroom Curry

INGREDIENTS *serves 2-4*
4 tbsp butter or ghee
1 large onion, chopped
2 cloves garlic, chopped
1 cup trimmed green beans cut into 1-in
  pieces
2 cups sliced mushrooms
3 tomatoes, peeled and chopped
1 tbsp lemon juice
2 slices fresh ginger root
$\frac{1}{2}$ tsp turmeric
$\frac{1}{2}$ tsp ground coriander
$\frac{1}{2}$ tsp curry powder
fresh cilantro or parsley

METHOD
Place the butter in a bowl and cook on full
power for 1 minute. Add the onion and
garlic and cook on full power for 3 minutes.

Stir in the rest of the ingredients, except
the fresh cilantro or parsley. Cover and cook
for 8-10 minutes, stirring twice.

Garnish with fresh cilantro or parsley.

Black-eyed Peas with Mushrooms and Cilantro

INGREDIENTS *serves 4*
2 tbsp butter
1 large onion, chopped
2 cloves garlic, chopped
$2\frac{1}{4}$ cups cooked black-eyed peas
$1\frac{1}{2}$ cups canned tomatoes, drained and
  mashed
1 slice fresh ginger root
salt and freshly ground black pepper
Garam Masala (see page 126)
fresh cilantro

METHOD
Put the butter in a dish and cook on full
power for 45 seconds. Add the onion and
garlic and continue to cook, covered, for 3
minutes.

Add the black-eyed peas, tomatoes and
ginger and cook on full, covered, for 4-5
minutes until hot through, stirring once.

Season to taste with salt, pepper and
Garam Masala and stir in plenty of
chopped cilantro leaves. Eat hot or cold
with rice.

Couscous with Vegetables

INGREDIENTS *serves 4*
$\frac{1}{2}$ cauliflower, cut into flowerets
$\frac{1}{3}$ cup diced carrots
1 large parsnip, diced
3 tbsp water
2 cups canned garbanzo beans, drained
$1\frac{3}{4}$ cups canned peas, drained
Tomato Sauce (see page 219) made with
  chili powder to taste instead of basil
2 cups couscous
2 cups boiling water
salt
2 tbsp butter

METHOD
First prepare the vegetable topping. Put the
cauliflower, carrots and parsnip into a dish
with the water, cover with vented plastic
wrap and cook on full for 5 minutes, stirring
once.

Stir in the garbanzo beans and peas and
cook for a further 4 minutes, stirring once.
Drain and keep hot.

For the couscous, put the grain in a deep
pot, cover with the boiling water, add a
pinch of salt and cook on full power for 4
minutes. Stir in the butter.

Re-heat the Tomato Sauce for 3 minutes.

Serve the couscous topped with the spicy
vegetable mixture and allow guests to serve
themselves with the sauce.

Broccoli and Cauliflower Cheese

INGREDIENTS *serves 4*

1lb fresh broccoli, washed, or 12oz
    frozen
1 cauliflower, washed
2 potatoes, peeled
2½ cups Béchamel Sauce (see page 219)
2 tbsp butter
salt and freshly ground black pepper
¼ cup milk
4 slices cheese
1tbsp crisp bread crumbs

METHOD

Arrange the broccoli in a round dish with the spears facing in to the center and stems out. Add 4 tsp salted water and cook on full power for 5 minutes, covered.

If using frozen, thaw first and only cook for 3 minutes at this stage.

Arrange the cauliflower flowerets in the same dish in a ring when the broccoli is finished and remove to a plate. Cook on full power for 5 minutes and then allow to stand for 3 minutes.

While the vegetables are cooking, slice the potatoes thinly, use the food processor if you have one. Make up the Béchamel Sauce.

Arrange the potatoes on the bottom of a buttered deep dish. Add salt and pepper to the milk, pour over the potatoes, partially cover with a lid or with plastic film. Microwave on full power for 5 minutes, allowing longer if the potato slices are chunky. Stand for 3 minutes.

Arrange the broccoli spears facing in to the center in a ring, alternating with the cauliflower.

Pour over the well-seasoned Béchamel Sauce and microwave for 10 minutes on full power. Sprinkle with freshly ground pepper and cover with the slices of cheese. Microwave on full power for 2 minutes or until the cheese has melted. Sprinkle with the bread crumbs and brown under the broiler, if liked. Allow to stand for 2 minutes and then serve while the cheese is still soft.

▲ ▶ Broccoli and cauliflower cheese
▶ Leek parcels

Baby Onions Escoffier

INGREDIENTS *serves 4*
4 cups baby onions
1 tbsp oil
1 bay leaf
1 thyme sprig
1 tsp fennel seeds
$\frac{1}{2}$ cup golden raisins, soaked
3 tbsp dry white wine
1 tbsp brandy

METHOD
Peel the onions, but leave them whole. Put them in a dish with the remaining ingredients, cover with vented plastic wrap and cook on full power for about 10 minutes, shaking the dish twice.

Serve with lamb, beef or game.

Leek Parcels

INGREDIENTS *serves 4*
3 tbsp polyunsaturated vegetable
    margarine or butter
6 tbsp all-purpose flour
1$\frac{1}{4}$ cups milk
$\frac{1}{2}$ cup grated Edam cheese
1-2 tsp mustard (optional)
salt and freshly ground black pepper
4 leeks
2 tbsp water
4 slices ham

METHOD
First make the sauce. Put the margarine or butter in a bowl and cook for 1 minute on full power. Stir in the flour. Pour on the milk. Cook for 3 minutes, beating after each minute. Stir in the cheese and mustard, if used. Cook for a further minute and beat again. Season to taste with salt and pepper. Keep the sauce warm while you cook the leeks.

Trim the leeks and wash thoroughly. Put them in a dish with the water, cover with vented plastic wrap and cook for about 8 minutes, rearranging once, until done.

Drain the leeks and cut off a few rings for the garnish. Wrap each in a slice of ham, lay side by side in the dish and pour the sauce over. Cover and cook for 2-3 minutes until hot through. Serve at once.

Glazed Onions

INGREDIENTS *serves 4*
8 small onions, peeled but left whole
2 tbsp honey
2 tbsp butter
2 tbsp hot water

METHOD
Put the onions in a dish.

Cream the honey and butter with the water and pour over the onions. Cover with vented plastic wrap and cook on full power for 8-10 minutes, until the onions are tender, shaking or stirring the dish once.

Serve hot. This is particularly good with pork chops and mashed potatoes.

Russian Beets

INGREDIENTS *serves 4*
6 tbsp butter
5 medium uncooked beets, diced
2 tbsp red-wine vinegar
$\frac{1}{2}$ tsp dried dill
$\frac{1}{2}$ tsp dried fennel
salt and freshly ground black pepper
3 tbsp cornstarch
2 tbsp milk
fresh dill or fennel
sour cream

METHOD
Place butter in a bowl and cook for 1 minute. Stir in the beet, vinegar, herbs and seasoning. Cover and cook on full power for 8 minutes or until beets are tender.

Place cornstarch and milk in a small bowl and mix until smooth. Stir mixture into beets and cook, covered, for about 4 minutes until thickened.

Allow to stand, covered, for 2 minutes. Garnish with fresh dill or fennel and serve hot or cold, with sour cream, to accompany cold meats.

Roman Spinach

INGREDIENTS *serves 4*
2lb fresh spinach
$\frac{1}{2}$ tbsp oil
$\frac{1}{2}$ tbsp butter (approx.)
$\frac{1}{3}$ cup pine nuts
$\frac{1}{3}$ cup golden raisins
1 clove garlic, crushed
salt and freshly ground black pepper

METHOD
Wash the spinach and discard tough stems and discolored leaves. Put it in a roasting or boiling bag and tie loosely. Cook on full power for about 6 minutes, shaking the bag once, until the spinach has collapsed.

Put the oil and butter in a dish (use more if you want a richer taste), and add the pine nuts, golden raisins, and garlic. Cook for 1 minute.

Meanwhile, shred the spinach. Add it to the dish and toss well. Season with salt and pepper to taste.

Cook for a further minute, covered with vented plastic wrap, to heat through.

Perfect Asparagus

INGREDIENTS *serves 4*
12oz asparagus spears
3 tbsp water
3 tbsp butter
2 tbsp Parmesan cheese

METHOD
Trim the woody ends from the asparagus spears so that they are all the same length. Lay them in a dish arranged top to tail and pour on the water. Cover with vented plastic wrap and cook on full power for 5-7 minutes, depending on the size of the .spears.

Drain the asparagus and keep warm.

Put the butter and Parmesan in a jug and cook for 1 minute.

Serve the sauce separately.

Brussels Sprouts with Water Chestnuts, Garlic and Mushrooms

INGREDIENTS *serves 4*
1 tbsp butter or margarine
1 clove garlic, crushed
5-6 cups baby Brussels sprouts, trimmed
2 cups sliced mushrooms
1 cup canned water chestnuts, drained
soy sauce

METHOD
Put the butter in a dish and cook on full power for 30 seconds. Add the garlic and cook for 1 minute.

Add the sprouts, mushrooms and water chestnuts, with 1 tbsp of the chestnut liquid.

Cover and cook for 3-4 minutes, until hot through.

Season with soy sauce and serve.

Italian style Zucchini

INGREDIENTS *serves 4*
3½ cups sliced zucchini
1 small onion, chopped
1 clove garlic, crushed
3 tbsp water
1¾ cups canned tomatoes, drained and blended
salt and freshly ground black pepper
3 tbsp grated Parmesan cheese

METHOD
Put the zucchini in a dish with the onion and garlic. Add the water. Cover with vented plastic wrap and cook on full power for about 7 minutes, until nearly done.

Stir in the tomatoes and season with salt and pepper. Cover and cook for 2-3 minutes, until hot through.

Sprinkle with grated Parmesan cheese and serve.

VARIATION
You can layer the zucchini with sliced Mozzarella cheese and tomato sauce instead of serving them with Parmesan.

▼ Brussels sprouts with water chestnuts, garlic and mushrooms

Parsnips and Mushrooms in a Cheese Sauce

INGREDIENTS *serves 4*
1lb parsnips
3 tbsp water
1 tbsp lemon juice
4 cups mushrooms, wiped and sliced

SAUCE
3 tbsp butter
6 tbsp flour
$1\frac{1}{4}$ cups milk
$\frac{1}{2}$ cup grated cheese
salt and freshly ground black pepper
nutmeg

METHOD
Peel the parsnips, trim them and cut into eighths. Cut away any very woody cores. Put them in a dish with the water and lemon juice. Cover with vented plastic wrap and cook on full power for 7 minutes, stirring twice.

Stir in the mushrooms. Cover again and cook for a further 3-4 minutes, until the vegetables are done. Keep hot.

Make the sauce. Put the butter in a dish and cook for 30 seconds. Stir in the flour. Pour in the milk and cook for 3 minutes, beating after each minute. Stir in the cheese. Cook for a further minute, then beat again. Season to taste with salt, pepper and nutmeg.

Drain the vegetables and pour the sauce over them. Reheat for a minute if necessary.

Fennel with Parmesan

INGREDIENTS *serves 4*
2 bulbs fennel
$\frac{1}{4}$ cup butter
1 tbsp lemon juice
salt and freshly ground black pepper
2 tbsp Parmesan cheese
2 tbsp chopped fresh herbs (optional)

METHOD
Remove the tough outer leaves of the fennel. Trim the bulbs, but reserve the feathery fronds. Slice the bulbs.

Put the butter in a dish and cook for 1 minute on full power. Add the fennel and turn in the butter to coat. Cover with vented plastic wrap and cook for about 10 minutes, stirring the dish a couple of times, until the fennel is tender.

Sprinkle on the lemon juice, season with salt and pepper and spoon over the Parmesan cheese.

Garnish with the fennel fronds, chopped, or fresh herbs.

▲ Fennel with Parmesan

217

Hot Oatmeal Potatoes

INGREDIENTS *serves 4*
2lb new potatoes, scrubbed
¼ cup butter
6 scallions
½ cup quick-cooking oatmeal flakes
¼ cup heavy cream (optional)
1 tbsp chopped fresh parsley

METHOD
Prick the new potatoes several times with a fork. Place in a deep dish with 1 cup salted water. Cover with a lid or plastic wrap and microwave on full power for 10 minutes. Allow to stand for 3 minutes.

Test the potatoes, if they are not quite cooked, give the dish a quarter turn and cook for a further 3 minutes. Drain, and then cut the potatoes into even slices.

Melt the butter in a dish. Add 4 chopped scallions, stir well, and mix in the sliced potatoes and the oatmeal. Cook on full power for 5 minutes. Add ¼ cup cream to the potatoes if liked.

Sprinkle with the remaining 2 chopped scallions and the parsley.

Corn-on-the-Cob

INGREDIENTS *serves 4*
4 corn-on-the-cob with husks
4 tbsp butter
1 tbsp green or ripe olive pieces
1 tsp capers, chopped
2 scallions, chopped
½ red bell pepper, deseeded and diced
1 cup sliced mushrooms
salt and freshly ground black pepper

METHOD
Microwave the corn in the husks with ½ cup water, covered, for 5 minutes. Allow to stand for 2 minutes.

Melt the butter in a bowl on full power for 1 minute. Add all the other ingredients and cook for 3 minutes.

Remove the husks from the corn. Pour the butter mixture over the corn. Season well.

◀ ▲ Hot oatmeal potatoes
◀ Corn on the cob

Turnip and Potato Bake

INGREDIENTS *serves 4*
2½ cups peeled and thinly sliced turnips
3 cups peeled and thinly sliced potatoes
butter
salt and freshly ground black pepper
4 tbsp light cream
chopped fresh chives

METHOD
Layer the turnips and potatoes in a round dish, dotting each layer with butter and seasoning with salt and pepper. Cover with waxed paper and press well down.

Stand the dish on an inverted plate. Cover and cook on full power for 9 minutes, turning once.

Slowly pour over cream so that it seeps betwen the layers. Brown slightly under the broiler, garnish with chives and serve.

Tomato Sauce

INGREDIENTS *makes 2½ cups*
2 tbsp oil
2 onions, peeled and diced
1 clove garlic, crushed
1 carrot, scraped and grated
5⅓ cups chopped tomatoes
1 tsp sugar
1 tbsp chopped basil
1 bay leaf
1 bouquet garni
salt and freshly ground black pepper
½ cup white wine

METHOD

Heat the oil for 1 minute in a casserole or bowl. Add the onion and garlic and cook for 2 minutes. Add the carrot and cook on full power for a further 2 minutes.

Stir in all the other ingredients, mix well and cook, covered, for 10 minutes. Allow to stand for 5 minutes. Remove the bay leaf and bouquet garni.

Strain the sauce to remove the tomato skins. Use as required.

VARIATION

If a rough texture is preferred, peel the tomatoes before cooking. The sauce can then be put through a blender or food processor. If using canned plum tomatoes, add 2½ cups or 2×14oz cans.

Béchamel Sauce

INGREDIENTS *serves 4*
2½ cups milk
¼ onion, peeled
1 bay leaf
1 bouquet garni
1 slice carrot
3 tbsp butter
½ cup all-purpose flour
salt and freshly ground black pepper

METHOD

Put the milk in an ovenproof glass measuring pitcher with the onion, bayleaf, bouquet garni and carrot. Cook on full power for 3 minutes and allow to stand, covered, for 10 minutes.

Heat the butter in a bowl for 2 minutes, remove from the oven and stir in the flour. Gradually add the strained milk and beat

the mixture until smooth. Season well.

Reheat in the oven at full power for 2 minutes, then remove and beat. Return to the oven at full power and cook for a further 2 minutes, then beat again. Cook for another minute, allow to stand for 2 minutes, beat and leave to stand.

Use for vegetable dishes with or without first adding herbs and cheese.

VARIATION

Add ½ cup grated cheese before the last 2 minutes cooking time, then beat and leave to stand.

Hollandaise Sauce

INGREDIENTS *serves 4*
¾ cup butter
2 tbsp wine vinegar or
   2 tbsp lemon juice
2 egg yolks
salt and freshly ground black pepper

METHOD

Melt the butter on full power for 2 minutes.

Beat the vinegar or lemon juice in a small bowl with the egg yolks and seasoning.

Pour the melted butter into the bowl, gradually beating as the butter is added. When half the butter has been incorporated, cook in the microwave oven for 30 seconds; remove and whisk again.

Beat in the remaining butter and cook for 30 seconds. Beat and, if necessary, cook for a further 30 seconds. Serve immediately.

VARIATION

Allow the Hollandaise Sauce to cool slightly and fold in 1 cup whipped heavy cream. Serve with any crisp vegetable for a special occasion. For another variation: Add 1 tbsp chopped gherkins or capers for extra flavor.

▲▲ Tomato sauce
▲ Hollandaise sauce

Mango Chutney

INGREDIENTS *makes about 3¼ cups*
2 (about 1½lb) mangoes, peeled and
    diced
1 large onion, chopped
⅓ cup raisins
⅓ cup chopped dried apricots
1 tbsp rum
1¼ cups wine or cider vinegar
sugar
½ tsp ground allspice
½ cinnamon stick
1 piece fresh ginger root
1 small green chili pepper, deseeded

METHOD

Mix the onion with the mangoes and cover
with 1¼ cups of water in a large bowl. Cook
on full power for 5 minutes.

Soak the raisins and apricots in the rum.

Drain the mangoes and weigh the fruit.
Use the same weight of sugar as fruit for the
chutney.

Pour the vinegar into a pitcher and add
the sugar and spices. Microwave on full
power for 4 minutes to melt the sugar.
Check to see if sugar is completely dissolved
and, if not, cook for a further 2 minutes.

Return the mangoes to the bowl with the
vinegar and sugar mixture and stir in the
raisins, apricots and chopped chili. Cook at
full power for 10 minutes and then stand for
5 minutes. Cook for a further 10 minutes on
full power or until the mixture becomes
thick.

To test it, put a spoonful on a cold plate,
leave to cool and see if it wrinkles when
pushed. If the mixture is still too runny,
cook for another 2-3 minutes.

Bottle in sterilized jars. Seal and label.

This chutney is an excellent accompaniment to spicy dishes and curries. It can
also be served with vegetarian cutlets and
nut roasts.

▲ ▶ Mango chutney
▶ Fruit chutney

Fruit Chutney

INGREDIENTS *makes 6 jars*
2¼lb apples, peeled, cored and sliced
2¼lb onions, peeled and sliced
grated peel and juice of 2 lemons
½ cup chopped dried apricots
6 cups brown sugar
2½ cups malt vinegar
1 small green chili pepper, deseeded
1⅓ cups golden raisins
1⅓ cups raisins

METHOD

In a large bowl, microwave the sliced apples
and onion rings, covered, for 5 minutes on
full power.

Add the lemon peel and juice, stir them
and then add the apricots and sugar. Mix
well.

Cook for 10 minutes on full power,
stirring to dissolve the sugar. When it is
dissolved, add the vinegar, chopped chili
pepper, golden raisins and raisins.

Cook on top of the stove, uncovered, for
1-1½ hours until thick. Ladle into sterilized
jars, seal and label.

Three Fruits Marmalade

INGREDIENTS *makes 6 jars*
1lb oranges
1 grapefruit
2 lemons
7 1/2 cups water
3lb sugar

NOTE
This easy, cleaner way of making delicious marmalade only needs stirring occasionally. However, it is essential that the sugar is dissolved by stirring before boiling for a second time.

METHOD
Cook the fruit in 2 batches in the microwave oven on full power for 3 minutes each.

Cut the fruit in half and squeeze out the juices. Slice the skins with a sharp knife or the small slicing blade for a food processor. Put the pits in a piece of cheesecloth or fine rinsed cloth and tie the top of the bag securely.

Use a large bowl or 4-qt casserole. Place the pits, sliced skin and water in it, turn to full power and heat the water for 45 minutes.

Stir in the sugar until it is dissolved. If necessary, give it a 3 minute burst of full power, remove and stir to dissolve the sugar. Use oven mitts, as the bowl of fruit will be hot and needs handling carefully.

When the sugar has dissolved, replace the bowl and microwave at full power for 1 hour. Stir after 10 minutes, skim any foam from the surface and continue cooking.

Test for setting on a cold plate: if a spoonful of marmalade wrinkles after 1 minute, it has reached setting point and is ready.

Ladle into warm sterilized jars, seal and label.

VARIATION
To make orange marmalade use 2lb Seville (bitter) oranges and 1 lemon. Make as above.

▲ ▶ Three fruits marmalade
▶ Strawberry jam
▶ ▶ Lemon curd

Strawberry Jam

INGREDIENTS *makes 4 jars*
5 1/2 cups strawberries, hulled
juice of 1 lemon
4 cups sugar

METHOD
Put the fruit in a large bowl or casserole with the lemon juice and cook for 5 minutes on full power. Mash the strawberries slightly with a wooden spoon.

Add the sugar and stir well. Cook for 3 minutes on full power and stir again. Cook on full for a further 3 minutes and stir to check the sugar is dissolved. If necessary, cook for a further 2 minutes on full power.

Cook for another 6 minutes on full power, stir around thoroughly and cook for a further 6 minutes on full power.

Test on a cold plate; the jam should wrinkle after 1 minute. If not, cook for another 2 minutes on full power.

Pour or ladle into sterilized jars, seal and label.

Lemon Curd

INGREDIENTS *makes 1 1/2 lb*
2 1/4 cups sugar
grated peel and juice of 4 lemons
3/4 cup butter
6 eggs, beaten

METHOD
Put the sugar in a glass bowl.

Mix the butter into the sugar and cook on full power for 1 minute.

Add the peel and juice of the lemons to the butter and sugar and mix well. Strain in the beaten eggs, beating the mixture well.

Cook on full power for 2 minutes, remove and stir well. Return to the oven and cook for a further 6 minutes, removing every 2 minutes to stir.

Test the mixture to see that it is smooth and thick. Pot in sterilized jars and store in a cool place.

Lemon curd has a limited shelf life and is best eaten within 2 weeks unless kept in the refrigerator.

INDEX